W9-CZT-689

CRITICAL INCIDENTS IN CHILD CARE

HV
881
B43

126876

CRITICAL INCIDENTS IN CHILD CARE

A Case Book for Child Care Workers

By
Jerome Beker

Jewish Board of Guardians, and
Editor *Child Care Quarterly*

in collaboration with
Shirle M. Husted

and

Paul M. Gitelson
Jewish Board of Guardians
Philip Kaminstein
Berkshire Farm for Boys
Lois Finkel Adler
Lakeside School

BIP '86

Behavioral Publications   1972   New York

GOSHEN COLLEGE LIBRARY
GOSHEN, INDIANA 46526

Library of Congress Catalog Card Number 74174272
Standard Book Number Paper: 87705-074-0
Standard Book Number Cloth: 87705-061-9

Copyright ©1972 by Behavioral Publications
All rights reserved. No part of this work may be reproduced or
utilized in any form or by any means, electronic or mechanical,
including photocopying, microfilm and recording,
or by any information storage and retrieval system
without permission in writing from the publisher

Printed in the United States of America

BEHAVIORAL PUBLICATIONS, 2852 Broadway
Morningside Heights, New York, New York 10025

Library of Congress Cataloging in Publication Data

Beker, Jerome.
    Critical incidents in child care.

    Bibliography: p.
    1. Children--Institutional care--United States.
2. Child welfare--Study and teaching. 3. Social
work education. I. Title.
HV881.B43   362.7'32   72-2560
ISBN 0-87705-074-0 (pbk.)
ISBN 0-87705-061-9

For Emmy

CONTENTS

Part One

Institutional Child Care Practice and the Case Study Method

Part Two

The Cases

UNIT ONE—THE CHILD CARE WORKER

UNIT TWO—HELPING DIFFICULT YOUNGSTERS

PREFACE

Among the many things that are needed in the residential care and treatment of children is a technology of practice for child care workers. At a future stage in the development of such a technology, a child care worker might have a systematic repertoire of care and treatment techniques with which to help individuals and groups of children with behavior problems. Were such a technology to become highly developed, not only would the child care worker's techniques be detailed but specific cues would indicate which techniques ought to be applied to which problems.

With such a technology of child care practice spelling out and integrating a variety of techniques, problems, and cues, one might even look forward to predictable outcomes from the actions of child care workers. However, until such a technology is developed, sophisticated curriculum materials used by sensitive instructors and supervisors can help child care workers move toward the most advanced level of practice of which they are capable.

This book makes a distinct contribution to developing a technology of child care practice and to helping child care workers refine their current skills, many of which are highly intuitive. The contribution of Dr. Beker and his colleagues takes the form of a series of cross-sectional glimpses at actual problem cases, typical of the kinds faced by child care workers in their daily work.

The first contribution, directed toward the development of a technology, is reflected in the implicit use of intrapsychic, interpersonal, and sociocultural concepts in the organization of the case materials. This relating of concepts and real cottage situations is the beginning of bringing order to the myriad details to be dealt with in complex cottage situations.

The second contribution, directed toward helping child care workers to improve the level of their practice, is the presentation of much-needed curriculum materials in the form of the cases, the suggested procedures for analysis, and the discussion questions. The case materials, although vivid, clear, and to the point, are not all-inclusive case studies. Rather, they are open-ended vignettes which invite, indeed at times compel, the reader's involvement, encouraging him to consider the case, particularly its problems and opportunities, and to project solutions or possible next steps for the child care worker. The reader may also consider what should, or could, have been done in the described circumstances to foresee and prevent the crisis portrayed. Consideration of the cases in group discussion would undoubtedly enhance their value, as the child care workers would thus have the opportunity to exchange ideas, criticize one another's opinions, interpretations, and solutions, and generally contribute to one another's learning experiences.

In seeking to make child care and treatment more helpful, we have undoubtedly been asking too much of child care workers. Often, they have barely held their own in working with difficult and large groups of children. *Critical Incidents in Child Care,* if used skillfully, will provide concrete help to child care workers in their exceptionally important human undertaking of caring for and helping children.

GEORGE H. WEBER

IN APPRECIATION

A number of years ago George H. Weber broached the idea for the project that has culminated in this book, and his encouragement, advice, and support have been of particular value throughout the course of the work. My father, Harold Beker, has contributed substantially from his long experience and great insight and skill in closely related fields. Jerome M. Goldsmith, Executive Director of the Jewish Board of Guardians, has been a continuing source of support both personally and by making the resources of the agency available to the project. He, Jack A. Kirkland, Harry Krohn, Braulio Montalvo, and other individuals too numerous to mention and sometimes, undoubtedly, unrecognized by us have offered specific case ideas and general principles and have helped us attain what insights may be reflected in the book. We are most appreciative.

The project was supported primarily by the National Institute of Mental Health through its Grant No. MH 14784. Supplementary assistance was given by the Ford Foundation through the Syracuse University Youth Development Center and by the field settings in which we worked. In addition to providing material resources, the latter opened themselves to project personnel who, as formal and informal observers, gathered much of the raw material for the cases. We are grateful for their cooperation and for that of their staff members and youngsters. These agencies included Berkshire Farm for Boys, which was the original field setting for the project and participated over an extended period, the Hawthorne Cedar Knolls and Linden Hill Schools of the Jewish Board of Guardians, Camp Arthur of the Jewish Y's and Centers Camps of Philadelphia, and an independent boarding school. In addition to the authors, the observers included Lloyd M. Sundblad and James B. Victor.

I also want to express my gratitude to the contributing authors, each of whom provided cases and case ideas which were often based on personal experiences at the agencies just named and elsewhere. In addition, Philip Kaminstein was actively involved in the project from its inception, and he and Paul Gitelson offered suggestions on all the cases in draft form, proposed discussion questions, and assisted in conceptualizing the work as the book neared completion. They gave most generously of their time and enthusiasm and contributed significantly to the quality of the material.

I cannot say enough about Shirle Husted, whose talent propelled itself into recognition despite her great modesty about it. She began work on the book as my secretary and has become not only a contributing author, but also an active partner and collaborator every step of the way. Of course, along with the final decisions the responsibility for any failures in the book is mine.

Our typing was done quickly and efficiently by Molla Hamblet and Bette Weber, and Karnit Breite's assistance with administrative, editorial, and clerical details in the later stages of the work was indispensable. We all appreciate their contribution and those of the many other individuals who helped from time to time.

As in all my work, my greatest spiritual debt is to my wife, Emmy, who helped in many concrete ways as well. Her substantive contributions are, in most cases, too closely intertwined with mine to be listed separately. Our young sons, Joshua and David, have seen less of their father in recent months than any of us would have preferred. I hope that their sacrifice and Emmy's will be repaid by the contribution of this book to the lives of youngsters who may be less fortunate than they.

J. B.

BIOGRAPHICAL NOTES

Jerome Beker, Ed.D., has recently been appointed Director of Child Care Studies at the Institute for Child Mental Health in New York City and is Editor of *Child Care Quarterly.* A graduate of Swarthmore College and Teachers College, Columbia University, he has been an NIMH Postdoctoral Fellow and Research Psychologist at Berkshire Farm for Boys, Senior Research Associate at the Syracuse University Youth Development Center, and Director of Residential Research at the Jewish Board of Guardians. He has also served in child care, supervisory, and administrative roles, and as a consultant in residential settings. His previous publications include a case book for training camp counselors and numerous articles. Dr. Beker is a member of the Board of Directors of the American Branch of the International Association of Workers for Children and served on the Child Care Advisory Committee of Rockland Community College and the Editorial Advisory Committee of *Psychosocial Process: Issues in Child Mental Health,* the Journal of the Jewish Board of Guardians.

Lois Finkel Adler is a graduate of the master's degree program in child care counseling offered by Tufts University in collaboration with the Judge Baker Guidance Center. She was involved in the project as a research assistant with the Jewish Board of Guardians and is currently a child therapist and caseworker at the Lakeside School of the Edwin Gould Services for Children and an instructor in psychology at Rockland Community College. She has also been therapy coordinator at Bethlehem Children's Home, Staten Island, New York, and an instructor in the child care curriculum at Staten Island Community College.

Paul M. Gitelson, ACSW, holds a master's degree from the Columbia University School of Social Work and is Executive Assistant at the Hawthorne Cedar Knolls School of the Jewish Board of Guardians, where he previously served as Director of Child Care Training, as a social worker, and as a professional child care worker in an experimental project. A former Director of Child Care at Abbott House, Mr. Gitelson served on the Rockland Community College Child Care Advisory Committee and has been an Instructor in its Human Services Program and a Field Work Supervisor at the Fordham University School of Social Work.

Shirle M. Husted served the project as research assistant with the Jewish Board of Guardians. Her background includes college-level course work in sociology and experience as a newspaper columnist. She has also been associated with the Northwest Mental Health Clinic in Illinois and has been a Girl Scout camp leader. As the only contributing author with children above the age of six—she has three teenagers—Mrs. Husted brought parental experience with youngsters of all ages to the project along with her many talents.

Philip Kaminstein, Training Coordinator at Berkshire Farm for Boys and the Berkshire Farm Institute for Training and Research, holds a master's degree from New York University. He has also served as a caseworker for youthful offenders at the Minnesota State Reformatory, as Superintendent of Thistledew Camp operated by the Minnesota Department of Corrections, and as Director of the Minnesota Reception Center for Youthful Offenders. Mr. Kamistein has authored and coauthored several publications and an audiotape series on child care training as well as numerous tapes on drug abuse.

INTRODUCTION

As this is written, about 300,000 young people in the United States and many thousands in other countries are living in institutional settings rather than with their families. Most of them have been institutionalized because they are mentally, physically, or emotionally handicapped, because they have violated the law, or because they have no families willing or able to care for them.

In each of the various types of institutions serving young people of school age, there are staff members assigned to supervise and work with the youngsters during the day-to-day routines of living. These personnel, referred to in this book as "child care workers," normally perform many of the functions of parents in family situations and are usually expected to contribute to the rehabilitation process as well. Despite the importance and complexity of the tasks involved, there is relatively little training material available for child care workers and even less that is directly and specifically oriented to their needs. The purpose of this book is to provide such resources for use in formal training programs in community colleges, universities, and elsewhere, in pre- and inservice training within institutional settings, and in supervision on the job.

Case studies provide a particularly appropriate way to approach this task, as has been shown in leadership training programs in such related fields as education and social work. Effective practice in all these fields depends on the development of similar interpersonal attitudes, insights, and human relations skills, even though the specific kinds of situations encountered and the roles of the adults involved may vary. Training for these kinds of work appears to require supervised experience in evaluating and choosing among concrete alternatives in specified circumstances rather than memorizing specific formulas or abstract principles, and case studies provide particularly appropriate resources for this process.

The cases themselves, 115 in all, are relatively short vignettes illustrating a wide range of the categories or kinds of situations that tend to arise in child care work. The incidents portrayed were selected and classified on the basis of an examination of child care practice in several settings by the authors and their colleagues, including child care workers and supervisory personnel. Each case is intended to represent, in concrete terms, a class or kind of situation that seems to arise regularly. Although not all possible situations can be portrayed, of course, it is hoped that the cases reflect all the types of situations that normally occur in the course of institutional child care.

Although the reader may have to make appropriate adjustments in some instances, most of the cases can be applied to youngsters of a wide age range. Therefore ages are usually not specified in the cases. Whereas most of the characters are portrayed as male, the issues raised are usually relevant to work with youngsters of either sex. Also, the book does not assume any single view of the role of the child care worker, such as "substitute parent," "milieu therapist," "behavior modification specialist," and so on. The reader can analyze the cases in terms of his own needs and point of view.

The book does, however, reflect the position that child care work is more than custodial, more than simply a matter of keeping youngsters reasonably healthy and under control. Our view is that promoting personal and social development is an essential part of effective institutional child care. Therefore the cases are focused on "opportunity events," incidents that appear to offer crucial opportunities for child care workers to contribute to the development of the youngsters in their care as well as to meet basic needs. Less attention is given to other aspects of the child care job, those that do not involve interpersonal interaction and relationships. These functions, largely routine and administrative in nature, are not only less appropriate for teaching by the case method, but also more likely to vary according to the policies of individual institutions. They are therefore probably better left for staff manuals or other text material and on-the-job orientation.

The cases are "open-end," stopping at a point where a decision must be made and action taken, usually by the child care worker. Thus they present problems for readers to think about and discuss prior to making actual decisions. Although such decisions on the job must usually be made immediately, without the luxury of time for reflection, it is anticipated that experience with case analysis will help practicing and prospective child care workers develop the ability to understand a wide variety of situations quickly and to respond in an appropriate way. Neither specific simplistic rules or recipes that would be difficult to apply flexibly in new situations nor broad general principles of human relations that need to be translated for application on the job can provide this ability. Rather, it depends on the active personal involvement of the learner in situations such as are portrayed in the cases. The specifics of this process are described and discussed in Part One, Institutional Child Care Practice and the Case Study Method.

Part Two, The Cases, has been organized so as to present related issues together and to provide quick, easy access to material desired by readers. The individual chapters represent the topics with which the cases are concerned, as described briefly in the table of cases preceding each chapter, while the units represent broader areas that may be helpful for teaching purposes. A brief description of each case and its focus is also included in the appropriate table of cases to facilitate access to the material. Although the cases are largely based on actual occurrences or combinations of occurrences, all names have been changed. Therefore, any resemblance between names appearing in the cases and those of real people, places, etc., is coincidental.

The cases in Unit One are focused on the child care worker, first as an individual whose personal needs and emotions often become involved in his job for better or for worse, and then as a worker in a responsible, essentially professional role. This material is presented first because it appears to underlie successful child care practice. The individual who cannot handle the substantial personal pressures of this kind of work or cannot accept and meet his responsibilities to the youngsters in his care and to the organization which employs him is a poor candidate for a child care position. Thus, in addition to helping lay the groundwork for success, the cases in Unit One may help uncertain individuals determine more clearly whether the work seems appropriate for them.

In Unit Two, the emphasis shifts to the youngsters—as individuals, in groups, and as they relate to child care workers. Unit Three is concerned with the institutional setting and the formal and informal program that provides the context for the work of child care personnel. Unit Four focuses on staff relationships with particular emphasis on the child care worker as he interacts with colleagues, supervisors, and administrators. The cases in Unit Five portray the child care worker's contacts with people outside the immediate institutional environment, primarily parents and individuals encountered during activities off grounds.

Part Three provides discussion questions for each case. These are designed to broaden and deepen the reader's understanding of the issues. For best results they should not be consulted until after an attempt has been made to identify and analyze the major issues in a case, so they are presented separately from the cases. The list of references at the end of the book suggests a variety of materials that may be of interest and value to readers responsible for the training and supervision of child care personnel as well as to child care workers themselves. Several of the references relate specifically to the case study method as it has been developed and applied in other fields.

There is a considerable degree of variation among institutions in the terminology used to designate particular categories of individuals, living facilities, and so on. As indicated above, we have chosen to refer to the people who work with youngsters in their living groups and oversee such daily routines as getting up, eating, and bedtime as "child care workers." Although this appears to be the most widely used designation, other titles that may refer to essentially the same role include cottage parent, counselor, supervisor, aide, child care specialist, child care technician and, particularly in other countries, "educateur."

In many institutions the term "supervisor" refers to the person who supervises child care personnel rather than to individuals who work directly with the youngsters. Child care personnel may also be supervised by the child care director, child care coordinator, cottage coordinator, or someone with a different title, but the supervisors of child care workers are usually referred to in the cases as supervisors or child care directors. It should be noted that the term "supervisor" is not used in this book to refer to those who work directly with youngsters, as in the case in some (particularly correctional) institutions.

The institutionalized young people are referred to most frequently in the cases as "youngsters," the term that seemed to offer the greatest flexibility in terms of age, sex, and kind of institution. Living units are usually referred to as "cottages" and sleeping areas as "dorms," since these appear to be among the most common designations and are least specific to any particular type of institution. The terms "caseworker" and "therapist" are generally used interchangeably in the book, as is often the case in institutional settings, although practice on this varies widely.

Institutional policies regarding how youngsters may address child care personnel vary. Probably most frequently the use of a title (for example, Mr. Jones) is expected, although this is optional in many institutions. Certain staff members acquire special titles (for example, Mr. J.; Pop), and first names are often used where they are permitted, particularly with older youngsters and younger child care workers. In this book first names are used in some situations and formal titles in others. Of course, the reader will want to translate these usages to reflect whatever policy or custom exists at an institution where he may be working and/or to reflect his own preferences in this area.

Finally, we have attempted in the cases to convey the flavor of institutional life and the incidents portrayed as clearly as possible. This requires the use of language often not put into print, but it is printed here because it is essential. Although such language is probably used less frequently in the cases than in most institutions, it appears to the authors that the extent and manner of its use here faithfully reflects the feeling qualities that are essential to the effective use of the material.

The authors hope that this material and the consideration it stimulates will not only be helpful to prospective or practicing child care workers and, through them, to the youngsters in their care, but will also contribute to readers' understanding of themselves and the full range of their interpersonal relationships.

Part One
Institutional Child Care Practice
and the Case Study Method

TOWARD EFFECTIVE
INSTITUTIONAL CHILD CARE

THE JOB OF THE CHILD CARE WORKER

Although the specific tasks and responsibilities of child care workers may be defined somewhat differently in different institutions, many basic elements appear to be common to most institutional settings. Based on a study of a variety of such situations, it has been suggested that most child care positions include the following areas of responsibility:

1. Participating personally in the planned, daily routine of group living, including awakening the children in the morning and putting them to bed at night, and—depending on the diagnosed degree of dependency of individual members of the group—supervising, guiding, and encouraging socially acceptable habits regarding body hygiene, personal grooming, toilet training, table manners, and dealing with others.
2. Supervising the provision of food, clean clothes and bedding, and other items and services needed to meet the requirements of reasonably comfortable and socially acceptable group living, as well as the special needs of individual children as determined by their therapists.
3. Providing first aid and nursing care—under medical supervision—for the child who is injured or sick.
4. Providing and symbolizing security to the children in care by maintaining discipline and order in and around the living quarters and on outings as well, keeping the demands of individual children in balance with the needs of the group as a whole.
5. Participating with the children in both planned and casual recreation and other activities such as household chores and other work projects designed to promote a healthful peer experience

for the children and to provide them with a meaningful and socially acceptable outlet for accumulated physical energy and pent-up emotions.

6. Stimulating the children to seek knowledge and orienting them toward the social norms that govern life both within and outside the institution.

7. Interpreting, facilitating, and enforcing the institution's policies and providing information to and consulting with other staff members about individual children.*

As the central importance of child care work to the overall success of institutional programs has become clearer, however, new concepts of the child care worker's job that go beyond these specifics have emerged. Increasingly child care personnel serve as the coordinators of youngsters' lives in the institution. Thus it has been suggested that,

> In a residential unit, the child care workers should be able to hold the child's ongoing life all of a piece while the child is being educated, receiving psychotherapy, speech therapy, dance lessons, or whatever. Further, the child care worker should be respected as the coordinator of the child's day, determining where he is able to go and when, to keep him from being fragmented by services and servers.†

From this perspective the child care worker is the person to whom institutionalized youngsters can look for the stability, order, and security that are so often missing from their lives both in the institution and outside. Although this concept of the job has not been broadly

*Hromadka, Van G., *Child care worker on the road to professionalization.* Hawthorne, N. Y.: Hawthorne Center for the Study of Adolescent Behavior, Jewish Board of Guardians, 1967 (mimeo.), pp. 9-10.

†Chambers, Guinevere S., Opening Address. In Virginia E. Besaw (Ed.), *Proceedings and discussion: National Conference on Curricula for the Career Ladder in the Child Caring Professions.* Pittsburgh: Department of Child Development and Child Care, School of Health Related Professions, University of Pittsburgh, 1969, p. 14.

implemented to date, it appears to hold the promise of more effective institutional programs in the future. In addition to the specific kinds of duties listed above, in this view,

> ... the special function of child care in the residential treatment center is to help the children negotiate the various complex systems that they must mobilize for their own use in order to get better and get out. Each of these systems—the cottage, the school, the clinic, and others—presents the child with certain demands and opportunities designed to add its special function to the total pattern of treatment; and the child care worker is strategically placed to assist both the child and the system to do what they are supposed to do together. Oriented thus to the *encounter* between the children and their systems, the worker moves to facilitate the work between the two and finds it unnecessary to choose between them or to declare his loyalty to one or the other. Instead, he acts from the assumption that the child and the institution have a common stake in the treatment process, that the network of treatment systems is complicated and difficult to negotiate, and that his assigned function is to mediate these transactions. Thus, in any given encounter between a worker and a child, the central question is, What system are you trying to help him use? And in every contact with a system representative, the central question is, How are you helping this system reach out and incorporate which children into its part of the treatment pattern?*

It should be noted that this view refers not only to helping youngsters and adult specialists work more effectively together but also to facilitating productive kinds of interaction among the youngsters themselves. The effective implementation of this approach, which views child care as the key, central institutional staff position, depends in part on having the support of the institutional structure and supervisory personnel. There is, however, much that child care workers can do on

*Schwartz, William, *"The practice of child care in residential treatment."* Paper presented at the Bellefaire Centennial Symposium, Cleveland, May 24, 1968 (mimeo.), p. 11.

their own if they can establish effective working relationships throughout the institution.

It is the tasks cited above that normally define the child care worker's function, and the way he carries them out largely determines his impact on the youngsters in his care. "Treatment" impact can perhaps best be viewed as healthy development, a particularly complex and difficult goal for institutionalized youngsters. Thus each part of the job as described above has dual significance, its immediate objective and its potential for promoting healthy development; and each contact between a child care worker and a youngster has treatment implications. Effective child care work, therefore, entails consideration in any given situation of both the immediate objectives and the opportunities for longer range treatment impact on those involved.

Many youngsters have enough zest, spirit, and positive motivation to help adult leaders who are working with them. In many institutional settings, however, the youngsters may appear passive and defeated or actively negative, thus requiring child care workers to bring substantial personal strength and conviction to the task.

In summary, the frequent designation of child care personnel as "cottage parents" or "house parents" reflects the fact that all the duties described above are closely related to the kinds of things parents do with and for their children in healthy, intact family situations. Thus although child care workers do not function as true parents, they do supervise the routines of living, helping the youngsters to get up, washed, and dressed in the morning, eating with them, making sure that the cottage is cleaned, helping them get to bed at night, and so forth. Like parents, they help to provide for youngsters' less tangible needs by, for example, helping with schoolwork, listening to problems, providing adult companionship, stimulating activities, sharing joys and sorrows, establishing limits, fostering a healthy climate or atmosphere in the cottage, and setting a good example. Like parents, they also help to organize the youngsters' lives so that various experiences, such as school, can be utilized as effectively as possible, and they try to support growing maturity and independence by providing increased freedom and autonomy as youngsters are able to handle it. Each of these experiences provides an opportunity for the child care worker to facilitate the healthy development of the youngsters in his care.

TOWARD A PHILOSOPHY OF INSTITUTIONAL CHILD CARE

We have just examined briefly what the child care worker does. His philosophy and that of the institution in which he works do much to determine how he does it. Each institution has its own philosophy, whether it is stated explicitly or is implicit in the way the institution is operated, and the philosophy does much to determine the institutional atmosphere or climate. It includes the beliefs and values according to which life in the institution is organized and the child care techniques are used or rejected. Most institutions today share a common philosophical core including such values as commitment to rehabilitation of youngsters rather than custody alone, the rights of individual youngsters, respect for their natural families and home backgrounds, the avoidance of unnecessarily harsh punishment, and the like. They may differ, however, in preferred modalities of treatment, program emphases, expectations for youngsters and staff members, and so forth.

Since child care workers are usually happiest and most effective in settings whose philosophy mirrors their own, candidates for child care positions would do well to think through their own philosophies and to ascertain those of the institutions in which they are interested before accepting employment. The importance of an institution's philosophy to the development of the youngsters in its care is reflected in Plato's observation that, "What is honored in a land is cultivated there."

SIX REQUIREMENTS FOR EFFECTIVE CHILD CARE WORK

1. The effective child care worker is clear about his **goals.** At every stage it is important that specific goals or objectives be developed for the group and for individual youngsters—with their participation, if possible—to guide the child care worker and other institutional personnel in their work. Goals provide a focus for consistent staff efforts and a standard for evaluation and thus are fundamental to the success of the program.

2. The effective child care worker uses **relationship.** Much as the sculptor works with clay and the writer with words, the child care worker utilizes relationship as the basic substance or medium with which he works. Having a relationship with the youngsters in his care not only eases the worker's tasks in getting the necessary routines of group living accomplished—such as getting the cottage clean—but also appears to be essential if such experiences are to have treatment impact. To clarify the point, we need only compare how we, ourselves, are likely to respond to personal advice or criticism offered by a casual acquaintance with our likely response if it comes from a trusted, respected friend. This principle operates in our interactions with other staff personnel as well as with the youngsters: Relationship increases the potential effectiveness of our work, and it appears to be essential if we are to have a lasting impact on the youngsters in our care.

3. The effective child care worker is an **adult.** Although the child care worker does many of the kinds of things that parents do, he is not really a parent to the youngsters in his care, and this distinction is often an important one. But he must, nonetheless, function as a responsible adult, allied with the general policies and practices of the institution and charged with the duty of meeting many of the needs of the youngsters in his care. Therefore the relationships he establishes with the youngsters are not between peers or equals, although it is good practice to give youngsters as much freedom and control over themselves as they can effectively handle, but between adults in authority and youngsters in their care. The child care worker should retain the initiative and control over both himself and, when necessary, over the youngsters. In particular, he should attempt to elude two kinds of "traps" often prepared, whether consciously or not, by youngsters for unwary adults—becoming caught up in fruitless battles of will or succumbing to the standards and values of the group. In either case he would be functioning on the level of the youngsters.

4. The effective child care worker functions as a **professional.** Although they may lack the formal training generally associated with professional service, child care workers are charged with the complex, essentially professional task of working with usually troubled youngsters toward the achievement of treatment goals. They are

expected to apply the developing body of knowledge in this area, not routinely but differentially, as seems appropriate with various children in a wide variety of situations that may arise on the job. As a professional the effective child care worker should also try to be aware of his own behavior and the reactions of others on the job and to use himself and his relationships planfully to accomplish the objectives of his work. This is perhaps the greatest challenge, since the worker must attempt to be spontaneous and genuine in relating to the youngsters in his care while not permitting his emotional involvement to impede his professional judgment. This is a key problem that child care work shares with psychiatry, social work, teaching, and related fields.

5. The effective child care worker is a **generalist.** An institution may have many specialists working with the youngsters in its care—psychiatrists, social workers, teachers, recreation workers, nurses, and others—each of whom may be more skilled in his own field than the child care worker could be. But the child care worker alone is responsible for youngsters "across the board." Within an hour, his work may range from calming a troubled boy, to helping another with his schoolwork, to umpiring or joining with his group in a softball game, to providing first aid, to judging that the help of one of the specialists is needed and interpreting the situation to him. As a generalist the child care worker provides the closest approximation to a complete model of adult functioning that is available to the youngsters. They see him at work, at play, and at rest, and they relate to him in a wide variety of situations which he should be equipped to handle either directly or by referral. When referral is necessary, the process should be handled in a way that will increase youngsters' confidence both in the child care worker and in the special services with which they will be involved. Of course, the child care worker also functions as a specialist in child care, and he may frequently be consulted as such, but he is a generalist in the overall institutional context in that he must be able to relate to each aspect of the situation and each specialty as it touches upon the youngsters' lives and progress. He is also their most direct link with the reality of life's demands and opportunities as reflected in the institutional program.

6. The effective child care worker is a member of a **team.** Overall

treatment processes in the institution, including goal setting as well as implementation, are ideally carried out through the cooperative effort of the total institutional staff. The various specialists, although they may be concerned with the total personality of each child, tend to focus their efforts in limited areas. Teachers usually pay particular attention to academic and vocational learning, clinical personnel often focus on emotional problems, recreation workers are mainly involved with sports and hobby activities and associated skills, the medical staff looks primarily at physical health, and the like. It is often the case that only the administrator, who may necessarily be more remote from individual youngsters, and the child care worker are directly and centrally concerned with the full range of youngsters' relationships and development, although clinicians share this concern in many treatment-oriented settings. Therefore it is often the child care worker who is in the best position to help the various specialists to coordinate their work in the service of the child, and to help the child to integrate and use what the specialist can offer him. It is also the child care worker who can identify potential problems at an early stage to be referred for the attention of the appropriate specialists if that seems indicated. Finally, it is often the child care worker's task to help implement prescriptions developed by educational, psychological, medical, or other specialists. Thus the child care worker is a key member of the institutional team and must be able to work in a team relationship with his colleagues in various disciplines if the institutional program is to be maximally effective.

Although it would be impossible to include all the details of effective child care work in a single chapter, the general description of the job, the conscious development of a philosophy of child care, and the six basic requirements suggested above provide specific criteria that can be used by child care personnel to plan their own behavior when analyzing the cases to follow or "on the job." If a child care worker is clear on his *goals*, uses *relationship*, and operates as an *adult*, a *professional*, a *generalist*, and a member of a *team*, it seems likely that he will be doing an effective job. The specifics remain to be developed by workers and prospective workers in the process of supervised case analysis, as described on the following pages.

THE CASE STUDY METHOD

Effective child care work has an intangible quality that is difficult to communicate adequately in words. The best we can hope to do on a purely verbal level is to teach *about* child care; but merely knowing the facts does not make an individual an effective practitioner—just as one can "know" verbally all the facts about swimming without being able to swim a stroke. At least in part this is because effective child care practice involves subtle, nonverbal behavior and communication. Basic elements include comfort with oneself and awareness and acceptance of one's feelings and the impact of youngsters' behavior on them. Becoming an effective child care worker is therefore a process of personal development. Case studies can be helpful because they permit the direct, active, although vicarious, involvement of learners in realistic child care situations. The cases are appropriate for individual or group analysis, but learning is maximized when these approaches are combined. The basic purpose of cases, however, is to stimulate thought about them and their implications.

The cases presented in this book are narratives of significant situations that occurred, or could have occurred, in a variety of institutional settings. Many were handled unsuccessfully when they arose. Only the circumstances are given, with such background information as may be necessary for clarification. What was actually (or could have been) done and the outcomes are intentionally omitted. Thus the cases are "open end"; they present a situational and emotional context but stop at a point where a decision must be made by at least one of the people portrayed, usually a child care worker. The critical point may be an emergency requiring immediate handling or an opportunity for the child care worker to provide a constructive experience for the youngsters, his colleagues, and himself. It frequently combines both, since most crises contain within them the seeds of human growth. In this sense the cases can be viewed as "opportunity events" available to be seized and used by child care and other personnel. Whether they turn out to be stepping stones or stumbling blocks depends on how they are handled.

Although the cases typically present problems to be solved, readers should attempt to focus on total, multidimensional situations rather than simply on the "problem" presented by a particular youngster or staff member. Thus users should analyze the cases and make decisions about what they would do in terms of the complex human relationships involved and fundamental principles, beliefs, and values.

Just as is usually true in actual situations that arise in institutional work, the cases have no single "right" answers. Problems must be handled in accordance with the personalities and needs of the people involved, always in the light of basic values. In practice, solutions are frequently developed over a period of time. Of course, many of the cases do not illustrate the smoothness, warmth, and even tedium that may characterize a significant proportion of institutional life, since this is not their purpose. Readers with institutional experience may recognize many of the situations as similar to ones in which they have themselves been involved.

Careful study of the cases will reveal that there are various ways of looking at each. It will be seen that each of the characters in a given case may perceive the situation differently. From his own frame of reference the view held by each may be understandable. As this becomes clear to the reader he can begin to establish the habit of seeking a constructive solution to a crisis rather than merely seeking someone on whom to place the blame. This is much more difficult when one is actually involved in a situation, and case study helps learners (using "safe" somewhat impersonal materials) to develop the ability to stand back and observe situations objectively before making decisions. The cases provide a somewhat limited picture, of course, (just as in most actual situations not all the facts are evident,) and so it becomes necessary to identify the problems, make decisions, and take action based on partial knowledge. Thus efforts at analysis and inference can be stimulated, and operational meaning can be given to abstract verbal principles of child care practice.

Group analysis of cases through discussion in classroom and other settings, particularly after the individuals have considered the cases themselves, can help participants to broaden and deepen their understandings and insights. The underlying motivations of various characters and the consequences of alternative courses of action usually become clearer as some group members contribute insights that others have overlooked. As members identify, consciously or unconsciously, with the characters described, other group members may become better able to visualize the overall implications of the situations portrayed.

The case method places the primary responsibility for learning where it belongs—on the learner. This is especially true in group case analysis, where each individual is expected to contribute to the success of a group effort for the benefit of all, just as in the institution itself. In this way learners can begin to see themselves as collaborators with their instructors and supervisors, working toward common goals, rather than as "sponges" absorbing knowledge flowing from above. The latter process would hardly promote the maximum development of confident, effective child care performance.

In addition, effective child care work requires a feeling of camaraderie and joint responsibility for the realization of objectives shared by workers and the youngsters in their care. Only as prospective workers learn to function in this kind of relationship to those with authority over them will they be able to work comfortably and effectively as authority figures with youngsters, many of whom are likely to be confused in their own relationships with authority.

It is not only with regard to authority that group analysis of cases provides prospective child care workers with opportunities to improve their patterns of relationship and thereby their potential effectiveness on the job. On one level, group discussion of a case is centered on the content of the case itself. At the same time, however, the participants in the discussion are involved in a group situation and, consciously or unconsciously, are taking various roles and doing things that promote or impede the group's progress toward its goals. Such situations often resemble those of institutional life, where the effectiveness of the enterprise also depends on the effectiveness of the interpersonal behavior of the people involved. In this context the case material serves as the focus around which the group experience is centered. It is important that the group be aware of its own functioning if learning is to be maximized. The roles taken by each member at various times, and their appropriateness or inappropriateness, should be observed and discussed.

It should be noted that although agreement in the group on a given case may be more comfortable, it is not a required outcome of group case analysis. On the contrary, no individual should be pressured to join in a consensus of opinion as long as he believes himself to possess a significantly different and valid insight. On the other hand individuals are responsible to the group not to permit emotional or irrelevant personal factors to obstruct its actions. Although agreement on principal may not be complete, the group must strive to find agreement on action so that it will not be immobilized. It is here that the group discussion approach has its greatest usefulness, by providing group members with an actual human relations situation in which they can develop and practice interpersonal behavioral skills that will enable them to function effectively in a variety of situations on the job. Techniques of group case analysis are discussed more fully in the Appendix.

HOW TO ANALYZE A CASE

Eleven specific steps in the process of case analysis are presented below followed by a conceptual framework that may help readers get a "handle" on the case material. Both the steps and the concepts are illustrated in the sample case analysis that follows. It is sometimes helpful to make notes, however rough, in the course of developing a case analysis.

ELEVEN STEPS IN CASE ANALYSIS

1. Read the case carefully.
2. Identify the central issue or issues, both immediate and basic, that seem to be involved and the specific decisions that need to be made in order of priority.
3. Try to understand and put into words the needs and feelings of each of the characters portrayed or implied in the case and why each one does what he does.
4. Identify any characters whom you may favor, dislike, praise, or blame, and try to understand why you react to them in this way rather than more objectively.
5. Determine the present alternatives for action and the probable immediate and long-range consequences of each.
6. Decide what specific action, if any, should be taken, given the situation as presented, and why. It is important to select a concrete alternative—what you would do—even though it may be less than ideal, and to understand its pros and cons and your reasons for favoring it.
7. Consider how the situation might have been foreseen and the crisis prevented or directed in more constructive ways.
8. Consider the discussion questions provided for the case being

studied to see if they suggest any issues or insights that you may have overlooked.

9. Compare your analysis and conclusions with those of others, such as classmates, colleagues, or supervisors, preferably in a group discussion situation. Sometimes it is helpful if the individual participants analyze a case separately before group discussion; at other times the group may find it more appropriate to consider a case "cold." The focus of attention in group analysis of cases should be on the functioning of the group and its members as well as on the case itself. Role playing and other techniques may be helpful. Group analysis of cases is discussed more fully in the Appendix.

10. You may wish to use the chapter headings and the short descriptions of the cases in the Tables of Cases at the beginning of each chapter to identify other cases that raise related issues, perhaps in more complex form, for comparative purposes. Comparable cases from your own experience may also provide new insights.

11. Reconsideration of the same case after a lapse of time, preferably in comparison with a written or tape-recorded summary of the original analysis, may lead to broader and deeper understanding. Perhaps surprisingly, there can be marked differences, and one can often see evidence of his own growth in this kind of exercise. Any discrepancies should, of course, be studied until they are understood.

It should be noted that not all the cases lend themselves to each of the steps listed here, and the reader should adjust the process of analysis accordingly.

SIX BASIC CONCEPTS FOR CASE ANALYSIS

The six concepts presented here—opportunity events, interventions, outcomes, process, long-range impact, and messages—suggest a way of looking at the cases and provide a perspective for completing the steps just described. All of the significant considerations in case analysis and effective child care practice can be viewed in terms of one or more of these basic concepts.

The cases represent isolated segments of the stream of behavior in institutional life, incidents that we view as **opportunity events**—opportunities for child care workers to influence the stream of behavior and program impact. Opportunity events may consist of crises demanding that the child care worker step in and act, the apparent lack of anything "happening," or seemingly positive occurrences. Although crises are often the most dramatic opportunity events and the easiest to capture in case material, they are not the only ones and may not be the most important. In defining the central issue or issues of a case or situation, one is attempting to state the nature of the opportunity it contains.

The response of the child care worker to an opportunity event—what he does—is an *intervention.* It may involve staying out of a situation as well as the more frequent "doing something." The cases end at a point where the child care worker is called on to make a key intervention in this sense. The precipitating opportunity event may be an overheard conversation among the youngsters, a critical point in a conversation with a youngster, or a difference of opinion with a colleague. The task of the student, after he determines the potential significance of what is happening, is to decide what, if anything, he should do or say under the circumstances to help achieve the goals of his work. This is the intervention.

The immediate result of what the child care worker does is referred to here as the *outcome.* The outcome may be a significant change in the stream of ongoing behavior, such as when two youngsters who have been fighting are stopped. This can be accomplished in a number of ways—they can be physically separated and restrained, they can be spoken to, the fight can end spontaneously, and so forth. The child care worker can choose among a number of alternatives in most cases, hopefully on the basis of likely results over longer time spans, although immediate requirements of the situation, such as protection when youngsters are in danger, must be recognized as well.

The child care worker's sensitivity to *work in progress* (or *process*)—the ongoing development of the young people in his care—may influence markedly his handling of a given situation. For example, a youngster who is unable to control his temper and rages out of control when he is angry may need to be restrained physically, whereas it may be important to depend more on talking to a youngster who is consciously involved in the process of learning to control his tantrums.

Knowledge of this kind of background information permits child care workers to plan their interventions on an individualized basis so as to meet the particular needs of each youngster at a given time except when emergency situations prevent it. Work in progress can also refer to a child care worker's interactions with others on the staff, such as when he considers the timing of a request to his supervisor or wonders whether he knows a particular colleague well enough to offer a suggestion. A child care worker may also view his own professional development in this light, recognizing, for example, his increasing ability to avoid setting himself up for battles of will with the youngsters.

The major objectives of institutional programs are typically stated in terms of long-range goals for personal development, good citizenship, and so forth, and the child care worker's ultimate concern should be with the *long-range impact* of his work in those areas. We do not, however, have the kind of precise scientific knowledge in this field that would enable us to know or to predict with certainty the long-range impact of a particular kind of intervention. The variety of possible interventions, the meanings they have for the youngsters, the experiences encountered in the interim, and the possible long-range outcomes are all too numerous and complex. In the absence of scientific certainty we establish institutional objectives and an institutional "philosophy"—a system of beliefs about how the objectives can best be achieved.

Institutional philosophy is expressed in practice via specific policy guidelines, through which institutions provide child care workers with a frame of reference to organize their efforts to achieve long-range impact. Clearly stated policies also help child care workers provide a consistent environment with well-defined expectations for institutionalized youngsters, something that appears to be both essential for healthy development and often missing from institutionalized youngsters' backgrounds. Thus whereas a tantrum may need to be stopped so the worker can maintain group control, and while how he stops it may depend in part on considerations of work in progress with the individual youngster, the institutions's philosophy and policies provide a context that defines and delimits the child care worker's alternatives. For example, physical punishment may be contrary to policy in a given institution. Even though it might be effective at a given moment, it is excluded as an option because of its presumed long-range impact. It is important therefore that a child care worker have a clear understanding of the policies of the institution in which he works. In part they reflect the institution's implicit or explicit assumptions regarding the probable long-range impact of various kinds of possible interventions.

The consequences of interventions—whether in immediate outcomes, influences on work in progress, or long-range impact—depend largely on the *messages* that the interventions communicate to the youngsters. In other words how the youngsters or others perceive what the child care worker is doing does much to determine its influence. Child care workers must therefore try to make sure that their behavior communicates what they intend. How they say and do things may be at least as important as what they say and do. Misunderstandings are particularly likely with institutionalized youngsters, since they are often less able than most young people to interpret favorably what adults do. Also, anyone is more likely to misunderstand when he is under stress than when he is not.

Messages are often perceived by the recipient as mixed or conflicted and consequently may be confusing. This occurs most frequently when there is a disparity between what is said in words and what is conveyed nonverbally. The familiar line, "Do as I say, not as I do," implies this kind of difficulty, since youngsters tend to do what we do rather than what we say when there is a discrepancy. For example, it may be difficult for a child care worker who is dirty and unkempt to convince youngsters to keep themselves clean and neat. Likewise a worker can hardly expect to influence a group not to reject one of the youngsters if his own distaste for the scapegoat is apparent. It has been said that attitudes are "caught" rather than "taught," and this principle applies to most of what the child care worker is trying to convey. A good example is worth a thousand words.

Mixed messages can appear in more subtle ways as well. For example, a child care worker who encourages youngsters to bring their problems to him but appears to favor youngsters who are strong and self-sufficient may wonder why he hears about so few of the youngsters' problems. The worker who learns of an infraction "in confidence" will need to weigh the message he would give to the youngsters involved by ignoring the infraction against what he would say to them by reporting it and thus seeming to violate their trust. Will they trust him in the future? How important is it that they trust him? Will it affect their trust of adults in general? Their trustworthiness? How can such dilemmas be avoided, or handled before they force such a "lesser of two evils" kind of choice?

In summary, eleven specific steps and six concepts have been suggested as the basis for case analysis. *Opportunity events* are represented by the individual cases. *Interventions*, what the child care worker does, lead to immediate *outcomes*, which are often closely linked to the handling of emergency situations. Effective child care work is also concerned, however, with *work in progress* (or *process*) and *long-range impact,* as well as with *messages* conveyed by the child care worker in handling each situation.

In the process of case analysis, alternative interventions can be explored along with their probable consequences and the messages they appear to convey. The structure of the precipitating incident can be reviewed to determine whether and how earlier intervention might have permitted the situation to be restructured along more constructive lines and problems avoided. Consideration of the discussion questions, related cases, and reanalysis after a time lapse may add new insights.

AN ILLUSTRATIVE CASE ANALYSIS

A sample case, "Mr. Clean," is presented in this section, followed by examples or suggestions as seem appropriate for applying the eleven steps and six basic concepts that have been proposed above to analyze it. It should be noted that this analysis is only an illustration, designed to help make the methods and values of case analysis more concrete and meaningful to the reader. Therefore additional valid perspectives on the case are likely to present themselves to the interested, sensitive reader. As has been discussed above there are no single "right" answers, so it is usually most illuminating if each reader can add his own views to those of others, always in the context of basic objectives and philosophy, before a course of action is selected.

1. Read the case carefully:

MR. CLEAN

Just as John Evans was walking into the cottage recreation room, he heard a loud burst of laughter from the boys clustered in front of the television set. "What's so funny?" he asked, smiling. He was an experienced child care worker and he could sense that the boys were not just laughing at the program.

"It's that commercial," one of the boys replied. "They offered you double your money back if that cleaner didn't work, and Red said we'd pay triple if they'd just come out and use it on Chester."

"You've got to admit it's pretty bad, Mr. Evans," added Red, a little embarrassed. "Skip and I room with that slob, and it's getting hard to take. We tried everything. Yelling at him, freezing him out. We even tried to be nice to him, but nothing seems to work. He's a born pig! Even the staff can't make him shape up."

"Just a minute, Red," John replied. The television was forgotten by now and all the boys were looking at him. "Chester is new here. He'll learn. He's upstairs finishing his bed right now."

"Come on, Mr. Evans," persisted Red, beginning to push a little harder. "He's been here almost two months already, and you know he's a shithead. You wouldn't like to live with him, would you?"

"Maybe he does have some things to learn about keeping clean," replied John. "That could be one of the reasons he's here. Everybody's problems are a little different, but we try to work with you guys whatever your problems are. Let me see what I can do," he concluded, turning toward the door. As he left the room, he could hear the boys whispering among themselves.

John climbed the stairs and walked toward Chester's room. The boys have a point, he thought, as he walked through the door and got a whiff of the stale sour odor. Chester was on his bed leafing aimlessly through a comic book.

"I thought I sent you up here to make your bed, Chester," said John.

"I made it," the boy replied.

"It doesn't look made to me," said John. "It looks like maybe you pulled the blanket up a little, but that's all. Anyway, I'd like to talk to you for a while. Let's go down to the office."

Chester did not protest, and they walked downstairs and into the cottage office together. John was forced to admit to himself that there had not been much change in the situation since Chester's arrival almost two months before. Glancing again at the youngster, he noticed that Chester had been poking and squeezing at his face again, thereby turning a mild complexion problem into a full-blown, almost oozing case of acne. This poor kid is really a mess, thought John. The first thing we have to do to help him is to get him to care about being clean.

"Chester," John began after they had seated themselves, "would you find it easier to shower if we could arrange a special time when you'd be alone? Like now, when the guys are watching TV? We don't care much when you do it, but it's important that you keep yourself clean."

"What for?" asked Chester, almost casually. "I don't need it."

"I disagree," said John, more firmly this time. "I think you . . ."

Chester interrupted. "Look, Mr. Evans," he said, "my therapist said nobody could force me to, anyway."

Before John could reply, he heard sounds from the second floor. "I'll be back in a minute, Chester," he said, and walked quickly up the steps. When he reached the top, he saw Red and Skip pulling Chester's mattress through the door into the hall.

"What's going on here?" John asked sternly as he approached the boys.

"Look, Mr. Evans," Red answered, looking right at John. "We don't want no trouble, honest! But that pig's got our room smelling like a sty. He wets the bed, too, and he never cleans it up. That stink is everywhere. Let him sleep in the hall for a while. Maybe he'll learn to keep clean and get rid of that lousy smell out here."

Glancing back, John noticed that the other boys had apparently heard what was happening and were coming up the stairs. Chester was with them, and John could tell from his expression that he knew what was happening.

2. Identify the central issue or issues, both immediate and basic, that seem to be involved and the specific decisions that need to be made in order of priority.

In dealing with a case or an actual child care situation it is important first to determine where the significant problems and opportunities lie. Additional possibilities may, of course, present themselves during the course of analysis. In "Mr. Clean" the following problem areas may be identified, at least as possibilities, each of which may serve to define the case as an opportunity event:

(a) Chester's difficulty in keeping himself and his things clean
(b) Chester's relationships with the other boys
(c) The attitudes of the other boys toward Chester
(d) The boys' behavior in throwing Chester's bedding into the hall
(e) The child care worker's attitude toward Chester
(f) Cottage cleanliness
(g) Cottage morale

Can you think of others? Which decisions should be made now and which can be deferred for later attention? The reasons for the priorities established should be thought through and understood.

3. Try to understand and put into words the needs and feelings of each of the characters portrayed or implied in the case and why each one does what he does.

To work effectively with youngsters it is important to understand the reasons for their behavior, something they usually cannot tell us directly. In "Mr. Clean," John Evans suddenly finds himself faced with two of Chester's roommates angrily trying to throw the boy's things out of their room. His first inclination is simply to order Red and Skip to put Chester's bedding back where they got it, then to point out to Chester how his stubborn refusal to accede to cottage cleanliness standards is repeatedly getting him into trouble. There may be more to the situation than this, however, and the reader may want to consider the following possibilities, as well as others.

"He's a born pig! Even the staff can't make him shape up." Perhaps Chester simply has not had an opportunity to learn about cleanliness in the process of growing up, or perhaps it was of less concern in his family and neighborhood than it is to the other boys and to John. The boy may therefore be sincerely confused, wondering why everyone seems to be "picking on him" about such a small thing. On the other hand Chester may be using this to get attention and perhaps help, or to express his defiance, especially if he cannot accomplish these goals in any other way. Having seen Chester in a variety of situations, John should begin to be able to assess which of these factors and others may be combining to explain Chester's behavior.

"'Come on, Mr. Evans,' persisted Red, beginning to push a little harder. 'He's been here almost two months already, and you know he's a shithead. You wouldn't like to live with him, would you?'" Red may be voicing his own concern and that of others with Chester's personal habits. He may also be trying to enhance his own status in the group, trying to enlist John on his side in picking on Chester or, by taking matters into his own hands at the end of the case, expressing his own autonomy and independence as an adolescent and his impatience with John's handling of the situation.

". . . the other boys had apparently heard what was happening and were coming up the stairs." Perhaps they wanted to join in the "fun" of tormenting a scapegoat, or perhaps to see how John would handle the challenge to cottage rules and his authority that was implicit in the boys' behavior. They may have simply heard the commotion and welcomed the incident as a relief from the boredom and routine of institutional life. For whatever reason, they are there as an audience for whatever happens next, and John must consider them, too, in deciding what to do.

" '. . . my therapist said nobody could force me to, anyway.' " Therapists, too, have reasons for what they say, reasons that are normally based on youngsters' needs. Chester's therapist might, for example, have been attempting to ease the pressure on the boy, to win his confidence, or to let him experience the consequences of his behavior. There is also the possibility that the therapist never said what Chester claimed he did. Whatever the true situation is, it may not have been communicated to the child care worker, but now it seems important that he talk with the therapist. In any event John must consider the needs of the group as well as Chester's individual needs and find a way to reconcile them if they are in conflict.

It is often important also to consider the feelings of individuals who are not directly portrayed in the case, but whose existence and influence can logically be inferred. For example, John is clearly not a free agent. He is responsible to a supervisor who, presumably, is concerned about cottage cleanliness and its implications for both health and appearance as well as about the ability of the program to help the youngsters being served. Thus the attitudes of the supervisor might serve to limit John's alternatives in a real situation. A related factor is the influence of institutional policies. Fire regulations, for instance, might require that the hallway be kept clear at all times, so John could not let Chester sleep in the hall even if that seemed to be a reasonable temporary arrangement to ease the tension.

4. Identify any characters whom you may favor, dislike, praise, or blame, and try to understand why you react to them in this way rather than more objectively.

Inevitably readers will tend to like some of the characters in a case—just as they will tend to like some of the youngsters in a cottage—more than others. Some, for example, may see Chester as a hopeless "slob" and will tend to dislike and reject him for it. Others may feel that Red is unfair and unkind because, for whatever reason, he is taunting a youngster who appears beset with many problems. In this sense we cannot be fully objective. What we can do, however, is to examine and become aware of such feelings and how they may influence our behavior on the job. Otherwise we are likely to "act out" our feelings rather than to do what would be best for those involved. For example, his feelings alone might lead a child care worker to reject Chester or Red, but reflection might suggest that only a close relationship with an adult could help one or both of them. Once the worker recognizes and accepts his feelings, he is in a position to act with more objectivity to help meet youngsters' needs.

The same considerations hold for relationships with others on the staff. A child care worker might react with resentment to the idea that Chester's therapist may have told him that no one could force him to take a shower. If such a feeling is not recognized, it may lead the worker into a "battle of wills" with the therapist, as a result of which the worker might force the youngster to shower as a means of asserting his authority. If such resentment is recognized, the child care worker can handle it more effectively, perhaps by discussing it with the youngster's therapist in an attempt to reach some kind of accord. Too often in such situations youngsters are the victims as staff members act out their own feelings about each other at the youngsters' expense.

Finally, battles of will, whether with colleagues or youngsters, are rarely productive and should be avoided whenever possible. The responsibility for this lies primarily with the staff, since youngsters are often in the institution largely because they need help in just such situations, and it is the role of the staff to model more effective interpersonal behavior for them. Awareness of feelings is an important step in that direction.

5. Determine the present alternatives for action and the probable immediate and long-range consequences of each.

At this point in the analysis, one considers possible interventions and their likely outcomes, effects on work in progress, and long-range impact.

Perhaps the most obvious option available to John is to assert his authority by ordering Red and Skip to return Chester's things to his room and the other boys to go back to watching the television program. After warning Red and Skip not to try it again, he could then return to his interrupted conversation with Chester. The immediate outcome of such a course might be that the boys would obey and the crisis of the moment would be "solved." (If Red and Skip refuse, of course, there is a new problem to be dealt with.) In addition, however, John should be aware of the impact of his intervention on work in progress. Thus his concern is with such questions as these: What will this do to Chester's tenuous relationship with the rest of the group? How will it affect John's own relationships with Red and Skip? With Chester? By considering such questions as these, the reader can begin to evaluate the advisability of this and other alternatives. On the job, of course, this process must often be almost instantaneous; the cases provide the chance for learning under less pressured circumstances.

Some apparent alternatives will be eliminated due to considerations of long-range impact, which we have above related closely to institutional philosophy and policy. For example, John could conceivably throw Chester and his bedding outside, telling him not to return until he could keep himself and his things clean. It seems likely, at least in most situations, that this would not be a viable alternative because of its presumed long-range impact both on Chester and on the other boys, although something like it might be a planned approach in certain circumstances.

Among other alternatives available to John are the following: (a) He could send the other boys downstairs and talk the situation out with Red and Skip; (b) he could include Chester in such a conversation as well as Red and Skip; (c) he could call a cottage meeting to discuss the problem.

There are other options as well and multiple ways of approaching each of the above choices. For example, John could meet with Red and Skip to warn them not to repeat such behavior, to explain more about

Chester's problem to them, or to ask them how they think the problem might best be handled. A variety of the possibilities should be identified and their likely consequences explored.

6. Decide what specific action, if any, should be taken, given the situation as presented, and why. It is important to select a concrete alternative—what you would do—even though it may be less than ideal, and to understand its pros and cons and your reasons for favoring it.

It is at this point that the thought processes outlined above are combined into an intervention strategy planned to meet the immediate situation, to further work in progress, and to promote long-range impact. This makes the exercise more realistic and gives it focus, since in an actual situation a decision must be made. To vacillate and make no decision is, in effect, a decision in itself; in most crises it is a poor one that may lead to an even more difficult situation that will have to be confronted in the future.

The definition of the problem or central issue (2, above) is basic, of course. Given an understanding of the feelings of the characters involved (3, above) and the possible biases of the reader (4, above), it should be possible to choose an alternative (5, above) as the favored approach.

The child care worker may decide that the highest priority issues (after the immediate crisis is resolved) are Chester's cleanliness problem and the boy's relationships with the rest of the group (2). The worker may also feel that the other boys' rejection of Chester is at least partly justified and that Chester's slovenliness is the boy's way of avoiding the difficulties of close relationship with the others; it is his self-erected barrier (3). In these circumstances the worker might first try to end the immediate crisis by forcing Red and Skip to put the bedding back. Then he might "lecture" Chester on the importance of cleanliness both for health reasons and for his relationships with the other boys, perhaps threatening not to intercede the next time something like this happens as well as forcing the boy to shower. The message he would be communicating to the boy in this way might be more one of rejection than one of concern.

However, if the worker recognized that he, himself, felt repelled by Chester's personal habits (4), he might approach the problem differently, perhaps helping Chester to explore why he thinks his roommates did what they did (5). He might select another alternative in addition, such as seeking a conference with Chester's therapist, so that they could combine their resources to help. The message (not necessarily the words) could still be an honest one, "I do not like your behavior," or even, "Your behavior makes me feel angry or distant from you." But the other essential part of the message, "I am concerned and want to try to help," would be there as well.

This does not, of course, provide the "ideal" answer or the "perfect" solution, and there may, indeed, be none. We have presented one possibility among many. The example does, however, illustrate how significant concerns can be brought to bear on a problem and on the decision-making process. In a real situation, presumably, the child care worker would have more facts on which to base this decision as well, although the major considerations would probably be similar. Effective child care workers on the job are frequently forced to act in the face of uncertainty, however, and often with the feeling that they are selecting only the least dangerous or distasteful of a series of poor alternatives.

The case analysis method outlined is largely an organized procedure for arriving at the best decision possible given the circumstances, but in real situations there is rarely time to make detailed analyses before making at least tentative decisions. Thus it is important to develop the habit of analytic thinking so that it occurs almost automatically, and sound decisions can then be made in a crisis.

7. Consider how the situation might have been foreseen and the crisis prevented or directed in more constructive ways.

Most crises represent both a failure and an opportunity event at the same time. Consideration of how the crisis could have been foreseen and forestalled is essential, since it often appears that the present crisis has resulted from the neglect of an earlier opportunity. Particularly in institutional settings, in which contacts are so close and constant, interpersonal problems have a way of mushrooming; therefore prevention is of special concern. When a crisis develops, even optimum handling may leave a residue of negative feeling that can erupt in greater difficulties later. Once begun, a cycle of this sort is difficult to stop, since greater problems require more drastic action, which tends to leave even more potential for negative conflict than was there before. Thus many problems appear in a worsening series over time, and each appearance can be viewed as an opportunity to break the cycle.

Prevention may be considered on different levels, depending on how far back one goes in time and the point of view from which the situation is examined. For the child care worker, the primary question is what he, himself, could have done to foresee and forestall the crises. In "Mr. Clean" the immediate crisis could, perhaps, have been prevented if John had been able to "tune in" earlier and sense the tension in the group regarding Chester and had worked both with Chester and with the rest of the group on its causes. This might have involved helping Chester to adopt different personal habits, but the cleanliness issue may also, as we have seen, be an expression of deeper problems in the boys' patterns of group relationships or elsewhere. If so, it could have been anticipated that the problem would appear in other ways until the underlying issue had been met. Thus in the prevention of problems as well as in handling opportunity events as they arise (actually, two different perspectives on the same thing, since today's missed opportunities are tomorrow's problems), it is essential to try to recognize and deal with basic issues rather than with their surface manifestations alone.

At the same time it should be noted that affecting surface behavior can also help underlying problems; thus a cleaner, physically more appealing Chester would probably feel better about himself and find it easier to overcome relationship problems, since at least he would not repel others at first sight. His cleanliness would also carry the implicit message that he might be ready to try or to begin to explore relationships with others. Such intermediate steps are often necessary to overall progress.

Perhaps the most important point here is that most problems show themselves in a series of opportunity events, any one of which can be grasped and acted on; but the earlier the situation is recognized and handled, the easier and more effective the job tends to be.

There is a difficult paradox with regard to prevention that should also be considered. The key to prevention is anticipation—handling situations before they become problems and handling small problems before they become big problems or crises. On the other hand we may find ourselves victims of the "self-fulfilling prophecy"; by anticipating a problem, we may contribute to its development. In this connection youngsters often appear to meet our expectations. If we trust them, they may tend to be trustworthy; if we look for trouble, we often find it. Both parts of the paradox remain true: It is important to anticipate problems and just as important that we not create problems that would otherwise not exist. Whereas problems beneath the surface are often best exposed so they can be faced and handled, overanticipation may stimulate problems that would not otherwise have developed. There are no easy answers to this dilemma, but sensitive workers who are aware of it and attuned to it will be better equipped to decide when to anticipate problems and when to defer judgment or action.

8. Consider the discussion questions provided for the case being studied to see if they suggest any issues or insights that you may have overlooked.

Pertinent questions follow each case. They are provided as additional stimulants to thought and to help readers focus attention on basic underlying issues. They refer to significant aspects and broader implications of a particular case that might otherwise be overlooked, often including ethical considerations implicit in the situations portrayed. They are intended only as suggestions, however, and are not meant to precede or limit the process of analysis outlined here.

Example

The following question might have been among those listed for "Mr. Clean" had it been presented as one of the cases for analysis in this book.

Would it be a good idea for John to move Chester into a different room with new roommates to give him a "fresh start"? Why or why not?

9. Compare your analyses and conclusions with those of others, such as classmates, colleagues, or supervisors, preferably in a group discussion situation. Group analysis of cases is discussed more fully in the Appendix.

10. You may wish to use the chapter headings and the short descriptions of the cases in the Tables of Cases at the beginning of each chapter to identify other cases that raise related issues, perhaps in more complex form, for comparative purposes. Similarly, comparable cases from your own experience may help provide additional insight.

Compare and contrast the relevant issues raised in Case 2-10, Mixed Messages; Case 3-1, Teach me to Like Me; Case 3-8, Gracious Living; Case 4-4, Helping the Scapegoat; Case 5-2, On Their Own; and Case 11-5, Who Owns the Child?

11. Reconsideration of the same case after a lapse of time, preferably in comparison with a written or tape recorded summary of the original analysis, may lead to broader and deeper understanding. Perhaps surprisingly, there can be marked differences, and one can often see evidence of his own growth in this kind of exercise. Any discrepancies should, of course, be studied until they are understood.

Part Two
The Cases

UNIT ONE
THE CHILD CARE WORKER

1. THE CHILD CARE WORKER
AS A PERSON

To a greater extent than most other jobs, insitutional child care work makes personal, emotional demands on the people involved. The cases in this chapter illustrate a variety of such pressures and patterns of response, providing readers with an opportunity to explore the kinds of feelings that often cause difficulty for child care workers and their implications for performance on the job.

TABLE OF CASES

1.1 BLOWING UP: WHO PAYS THE PRICE?

Tom Owens was doing a slow burn. "Mike, I told you to turn off that radio," he said evenly. "I have something to say to the cottage and I want quiet." The other boys were standing around, waiting to see the outcome.

Mike was smirking and rock music was blaring from the small transistor radio in his hand. "This is our free time and it's my radio. If I want to listen to it, that's my business," he sneered. "If you want to talk to the cottage, I'm not stopping you!"

Tom saw red. It had been a long day and he was fed up with Mike's defiance. Although the youngster had made a lot of progress and Tom liked him, he had recently been challenging the staff at every turn, especially in front of the group; and he had always had a bad temper. "If you want to keep that radio, you'll turn it off now," Tom snapped.

"Says who?" Mike replied, trying to appear unconcerned. Tom advanced toward him. "Keep away from me," Mike muttered, half under his breath.

"Give me that radio!" yelled Tom, grabbing Mike's hand. Almost instinctively, Mike tripped him, and they both landed on the floor. Tom pulled the radio from Mike's hand and turned it off as they scrambled to their feet. "O.K.," Tom said, "get to your rooms, all of you. I want the lights out in twenty minutes, and I'll be up there to check." Slowly but without audible protest, the boys began to go upstairs. Mike glared at Tom but said nothing.

Still furious, Tom sat down at the desk in the cottage office to enter the incident in the cottage log. "At about 9:30," he wrote, "I called the group together to discuss the new cottage work schedule. Mike Grant refused to turn off his transistor radio and, after repeated requests and warnings, I tried to take it away from him. As I took it out of his hand, he tripped me and we both fell to the floor. No one was hurt and I got the radio, but I thought it would be best to end the incident so I sent the kids to their rooms. I think most of them were a little stunned, because they went quietly, even Mike. Mike seems to be getting increasingly difficult, and I think a special case conference might be helpful."

The rest of the evening passed uneventfully. Mike asked Tom when he could have his radio back and Tom told him he could pick it up in the morning, but neither of them mentioned the earlier incident. Before leaving the cottage, Tom wrote a note asking the substitute worker to give Mike the radio since Tom would be off duty in the morning. "Too bad about Mike," he thought on his way home. "He has no father and his mother doesn't seem to be much help. I think we may be just on the verge of reaching him, too. I'll make a point to spend some time with him tomorrow night."

When Tom came on duty the next evening, the group was sullen and Mike was missing. "What's wrong here?" he asked. "Where's Mike?"

"You know," someone muttered.

"Dammit, I don't know!" Tom snapped. "Now what's up?"

"Mike got shipped to the discipline cottage because some dumb child care worker reported him for nothing. Do you expect us to run up and thank you?"

"Mike got what?" gasped Tom. "There must be some mistake." He walked slowly to the cottage office to check the log. "Mike Grant," he read, "was assigned to the discipline cottage until further notice as a result of several incidents culminating in his knocking Mr. Owens to the floor last night, as reported by Mr. Owens." Feeling pained, Tom walked slowly out of the office and saw the boys standing around and glaring at him.

(Supplementary discussion questions, page 291)

1.2 TO CLEAR THE AIR?

Jeff Power stepped out of the child care office to stop Nat, his co-worker, who was on his way out of the cottage.

"What's up?" asked Nat. "You look as though something's wrong."

"Well, not exactly," replied Jeff. "I'm scheduled for my first supervisory session tomorrow. Doesn't that mean Mr. DeWolfe will be reviewing and discussing my log notes for the week?"

"Right," agreed Nat. "What's the problem?"

"I was just getting ready to write up my little encounter with Floyd this morning," said Jeff, "and I don't know exactly how to summarize it."

"It seemed pretty straightforward to me," replied Nat. "Floyd just didn't want to mop that floor, and nothing you said made a damn bit of difference to him. First he tried to con you and when that didn't work, he tried to make you look bad in front of the other kids. DeWolfe knows what Floyd's like when he gets in one of his moods. Just write it up the way it happened."

"I guess you're right. I wish I could have gotten him to do it, though. Boy, was I mad! Well, I'll see you later."

At the supervisory session the next afternoon, everything appeared to be going well. Mr. DeWolfe seemed pleased and complimented Jeff at several points for having handled situations well, particularly as a new child care worker. They had pretty much covered the events of the week when Mr. DeWolfe asked Jeff about the previous day's incident with Floyd. "Weren't you getting angry at him for not doing his job and for all the guff he was giving you?"

Jeff nodded. "I was furious!" he replied.

"Yes," Mr. DeWolfe said, "I can understand that. And sometimes it's a good idea to let kids know they can get us angry. What did you really feel like saying to him?"

Jeff smiled a little sheepishly. "Well, to tell you the truth, I felt like telling him he was 'full of shit.'"

"Perhaps you should have," said Mr. DeWolfe. Pausing a moment, he asked, "What do you think?"

(Supplementary discussion questions, page 291)

1.3 MY MISTAKE!

"Carlos," murmured Hal West to himself as he checked the trip roster at the front of the bus. "We're missing one kid and it's Carlos, of course. Mr. Big, himself!" He turned to John Harmon, the recreation worker who was going along as the staff representative on the volunteer-sponsored trip.

"I hate to keep the Volunteer Association ladies waiting," Hal said, "but I'd better check the cottage for Carlos. I'll be right back."

Hal was feeling less than kindly as he headed for the cottage day room where he saw Carlos sprawled on a couch in front of the television set. "Come on, Carlos," he said sternly, "let's get the show on the road. Everyone else is on the bus and ready to go. Move!"

"Not me, buddy," drawled Carlos, hardly bothering to look up from the television set.

Hal walked over and turned off the program. "Let's go, Carlos," he said. "On the bus! I'm not asking, I'm telling. I've had about enough of your bull."

Carlos held out his left arm. "See that wrist?" he asked. "The nurse says it may be sprained or even broken, and at 9:30 I'm supposed to go and get an X-ray. No bus tour with a bunch of cruddy old ladies for me!"

Hal scanned the morning report before he replied. "Carlos buddy, there's not one word in here about an X-ray scheduled for you, and the whole cottage is listed on the trip roster, so come off it."

Carlos shrugged. "All I know is I saw the nurse last night after I piled into the side of the infirmary. I was chasing that jerk, Eddie. My wrist hurt like hell, so I went right inside and she looked at it and said that it should be X-rayed this morning."

"Why isn't that in the cottage log, then?" asked Hal. "I read the log when I came on duty this morning."

"I guess because I didn't tell anybody when I got back." Carlos replied. "She gave me some aspirin at the infirmary and pretty soon after I got in, I went to bed. So what?"

"So, I think you're just trying to con your way out of this trip, Carlos. You spend more time and spin more stories to end up doing what you want to do than any other kid in the cottage. Let's see what the nurse has to say about it." Hal stalked to the telephone and dialed the infirmary number while Carlos, smiling to himself, turned the television on again.

Just then, Harvey Shore, one of the boys who had been on the bus, came into the cottage. "Mr. West," he called, "Mr. Harmon told me to find out how much longer you'll be. He thinks we better get started because it's a long trip."

The infirmary telephone was busy and Hal slammed down the receiver. "Tell him we'll be right there, Harvey," he said. As Harvey left, Hal turned off the television set again, pulled Carlos to his feet, handed him the jacket he had been sitting on, and began to propel him toward the door.

"Hey, stop it!" yelled Carlos angrily. "Get off my arm . . . that hurts . . . ouch! Look, I'm telling the truth. You gotta believe me!"

Hal did not answer as he continued to march the boy out of the cottage and onto the bus. With a terse, "O.K., you're set!" to John Harmon, Hal turned and walked back to the cottage without a backward glance. Still seething with anger, he hardly heard the bus drive away.

As he described this latest incident with Carlos in the cottage log, Hal wished he had not lost his temper with the boy. He had been trying hard to form a closer relationship with Carlos to help him realize that adults could be trusted and could be helpful, and he hoped this encounter would not prove to be a setback. Still, he felt it was good that he had not permitted the youngster to con him again.

Hal was finishing the log entry when the telephone rang. It was Mrs. Foster, the nurse.

"Please send Carlos Fisk over to the infirmary," she said, as Hal rolled his eyes toward the ceiling. "I'd like to send him out for his X-ray now."

Where do we go from here when Carlos gets back, thought Hal, as he began a little sheepishly to explain to the nurse what had happened.

(Supplementary discussion questions, page 292)

1.4 A LOSS OF FACE

It was Ted's first night on duty alone as a child care worker in Cottage 3 and he was a little nervous. Although he had worked for a week with Steve Garman, his predecessor, he wondered if he was really ready to handle this responsibility by himself. Still he felt he had learned a lot from the orientation and especially from Steve, who had been in charge of Cottage 3 for almost two years.

"The boys will try to test you a lot," Steve had told him, "especially at the beginning. It's very important that you establish yourself as the adult authority even if you make some mistakes at first. After that, things should get a little easier. But if the boys think you're weak and not really 'in charge,' they'll give you no end of trouble."

Ted had kept this in mind as he had watched Steve work. It appeared that Steve had a good relationship with the boys and only rarely had to exert his authority overtly, but when he did, he was firm and direct. Ted was doing his best to establish a similar pattern, and he felt that things had been going pretty well.

The evening had been relatively uneventful so far. Most of the boys were in the basement playing pool, a few were watching television, and the rest were reading magazines or talking. Ted was drifting between the two upstairs rooms when he heard loud shouts coming from the basement. From the top of the stairs, he could see that a fight had broken out between two of the boys who had been playing pool. The others had picked up cue sticks and were jabbing each other and the two who were fighting. As Ted hesitated in confusion, one of the boys picked up a pool ball and threw it across the room. Others followed suit, and Ted's shout of "What's going on here?" was lost in a crash as one of the balls went through a window. He rushed down the stairs and charged into the melee, hoping to disentangle the two boys who had apparently begun the fighting, but quickly decided that there was little he could do without help. Trying to keep calm, he ran to the phone and called the night supervisor.

"I need some help in Cottage 3—fast!" he said. "Can you come over?"

"Don't worry," Joe O'Brien replied, "I'll be right there."

Ted replaced the receiver and leaned up against a wall. The noise in the room below seemed to be subsiding, and he wondered if he should wait for Joe or try again himself. Just then Joe burst through the door and headed straight for the noise without giving Ted even a sideward glance. Ted walked toward the stairs. Joe's burly frame was planted squarely in the doorway.

"All right, you guys, knock it off right now!" he bellowed.

The boys looked up quickly and a hush fell over the room.

"Aw, shit, O'Brien's here," one of them said.

Joe paid no attention. "O.K., you've had your fun. Now get this place cleaned up and get upstairs on the double. You guys will never learn how to get along with each other, will you?"

The boys began picking up balls and cues and returning them to their racks. Alvin started to pick fragments of glass from the broken window. "Get that glass into a wastebasket!" shouted Joe.

"Up yours," Alvin muttered, but he did it anyway.

Finally, Joe seemed to remember Ted, who had been watching the performance in stunned silence.

"Well, I guess everything's under control now," Joe said, "Just call me again if you have any more trouble. That's what I'm here for."

"Thank you," said Ted, feeling a little stupid about it, and Joe left.

The boys were just finishing cleaning up, but Ted felt that the incident should not be allowed to pass unnoticed. "O.K., everybody," he said, "I want all of you in your rooms right now. The lights are going out in twenty minutes, and we'd better not have anything like this again!"

Somebody laughed. "Hey, you guys, look who thinks he's givin' orders now. Don't you think you should call O'Brien back to do that for you?"

(Supplementary discussion questions, page 292)

GOSHEN COLLEGE LIBRARY
GOSHEN, INDIANA 46526

1.5 ONE OF THE BOYS

"Looks good to me," said Roger as he scanned the room carefully, nodding with satisfaction. "The light won't show through, so we won't have to worry about the night watch unless there's too much noise. You guys did a good job."

The boys looked pleased. "It should work," agreed Tony, the acknowledged leader of the group. "Mr. Mantz makes his rounds, but he never comes in unless he hears us or sees lights on."

"Then they'll never know we all stayed up two hours past curfew to watch the late movie on TV," smiled Roger. "That'll be one of our Fletcher Cottage secrets."

"You're all right, Roger," said one of the younger boys with open admiration. "Even if you are a child care worker in this place."

"Thanks," replied Roger quickly, "but no more compliments. Just get finished with your Saturday chores. Tim, open those drapes and pull up the shades. The practice countdown is over. I'll go out to check those hall floors to see if they gleam, like the rule book says!"

The next day Roger was off duty, so he did not have time to think much more about the "after hours" television-watching experiment until he returned to the cottage on Monday. Everything had gone as he had expected. There had been no interference from the night watch, and the log confirmed that he had been unaware of any unusual lights or activity in Fletcher Cottage. The movie, a rousing Western, had left the boys on Cloud Nine, and Roger attributed about half the credit to the movie itself and the rest to the exciting, stealthy circumstances under which it had been seen. Most important, Roger felt, his idea of a "Secret Society" seemed to be taking hold in a way that would help to knit the boys into a closer, more involved group. As if to confirm this opinion, Roger noted that most of the routine cottage chores were being done without the usual need for his reminders. He exchanged knowing smiles with most of the boys as they left for school.

A few minutes later, the cottage telephone rang. It was Roger's supervisor, Mr. Conrad.

"Can you come over to my office for a few minutes?" he asked.

"Sure, Mr. Conrad," replied Roger. "Anything wrong?"

"I don't know," said Mr. Conrad. "I'll see you in a few minutes."

"What happened in your cottage on Saturday night?" Mr. Conrad asked when Roger had seated himself in the office. "One of your kids told someone in another cottage that you arranged for them to see a movie on TV after curfew, and a lot of the other kids around here are pretty upset about it. What's it all about?"

"Well, there really isn't much to tell, Mr. Conrad," replied Roger, smiling. "I set up a kind of 'secret club' for the cottage, to try to bring the kids together, with a few supposedly forbidden treats thrown in to make it a little more convincing. They're really starting to shape up, too, and I think this has a lot to do with it."

"But Roger," said Mr. Conrad, reddening. "How can you build anything worthwhile on that kind of a foundation? Most of these kids are here because they couldn't follow the rules outside. Now you're rewarding them for breaking the rules here, and even helping them. What are we teaching them about values if we 'buy' good behavior that way? And aren't you acting more like one of the kids than an adult leader?"

"Look," began Roger slowly, "what are we really talking about? Two hours of unauthorized time a month? We both know that some cottages waste more than that with fights and arguments that postpone bedtime almost every day! With my idea, all I have to do is act like I'm helping the boys put something over—it isn't hurting anybody—and I have the kids eating out of my hand!"

"I know Fletcher Cottage has a good record," Mr. Conrad replied, "and I know your boys think you're the greatest thing going. The question is, is that enough? And at what price?"

(Supplementary discussion questions, page 293)

1.6 CARING TOO MUCH?

Fred Dixon was relaxing in his room with the morning paper when he heard a tap at his door. "What is it?" he called out resignedly, wishing for a moment that he, like a taxi, was equipped with an Off Duty sign.

"Mr. D.?" came the whispered question.

Pulling himself to his feet, he opened the door to find a small, worried looking youngster standing in the hall.

"Mickey," said Fred in a concerned voice, "you're supposed to be at recreation. What are you doing here?"

"We were on our way to the ball field," explained the boy, "and I just ducked into the cottage for a second. I knew you were in your room. I gotta talk to you!"

"What's the matter?"

"It's about my mother's birthday card," Mickey replied, pulling an envelope out of his jacket pocket. "The one I made in art class. Could you please mail it for me? I got it stamped and everything."

"I thought we talked about that yesterday," said Fred. "You were supposed to take it to the administration building on the way back from school, so it could go out with the office mail. What happened?"

The boy hung his head. "I forgot," he said. "Please take it to the post office for me. It's Saturday and nobody takes any mail to town today, so if you won't take it, I know she won't get it in time. Please, Mr. D.?"

Looking down at the youngster, who seemed to be in genuine anguish, Fred nodded. "O.K., Mickey," he said, "I guess I can take it to the village this morning. I had planned to go out later, anyway."

With a sigh of relief, the boy handed the card to Fred. "Thanks a million, Mr. D.," he said. "I know nobody else would do this for me. I really appreciate it."

"Get back to the rec program, Mickey," said Fred, gently shoving the boy away from the door, "and don't worry about the card being mailed in time. I'll take care of it."

Closing the door, Fred swore softly to himself. "Dammit, why me? Because you're the only dummy who would do it," he thought dryly. "Also, because these kids need someone to feel that they're special and need a little extra attention."

An hour later, Fred had mailed the card and completed a few other errands. Heading back toward the institution, he saw Jess Bell, one of his younger co-workers, waiting at the town bus stop.

"Hey, Jess, like a ride back?" called Fred, bringing the car to a halt.

"Great!" replied Jess as he opened the door and slid into the front seat of the car. "But aren't you going anywhere on your day off?"

Fred glanced at his watch. "I'll be driving out to my sister's house later for dinner," he replied.

Jess nodded. "Been shopping in town?" he asked, noticing some packages on the floor of the car.

"Yes," replied Fred. "I got a few things for myself along with replenishing my bubble gum stock."

"I didn't know you chewed bubble gum," commented Jess with a grin.

"Hardly," laughed Fred. "I just use it as a miracle cure. You know, if the kids are getting upset or starting to stall around, a little thing like discussing the matter while everybody is unwrapping a piece of bubble gum is often very helpful. There were only a couple of pieces left," Fred continued. "It's a good thing I remembered to check before I came into town to mail that birthday card for Mickey. You know, he worked all week to make a hand-painted birthday card for his mother and then forgot to mail it yesterday. The only way she could get it in time for her birthday was for me to take it to the post office before the last mail went out at noon today. Guess kids would forget their heads if they weren't tacked on!"

After a moment's pause, Jess said slowly, "You made a special trip into town to mail a card for Mickey on your day off? You really spoil them, Fred!"

Shaking his head, Fred responded, "No, I don't think so. These kids need someone who really cares about them. After all, we're like their family while they're here."

"But that can be overdone, too," Jess persisted. "Just yesterday, Tommy was talking about how you stayed over in the gym, on your own time, to help him repair that volley ball net he ripped up. He was bragging a little, I think, about not being punished because the job got done in one afternoon."

"Oh, I doubt that Tommy was bragging," replied Fred easily. "It's just that Mr. Brownell was angry about the net being ripped and said that if Tom couldn't get it fixed before the next game was scheduled to start, he'd have to miss recreation for a couple of days. I didn't have anything in particular to do, so when Tommy asked me to help him out, why should I refuse? I just see that as part of my job."

Jess sighed before he spoke. "I don't know, Fred," he said. "There's no doubt about how much you like the kids, and they like you, too. But why are you always bailing them out? How are they ever going to learn to stand on their own two feet and accept the consequences of what they do or don't do, if you're always standing there ready to rescue them?"

(Supplementary discussion questions, page 294)

1.7 CULTURE SHOCK

As he approached the infirmary, Vic Dawson could hear the nurse's voice. He thought Mrs. Drake sounded pretty upset and wondered what Miguel had done.

"That's quite enough, Miguel!" he heard her snap. "Your child care worker should be here any minute to march you right back to the cottage."

"I can hardly wait, you bitch!" retorted the boy.

Vic pushed the infirmary door open and glanced at Miguel, who was quivering with anger. "What's up, Mrs. Drake?" asked Vic. "Mr. Ross said you called."

"I'm reporting Miguel and asking that he not be permitted to serve as interoffice messenger," she replied. "When he brought over my log book a few minutes ago, I asked him to please help me get some supplies down from the storage cabinet. He started shouting obscenities. . ."

"I told her to go screw. . ." interrupted Miguel hotly.

"O.K., Miguel, that's enough," said Vic firmly. "Let's go!" Turning briefly to the nurse, he added, "I'll get back to you, Mrs. Drake."

After several unsuccessful attempts to convince Miguel to explain his behavior, Vic dropped the still-defiant boy off at the cottage. Puzzled and annoyed, he decided to try to see his supervisor about the episode. A few minutes later he was in Mr. Bridges' office describing the infirmary incident.

"I know," said Mr. Bridges, "I was just scheduling a case conference for Miguel. Look at this report the school sent over," he added.

Vic scanned the two typewritten pages and shook his head. "Whew! I knew Miguel was having some trouble in school, but that's quite a record for a kid who hasn't been here two weeks yet. It sounds like he's constantly mouthing off at the teachers. I really don't understand it," he continued, shaking his head. "Miguel's behavior has been fine in the cottage. He seems to be getting along well with the other boys, and the kid described in this report just doesn't sound like him."

Mr. Bridges nodded thoughtfully. "You know, the problem may be women."

"Women?" echoed Vic. "I don't understand."

"Well," explained Mr. Bridges, "Miguel is Puerto Rican, and his family has only been in this country a few months. In traditional Puerto Rican homes the woman takes a very secondary position—the man is boss. In fact if the father dies, it's the oldest boy who runs the household, not the mother. Women have virtually no power. Maybe you noticed in this report," he continued, "that each time Miguel got into trouble at school, it was because of the way he reacted to an order or a request by a female teacher. And today, it was the nurse. If he's been raised in a culture where a man never takes orders from a woman, that could be why he gets defiant when a female tries to tell him to do anything."

"Well," Vic responded slowly, "he's here now and he's going to have to adjust to the way we do things. Otherwise he'll never make it. We just don't live that way!"

Just then the telephone on Mr. Bridges' desk began to ring. "He'll have a rough time," Mr. Bridges nodded as he picked up the receiver. He listened, then replied, "I'll be right over." Hanging up the telephone, he turned again to Vic. "Sorry, Vic," he said, "I've got an emergency in Cottage Four. We'll have to pick up on this later. Meanwhile, give it some thought."

Vic followed Mr. Bridges out of the office and, shaking his head, walked toward the cottage, where he recounted the discussion to his co-worker. "Well," he concluded decisively, "I'm going to find Miguel right now and talk to him about this. If he really feels that way about women, we'll have to find a way to straighten him out and see if he's going to cooperate with us. Any ideas?"

(Supplementary discussion questions, page 294)

1.8 "DID YOU?"

Tod Adams tried to suppress a yawn as he sat down with two of the boys to help them work on their model airplane. He was really exhausted and wondered whether most of it was because of the touch football game that afternoon or the fact that he had stayed out so late the night before. Probably the latter, he thought. His date, Liz, was probably spending today resting. She was off on weekends because she worked in the institution's business office.

Tod suddenly realized that one of the boys was talking to him.

"Does this piece go here, Mr. Adams?"

Tod shook his head momentarily and looked at the parts Jay was holding. "Looks good to me," he said. "Did you compare it with the other side? It should be the same."

"Hmm," said Jay, holding the pieces against the other side, where they had completed a similar section the week before. Tod had to force himself to keep his eyes open.

The other boy, Donald Frost, was less absorbed in the model and had been watching Tod. "Are you sick, Mr. Adams?" he asked. "You look like you're somewhere else."

"Just a little tired," answered Tod with a grin. "I didn't know it showed."

"Did you have a big weekend?"

"Kind of," nodded Tod, leaning back and momentarily forgetting the model.

Donald gave a knowing laugh. "Hey, man," he said, "I'll bet you got a date with that chick in the office I saw you talking to last week. The one with the long black hair. Right?"

"Yeah," laughed Tod in agreement. "That's the one."

Jay had looked up from the model by now, and both boys leaned forward expectantly, tossing questions at Tod.

"Was it your first date?"

"Where did you take her?"

"Did you see a movie?"

"Do you like her?"

"You going to take her out again?"

Tod held up his hand as if to ward off the crossfire of questions.

"Look," he said, smiling. "It wasn't any big deal. I asked her out to a party a friend of mine was giving. It turned out to be a real blast and we ended up staying too long. O.K.? Come on," he concluded, "let's get back to the model or we'll never get it done."

"All right, Mr. Adams," said Donald knowingly. "But keep us posted, will you? We got to look out for our staff members." He winked at Tod and turned his attention back to the table.

Jay was still looking at Tod. "Mr. Adams," he finally said, quietly. Tod looked at him. "Did you get to lay her?"

(Supplementary discussion questions, page 295)

1.9 A CASE OF BLACK AND WHITE

Earl Dunton shook his head vehemently. "No, Mel, I won't change a thing on this report. This kid," he continued, indicating the dejected Negro youngster sitting in front of him, "stole a wristwatch from Reuben Hill and he has to learn his lesson. That's what we're here for, Mel. You should be able to see that." Turning to the crestfallen Bill, he added, in a milder tone, "Boy, go get your dinner. It's not the end of the world."

As soon as the door of the lounge closed behind the youngster, Mel

Steele exploded. "You called him 'Boy!' Oh, Earl, you really are something else. You busted one of your own people! You know he'll be on restriction now and he won't have a chance to get into the Opportunity Program. Why couldn't you accept his alibi when he said he was only borrowing Reuben's watch? You 'Uncle Toms' make me sick!"

Earl's dark face was impassive as he replied, speaking slowly. "I've been a child care worker for twenty years and I've learned not to let two things bug me," he said. "Smart-ass young kids and wild-eyed young workers. And I've been black all my life, so don't try to tell me what that's all about. My attitude toward my people and toward all people is based on fairness. The only way kids like Bill are going to make it when they leave here is by learning to work with the world the way it is. That doesn't mean I want these kids to have a good life any less than you do."

Mel walked toward the door. The contempt in his voice was thinly veiled. "Don't worry about fairness, Earl, baby. This place and this whole damn society will screw your brothers plenty without your help!"

"Tell me," asked Earl, grinning, "how much chittlin' and fatback did you have to force-feed yourself to get all that soul? My experience says this is one of the places where blacks do get a fair shake. That's one reason I stay here."

An hour later, as Earl sat in the administrator's office waiting to deliver his report on the theft and recovery of the wristwatch, he saw a list of youngsters who had volunteered for the Opportunity Program on the secretary's desk. It was generally felt that only the boys who made that program really developed job skills they could use when they were released from the institution. Idly scanning it, he noticed small checkmarks in pencil beside about half the names and realized that these designated the Negro boys on the list.

Earl then glanced at a small card clipped to the bottom of the page. "Please do not include more than four of the checked names," was written on the card. "They make the group too hard to supervise."

(Supplementary discussion questions, page 295)

1.10 ACCEPTING FAILURE

Jim Duncan stood at the open door to his supervisor's office and tentatively cleared his throat. Mr. Tate looked up from the report he was reading.

"Come in, Jim. Anything wrong?" he asked.

Sighing, Jim closed the door behind him and slipped into the chair beside Mr. Tate's desk. "Yeah, something's come up and I need to talk it over with you. I think I know what I want to do, but I'd like to have your support."

Mr. Tate leaned back in his chair. "Brian again?" he asked. Jim nodded.

"We had a big blowup in the cottage this morning because he wouldn't stop horsing around with a football. Finally, I had to tell him that if he didn't stop immediately and get to his chores, he'd be grounded. Then he slammed out the door yelling about adults constantly threatening and bossing him and how they couldn't get away with it."

"What happened then?" asked Mr. Tate.

"I started out after him, but just then the telephone rang. It was Mrs. Cooper," Jim continued, "checking on our laundry count. You know how she runs on, and by the time I could break in and explain that I'd have to call her back, Brian was coming back to the cottage. He walked past me, apparently very subdued, and went right to work on his chores. He even mumbled something that sounded like an apology."

"So far, it sounds like Brian's best day in a long time," commented Mr. Tate. "You've worked very hard with that kid, Jim, and you've done more for him than anyone could reasonably expect. He was on the verge of being sent away when you came and even though he's still hanging by a thread, you've somehow been able to sustain him."

"Thanks," Jim continued. "I only hope it makes a difference. Anyway, I thought the incident was over and done with until I went out to my car a few minutes ago and found that someone had broken off the side mirror. The side of the car was scraped up pretty badly, too, apparently with the jagged metal end from the mirror."

"Was it Brian?" asked Mr. Tate, frowning.

Nodding, Jim replied, "I'm afraid so. As I was looking at the car he ran up, repeated his apology in a really sincere, worried way, and ran back to the cottage. He looked near tears."

Mr. Tate shook his head. "I'm afraid you won't like it," he said, "but this really looks like the end of the road for Brian."

"Wait, Mr. Tate," replied Jim, earnestly. "Please hear me out. I know Brian has a bad record, but I honestly feel we've gained a lot of ground since I started working here three months ago. Right now he has more 'good' times than ever before. We seem so close to really getting through to him. Couldn't we just sort of ignore this?"

"I'm sorry," said Mr. Tate, kindly but firmly. "There comes a point where we can't afford the risk of keeping a boy any longer, and we've made exceptions for Brian already. It's not even good for him if he thinks he can avoid the consequences of his behavior."

"But don't I have anything to say about this?" asked Jim, anger beginning to show in his voice. "I've worked hard with this kid and you, yourself, have to admit that his outbursts are less frequent than before. Besides it's my car and I'm willing to have it fixed . . ."

"That's not the point, Jim," interrupted Mr. Tate. "Sure, all the one-to-one time you've put in with Brian seems to have helped, but you've read the records and you know what he can do when he loses his temper. Scraping up your car is just another example, and there's an element of danger there that I can't ignore. Besides, although it's true that there are fewer outbreaks in the cottage, there's still a great deal of concern about his behavior elsewhere in the institution. I have to consider that, too."

"But couldn't we just wait a little longer?" asked Jim. "I think we might be getting close to a major breakthrough with him."

Again Mr. Tate shook his head. "You know what kind of a setting we have here, Jim," he said. "We're just not equipped to handle youngsters if it seems likely that they might seriously hurt each other. What if Brian had blown up at another boy and used that broken mirror in a fight?"

"He didn't. . ." began Jim.

"Not this time," stressed Mr. Tate. "Who's to say what will happen next time? No," he continued, "I'm afraid we'll just have to set up an appointment with Dr. Burke and see if Brian can be placed in a more appropriate setting. Just don't take it as your failure, Jim, because it isn't. We can't win 'em all.''

Despite Mr. Tate's reassurance, Jim felt lost and empty as he walked toward the cottage, wondering what he had done wrong. "Why not wait a little longer?" he asked himself. Should he have kept the latest incident to himself? What could he have done differently in working with Brian? Depression almost overwhelmed him as he reached the cottage, picturing Brian on the first step to a life of locked wards. "Maybe we can't win 'em all," he thought, "but can we give up and let a kid go down the drain?"

(Supplementary discussion questions, page 296)

2. THE CHILD CARE WORKER
ON THE JOB

The job of the child care worker includes a variety of responsibilities to the institution for which he works and to the youngsters in his care. These are often reflected in situations involving such issues as professional ethics and integrity, confidentiality, and institutional philosophy, policy, and goals. The cases that follow reflect the kinds of issues that frequently arise in this regard.

TABLE OF CASES

2.1 CONFIDENTIALITY

The screams echoed in the hallway. "Let me alone! Let me alone!" Mike Fitzpatrick walked quickly down the corridor and stopped at the second door. The night light was on, and Mike could see the sweat pouring down Tommy Burbank's face as he tossed in his bed.

"Wake up, Tommy, wake up," he said as he shook the boy gently.

Tommy sat up with a start. "Huh. . .what. . .where am I?" he murmured, glancing around the room.

"It's all right, Tommy. You were just having a bad dream," Mike replied. "You'll be all right in a few minutes." Mike held his hand on Tommy's arm while the youngster tried to focus on his surroundings. "Why don't you come into the other room for a few minutes before you try to get back to sleep."

"Say, Mike," the boy said as they sat down in the cottage living room, "did you ever have the same dream two nights in a row?"

"I think so," Mike replied. "Do you want to tell me about it?"

"Well, last night I had almost the exact same dream. Only last night I was with Jimmy and tonight I was alone. It was very late and we were walking down near the pond and two men started following us. We started to walk faster, but they walked faster, too. Then we started to run and they started to run. But they ran faster than we did and they kept yelling, 'Come with us, come with us.' They finally caught up to us and we were in a house and they kept dancing around and touching us and singing weird songs—and then I guess I woke up. Pretty weird, huh?" Tommy added, his usual bravado beginning to come back.

"Well, I guess that was a weird dream, Tommy," Mike said gently. "But I think you'll be O.K. now. You're very safe here, you know."

Tommy grinned wryly. "Yeah, I guess that's one thing you can say for this place. You won't tell anyone, will you Mike? Some people might make too much of it. You know how it is—after all, it was only a dream."

"Well, you weren't scared or anything, anyway," Mike said jokingly, trying to ease the boy's fear.

"Who me?" replied Tommy, smiling. "You know me better than that, Mike."

They said goodnight, and Mike watched Tommy disappear down the hall and into his room. He made an entry in the night report indicating that Tommy had been up after a bad dream and jotted a short note to Sharon Simmons, Tommy's therapist, describing the dream and how concerned Tommy was about it. Then he went back to the book he had been reading. The rest of the night was quiet.

When Tommy came into the cottage the next afternoon, he pointedly brushed past Mike without a word.

"What's eating Tommy?" Mike asked one of the other boys.

"He's pretty mad at you, but he won't say why. He just says he can't trust you anymore, and if he can't trust you, he can't trust anyone."

A light began to dawn. "Did Tommy see his therapist this afternoon?" Mike asked.

"I think he did."

"Thanks." Mike walked over to Tommy, who was sitting down looking unhappy.

"What's the matter, Tommy?"

"You're a damn liar like all the rest of them," Tommy sighed, apparently as much in sorrow as in anger. "You said you wouldn't tell anybody and I thought I could trust you. I'll know not to tell you anything next time. Why'd you have to go tell my stupid therapist about that dream?"

Stunned and feeling a little hurt, Mike pulled up another chair.

(Supplementary discussion questions, page 297)

2.2 THE MISSIONARY

Hal Sloane tapped the edge of his pipe on the ashtray. "So," he continued, "when this kid says he wants to have a trade like his uncle, I just nodded."

Jeff Stuart, another child care worker, had just entered the room. "Why?" he asked. "What does his uncle do?"

Hal grinned as he replied. "He works at a big used car lot, and part of his job is setting the mileage back on cars before they're resold. Like I always say, it's not our job to be missionaries. We're just here to take care of kids."

"I'm not sure you can limit it that way," said Ron Davies. "I guess it all goes back to the area of values. It seems to me that we stand for certain things which are pretty good, and part of my responsibility is to pass these on to the children we work with. Besides, we're teaching something about values whether we do it directly or not. Like they say, silence gives consent."

Before anyone could respond, the telephone rang and Hal picked it up. He listened for a few seconds, then said, "O.K., thanks." Replacing the receiver, he turned to the others and said, "The office called to say that the movie came."

"Good," said Ron, "I hear they managed to find a film which is still fairly new this time."

"Great!" commented Hal in mock seriousness, "the kids will really love a 'talkie'!"

Later that evening Ron and his boys were discussing the movie as they walked back to the cottage. It was a story about how an elaborate plot to commit a million dollar bank robbery was foiled. Ted, one of the younger boys, was excitedly flapping his arms as he tried to recreate one of the pivotal scenes in the story. "Boy, wasn't that something?" he yelped. "The part where all those guys were trying to get the money back outta that guy's basement?"

"That part was a pile of crap," said Jim, who was somewhat older, scornfully. "Nobody would turn down a cut of all that dough just because he decided to go straight! Those men who pulled the job knew him from prison—he used to be a con."

"So what?" asked Mike. "Not everybody who starts out in a gang has to stay in one. My brother went straight when he got out of jail."

"Then he never made the big time to begin with," scoffed Jim. "Once you get a taste of that easy money, you can't change." Most of the other boys shouted their agreement, and their conversation subsided as they reached the cottage.

Ron, who had been following this exchange among the boys closely but had not spoken yet, shook his head and took a deep breath as they walked through the door.

(Supplementary discussion questions, page 297)

(Supplementary discussion questions, page 297)

2.3 "CAN SHE DO THAT TO US?"

Tuesday was laundry day and the girls were sorting and counting their clothes and linens before putting them into the cottage laundry bags.

"Hey, girl, keep your crap out of this bag," yelled Jean across the dorm to Cynthia Wallace. "You'll mess up our clothes."

"Look who's talkin'," replied Cynthia, tears welling up in her eyes. "Your stuff ain't so clean either, you know."

"I don't stink like you do," was Jean's retort. "You must piss in your bed or something."

The other girls began to snicker.

Crying, Cynthia stumbled across the room and dove at Jean, and they fell on the floor between the beds, tearing and scratching at each other. While they fought, the other girls in the dorm began to shout and throw the dirty laundry across the room at them.

Mary Green and Sue Owens, the two child care workers, were across the hall collecting laundry in the other dorm when they heard the commotion.

"I'll see what's up," said Mary, dropping the laundry bag she was holding.

"What's going on here?" Mary asked after she had managed to restore quiet. The dorm was a mess, with dirty laundry all around. No one answered.

"What happened?" Mary asked again, the annoyance showing in her voice.

"Nothin' we can't handle, Miss Green," said Jean.

Mary turned to Cynthia, who was still crying. "Cynthia, are you O.K.?"

"It's nothing, Miss Green," the girl replied. "Just a little argument, but it's all over now."

The girls had been difficult lately and Mary's patience was wearing thin. She was particularly annoyed at the way they always seemed to delight in being cruel to Cynthia. Cynthia had been diagnosed as slightly brain damaged and seemed to be slower than the other girls, both mentally and physically.

"Is anybody going to tell me what happened?" Mary finally snapped.

"Guess not," someone mumbled from the other end of the room, and the girls all burst out laughing.

"That does it!" exclaimed Mary furiously. "You girls can put your laundry back. No laundry for you this week. If you want clean clothes, wash them yourselves. And there better be some changes around here, too!"

Mary turned to leave and Sue, who had just entered the room, followed her into the hallway.

"You were pretty rough on them," said Sue, as the two child care workers started downstairs.

"Maybe they'll learn," replied Mary. "I've had it with the way they torture Cynthia!"

"But why laundry?" asked Sue. "Is that something we should punish them with? We have enough trouble getting them to keep themselves clean and neat as it is."

"It was the first thing I thought of," responded Mary. "It seemed appropriate since that's where the problem came up. I had to do something they'd remember."

That evening, after Mary had gone off duty, the group was still angry and sullen, and Sue was still concerned about what Mary had done. She was sitting in the office when Jean and two of her friends knocked at the door. They came in, sat down, and looked at each other for a few moments before Jean spoke.

"Listen," she said, "we're all sorry for what we did upstairs this afternoon, and we probably should be punished for it. But Miss Green was really being a louse when she told us we couldn't get our stuff washed this week, wasn't she? Can't we please send our laundry in?"

(Supplementary discussion questions, page 298)

2.4 AFTERMATH

Ed Garrison stepped away from the soft drink machine in the staff lounge holding two cans of soda.

"Here," he said, handing one to his colleague, Stu Brooks. "O.K., what are you going to tell the kids about Ralph Carr being fired?"

Stu accepted the drink with a nod of thanks. "The truth, I guess," he replied. "I spoke with Mr. Holden when I heard the news and he said the truth was the simplest and the best way. I should just explain that Ralph was consistently late getting to work at the cottage, that he was warned frequently, and that unreliable people don't keep jobs. As much as I like Ralph, he did make life difficult for me that way. I never knew when I would get off duty."

Ed snorted in disgust. "Mr. Holden's a good guy, but he must be out of touch. What the hell kind of speech is that to make to kids like these? Gene and Freddy and some of the others—they were really close to him. They're the leaders in your group, too. They rapped with him all the time and he never put them off. So how can you tell those kids that we wrote him off because he couldn't always get out of the sack at six thirty in the morning?" he asked.

Stu nodded glumly. "I know, it's not going to be easy." He glanced at his watch and quickly finished his soda. "It's almost time for the kids to get in from school," he said. "I got to get back to the cottage and tell them about Ralph before they hear about it from someone else."

"Good luck," said Ed, shaking his head.

When the boys had all arrived at the cottage, Stu called them together in the common room and explained about Ralph's dismissal. There was a stunned silence. Freddy was the first to speak.

"Shit," he said angrily. "That's what always happens. We get to like a guy, someone we can really talk to, and they get rid of him because of some stupid rule."

"Everyone knows that Ralph was never that late, anyway," added Gene indignantly.

The other boys joined in an angry chorus of complaints. Bill Fletcher, one of the older boys in the cottage, finally raised his voice above the others. "Hey, Stu," he asked, "wasn't Ralph really a good guy?"

Stu nodded. "Of course. He's a close friend of mine."

"O.K.," replied Bill, looking him in the eye, "we all make mistakes. So he goofed, too. Can't you help get him back?"

(Supplementary discussion questions, page 298)

2.5 "GLAD YOU'RE HERE!"

Paul Reid was trying not to show how nervous he felt as George Robinson, the other child care worker in the cottage where he would be working, prepared to introduce him to the boys for the first time. George spoke to the table full of youngsters with an easy informality that Paul was certain only several years' experience could provide.

"Boys," he said, "I'd like you to meet Paul Reid. He'll be working here with us in the cottage."

The boys looked up from their lunches, some with interest and others with apparent suspicion. Most, however, responded to Paul's, "Hi." As they found places for themselves at the table, George suggested that the boys might introduce themselves. A youngster seated directly across from Paul spoke first.

"Andy Stone is my name," he announced. "You gonna remember that?"

"I'll try," replied Paul.

"My name's Harry Ward," said the boy seated next to Andy, "and I don't care if you remember it or not." He paused, and Paul realized that the boys were all looking at him.

"OK, but I'll try to remember it anyway," he said.

"What I really want to know is how long you're going to let us stay up after 'lights out,'" persisted the boy.

"What do you think, Harry Ward?" replied Paul, smiling slightly.

Harry's groan indicated what he thought and the appreciative laughs Paul heard from a few of the others at the table served to ease his tension a bit.

Near the end of the meal, George explained to Paul how the work detail was scheduled at meal time and Paul felt again that he was being tested when Andy Stone asked, "Hey, are you going to have the same crappy attitude about scrubbing pots and pans until they shine?"

"Only," Paul replied with mock gravity, "when they need it."

"See?" George laughingly told the group, "He's unshakeable."

When George went off duty that evening, Paul was left alone with the group for the first time. Some of the boys were at the gym and most of the rest were in the common room. Paul was in the cottage office getting acquainted with some of the files and recalling the concern he had felt earlier about being able to handle this kind of work. The interview for the position had been a difficult one, including a wide variety of personal questions about his likes and dislikes, his prejudices, his family background, even his sexual attitudes. The afternoon had gone well, however; he liked the people he had met, and he was beginning to feel more comfortable about the whole business of being a child care worker.

Paul's thoughts were interrupted by a voice from the open door.

"Mr. Reid, can we talk to you?"

He looked up and saw Andy Stone and Harry Ward standing in the doorway.

"Sure, come on in," Paul replied. "Andy and Harry, right? I want to be sure I have the names straight." The boys nodded as they sat down. "What's on your mind?"

"Nothing much," Andy said, apparently a little embarrassed. We just wanted to get acquainted. You know much about cars?"

"A little," said Paul. "Is that one of your hobbies?"

"Did you ever race?" Harry asked, enthusiastically.

Smiling, Paul shook his head.

"That's not my thing," he replied, "but I do know a little about engines."

That seemed to break the ice, and a lively conversation followed about cars, pro football, music, and where Paul had gone to school.

"You know," Andy interjected after about twenty minutes, "it's really going to be great having a white counselor in the cottage again. The white kids can't even talk to that black bastard, George. All he cares about is the other niggers."

(Supplementary discussion questions, page 299)

2.6 COMPLAINT DEPARTMENT

"It's not fair," announced Alfie, as he and Tommy stomped into the cottage child care office.

"What now?" asked Herb Penn, who had recently joined the staff, looking up from the desk at the two youngsters planted in front of him.

"The stinkin' rec schedule, that's what!" replied Alfie.

"Yeah," chimed in Tommy, "they messed it all up and now Cottage 4 gets the best time for outdoor rec, the best time for gym, the best . . . ."

"Hold on, boys," interrupted Pete Nelson, the cottage's other child care worker, who was seated in a corner of the office writing reports. "You know we switch schedules with Cottage 4 every second month. That means we've just had the 'best' times for everything, doesn't it?"

"So what?" retorted Alfie. "Come on," he said to Tommy disgustedly. "These guys all give you the same line." They both turned on their heels and walked out of the office.

"Those kids!" muttered Herb. "They're always groaning about

something. Never a day passes without someone in this cottage finding a new thing to complain about!"

"Come on, Herb," remonstrated Pete with a smile, "you mustn't interfere with the number one favorite pastime around here!"

"You mean griping?" asked Herb.

"Well, actually it's a blend of griping and groaning," explained Pete. "About half and half."

"You sound as though you approve," said Herb, somewhat surprised.

"Oh, I don't think it's always as bad as it sounds," shrugged Pete. "The kids need it for an outlet. It's like griping in the army." Glancing at his watch, Pete added, "We better get them moving toward the dining room. It's almost noon—we'll be late."

"Late for what?" asked Herb wryly. "The watery soup or the parboiled coffee? I can understand why the kids gripe about the food!"

In the dining room they stepped into the food line behind the boys in their group. "Look at that gunk, Pete," whispered Herb. "It doesn't seem possible, but every day it looks worse! You'd think they'd take special care to feed these kids well since they're so deprived in other ways."

Pete nodded. "You're right," he said. "I wish we could do something about the food situation, but every time we bring it up at a meeting, they just say 'budget' and the discussion ends right there."

"I guess the institution is satisfied that the kids are getting enough nutrition, and maybe that's all they can afford," replied Herb.

Most of the boys from their cottage were already seated when Herb and Pete arrived at the table. Alfie had just taken his first bite of stew, and he grimaced and looked up angrily at the two counselors.

"This stuff tastes like shit!" he spat. "What's your fancy explanation this time?"

(Supplementary discussion questions, page 299)

2.7 GIFTS

Charley Nash sank wearily into the shabby couch in the cottage day room. Glancing at the half-empty cup of coffee on the small table next to him, he sighed, "Whew, what a night!"

"Amen!" agreed his co-worker, Gary Jones, who was seated at the small desk across the room, making entries in the daily log. "Those kids were really wild!"

Charley started leafing through his pocket notebook and suddenly stopped. "Hey, what about Donald Gregg?"

"What about him?" replied Gary. "Something wrong?"

"It's his birthday tomorrow, and I bet he won't be getting a single present," answered Charley. "Nobody ever comes to see him or anything."

"It's rough, but there are other kids like that around here too," said Gary without looking up from the desk.

"Maybe in some cottages," said Charley slowly, "but the other kids in this cottage all seem to have at least one person who tries to keep in touch. Remember last month?" he continued. "Two of them had birthdays, and they both got cards and gifts."

"So?" countered Gary.

"Well, I thought maybe I could buy him a little game or something in the village, and . . ."

"You know the rules as well as I do," interrupted Gary, shaking his head. "No personal gifts from the staff. No way."

Charley thought for a moment before he spoke. "How about this," he began. "I could give him the gift anonymously. Then no one would know who it came from and . . ."

Grinning and shaking his head from side to side, Gary interrupted again. "Come on, Charley, who're you kidding?" he said. "You'd still be breaking the rules and you know it."

Charley slowly nodded his head in agreement. "Well," he concluded, "at least he'll get the standard birthday cake from the institution."

The following night, Charley was on late duty. Long after the boys had shared Donald's birthday cake and gone to bed, Charley heard noise coming from one of the dorms. He walked upstairs to check and found Donald sobbing in his bed. "Donald," he said softly, "what's the matter?"

"My birthday's all over, and I didn't get nothin'" was the choked reply. "I just wish someone had remembered."

The next morning, Charley told his co-worker what had happened. "Couldn't the institution give these kids birthday presents, Gary?" he asked. "It wouldn't have to be much."

"They used to do it," Gary replied, "but the kids preferred to have a special cake instead."

"I can understand that," Charley agreed. "But tell me, why would the institution object in a case like this if a staff member brought Donald a little gift?"

(Supplementary discussion questions, page 301)

2.8 MY BROTHER'S KEEPER?

Max Benson walked quickly down the steps of the administration building and turned toward the cottage. The mail had arrived a few minutes late and he had waited for it. He had left Sam Brodie, his co-worker, alone with the boys starting the Saturday morning cottage cleanup.

Despite the warm spring sunshine, the campus appeared to be deserted except for a few boys picking up papers near the cottages. As he passed Fred Nichols' cottage Max noticed two boys sprawled over the tailgate of Fred's station wagon, which was parked in the driveway.

"Hi, Mr. Benson," called one of the youngsters as Max approached. "You like this spring weather for a change?"

"Great!" replied Max, deciding that maybe the boys had permission to be in Fred's car. "You guys finish your jobs already?"

"We worked fast so we'd have time to soak up some sun," the boy answered. "It'll probably rain again tomorrow."

"No doubt," Max agreed as he hurried past toward his cottage.

About half an hour later, the cottage telephone rang.

"Hello, Max? This is Fred. Can you come over to my cottage for a minute?"

In the office in Fred's cottage Max saw that the two boys who had been in Fred's car were waiting for him with Fred.

"Max," said Fred, "these two boys somehow got into my car when they should have been cleaning the grounds around the cottage. They started fooling around, released the brake, and the car rolled down the incline and hit a tree. Luckily no one was hurt. But they're trying to tell me they thought it was O.K. because you saw them and didn't chase them away or anything." Fred turned to the boys. "Do you want to say that to Mr. Benson's face?" he asked angrily.

"Wait a minute, Fred," said Max, reddening with embarrassment. "I did see them stretched out over the tailgate."

Later, when they had salvaged the situation as best they could and the two child care workers were alone, Fred exploded. "Why the hell didn't you call me, Max?" he asked. "Those kids could've been killed!"

"Good Lord, Fred," exclaimed Max. "I'm sorry! I knew you were inside, and I thought you'd probably given them permission. I just didn't want to interfere. How do you decide when to butt in with someone else's kids?"

(Supplementary discussion questions, page 301)

2.9 VOICES OF EXPERIENCE

"Woody, is that you?" called Margaret from the kitchen.

"Yes, dear," said her husband, unlocking the door and stepping into the apartment. "I just finished in the cottage."

"Good, because dinner's almost ready," responded Margaret as she appeared in the doorway. "It's so nice to be able to eat alone with you on our nights off." She paused for a moment, then continued in a more serious tone. "On second thought, though, I guess we really won't be away from the cottage tonight."

"What happened?" asked Woody. They had been married for a great many years, and he knew almost instinctively that she was upset about something and wanted to talk to him about it.

"I want to talk to you about Terry Tobin," she replied.

"Terry Tobin. Isn't he the boy from Liz and Randy's cottage who was visiting our kids today with his guitar?"

"Yes. After he left and you had gone to that meeting, I noticed that his guitar was still in the common room. When I picked it up to give to one of the boys to take it back to him, a package of cigarette papers fell out. Just like the ones we were shown in that inservice training session on drugs! Several of the kids were standing around and they must have known what was going on. They seemed to freeze for a moment, then they acted as if they hadn't seen anything. I just sent the guitar back to Terry and put the cigarette papers in my bag."

"Were there any traces of marijuana?" Woody asked.

"No," replied Margaret, shaking her head. "Just the papers. Do you have any reason to think Terry might be on drugs?"

Woody, apparently lost in thought, did not reply.

"You know what they told us about reporting any evidence of possible drug use," Margaret continued, "especially because of the legal implications for the institution. Does this fall into that category?"

"It does look suspicious," Woody answered. He took a sip of water and shook his head. "It's almost uncanny," he said, "how close this hits to something that happened to me this afternoon."

"To you?" asked his wife.

"Well, something I overheard," Woody explained. "I walked into the child care meeting a few minutes early and you know how there are always small groups of people sitting around visiting and talking before Mr. Franklin arrives?"

Margaret nodded.

"Well, I happened to be sitting by myself going over the equipment list for the cottage, when I overheard Liz and Randy discussing a pot party they had attended last weekend!"

Margaret's mouth dropped. "Liz and Randy Clark? You can't be serious!"

"I'm afraid I am," replied Woody. "Apparently Randy had finished his midterm exams on Friday and they joined some other graduate students to celebrate. Margaret," he continued softly, "I gather they may have been trying some of the harder stuff, too."

"We've known those two young people for almost a year," said Margaret, "and I never would have guessed. They must stop in here for coffee as often as any of the other child care workers, and we think so highly of them. I really don't know what to say."

"I guess they don't use anything at the institution," Woody replied. "They certainly seem to do a good job with the kids, and I would have felt sure we would have heard about anything like that by now. We've even discussed what a shame it is that they plan to leave the institution when Randy finishes his studies. Now I'm not so sure, but I really feel bad about the whole thing."

"I can't understand it," said Margaret, shaking her head.

"Well, I guess times change," her husband suggested. "But our own kids are not much older than those two and I don't think they're involved with drugs. It still seems wrong to me, especially for people who are working with teenagers."

"Woody," Margaret asked, trying to understand, "do you suppose it's like the speakeasys we went to once or twice when we were young? Maybe pot parties are the same thing."

"No, Margaret," said her husband firmly, "this is more serious. After all, using and selling liquor . . ." Woody was interrupted by the ringing of the doorbell. "Are you expecting anyone?" he asked.

"Oh, I almost forgot. Liz said they might stop by for a few minutes this evening. She wanted to drop off those dress patterns she borrowed."

Margaret followed Woody to the door, and he opened it and invited Liz and Randy to come in. "Thanks for lending me these," Liz said, handing Margaret a large manila envelope. "I used the one I told you about."

An awkward silence followed and was finally broken by Randy. "What's wrong?" he asked. "You both look so strained."

Woody turned quickly, as though he had made a sudden decision, and said, "Please sit down for a moment. Margaret and I were just discussing something that came up today and it concerns you. We have a strong inkling that a boy in your cottage, Terry Tobin, may be smoking pot. We understand that you two have been experimenting with drugs, and I just don't know how you can work effectively with him under the circumstances."

(Supplementary discussion questions, page 301)

2.10 MIXED MESSAGES

Paul Sanders had had a bad day, and after dinner he asked Chuck Miller, the child care worker on duty in his cottage, if they could have a private talk. Chuck agreed and they sat down together on the front steps.

After a short pause, Paul began. "You know," he said, "sometimes I think I just can't win. This place is stacked against me."

Chuck thought about Paul's record for the day: three school detentions, two tantrums, his room a shambles, and a missed trip. "I guess you had a rough time of it today," he said.

Paul shook his head. "Bad ain't the word for it. And look what I'm left with. All those detentions, I have to pay for the stuff I threw out the window, and I didn't even get to go on the trip. Man, they don't ever leave you alone around here."

"I understand why you're upset," replied Chuck, "but you can't really expect to get away with the kind of things you did without any consequences, can you?"

"The thing I don't understand is that when I came here, they told me they understood my problems," Paul said, warming to the subject. "They said I should say whatever was on my mind and get everything out of my system, so I could kind of start over again. But now everyone acts like they expect me to be a model kid. If I could do that, they wouldn't have sent me here in the first place. Everytime I do something wrong, I get punished for it, even when I can't help it. Does that make sense?"

"But that's what therapy is for, Paul," answered Chuck. "That gives you a chance to express your feelings, and you can practice controlling yourself in the cottage and in school so you'll be ready to go back home to the city."

Paul was getting annoyed. "Bull shit! What am I supposed to do when I get angry and it isn't therapy time?"

Chuck had to admit to himself that Paul had a point. "But there have to be some limits," he said, "or we could never live together."

"Limits, limits. That's all I hear around here. I know we need rules so we don't hurt each other, but that's different from telling a kid that you're going to help him with his problems and then punishing him every time he acts like he has a problem! Like I said, if I was a model kid I wouldn't be here, but I'm doing my best to change and I get smacked down everytime I make a mistake. All the other guys have the same trouble. Oh well," sighed Paul, "at least you listen. Thanks, Chuck."

Paul stood up and went inside, leaving Chuck lost in thought.

(Supplementary discussion questions, page 302)

UNIT TWO
HELPING DIFFICULT YOUNGSTERS

3. YOUNGSTERS' PROBLEMS
WITH THEMSELVES

All youngsters face problems in the course of growing up and the child care worker should be prepared to deal with a variety of such situations. The cases in this chapter focus on the kinds of problems that appear to be "inside" individual youngsters more than between them and other youngsters or adults. Although it is not possible to illustrate each area of potential difficulty or handicap, a wide range is represented.

TABLE OF CASES

3.1 TEACH ME TO LIKE ME

Marshall Rice listened to the excited voices of the boys in his cottage as they hung their pictures on the walls of the corridor in the main building. "You never know what kind of a wild program idea will catch these kids' interest," he thought. "Would you believe a cottage art show?" They had gotten special permission to prepare the show on Saturday, when the building was usually empty, so it would be ready when the offices opened on Monday.

Marshall's smile faded as he heard Stewart Wood's piercing whine.

"Mr. Rice," Stewart called, "tell Bert not to hang his crappy picture next to mine!"

Red, one of the older boys in the cottage, spoke before Marshall could reply. "Shut up, Stewart," he snapped, "or we'll hang you instead of your picture."

There was an embarrassed silence and Marshall shuddered slightly, watching Stewart closely. The boys all remembered that Stewart had tried to cut his wrists in the cottage a few weeks before, and Marshall knew that this had not been the boy's first attempt. Except for occasional angry outbursts, Stewart usually seemed to be depressed, unhappy, and alone. Marshall had tried to draw him out but felt he had not been able to make much progress. After the latest incident, the institution's consulting psychiatrist had told the staff to watch the boy constantly, and Stewart seemed to be more miserable than ever.

"He feels completely worthless," Dr. Stillman had said, "and anything that might let him feel important would be helpful. He thinks he's no good and he's trying to punish himself for it."

Seemingly unable to respond to Red's verbal attack, Stewart turned and walked slowly toward the far end of the hall.

Meanwhile, Red looked at Stewart's picture on the wall and then at Bert's picture hanging beside it. "Hey, Stewart," he hooted, "I see what's eating you! You tried to paint the same thing Bert did. The only difference is that he can paint!"

The group broke into loud laughter and Stewart bolted down the hall and out the back door. Marshall quickly ran after him but, when he reached the door, Stewart was not to be seen. Worried, Marshall looked around and wondered where the boy could have gone. Mr. Olsen, the institution's driver, suddenly emerged from the nearby garage door and motioned to Marshall not to speak. "Are you looking for Stewart?" he whispered as he reached Marshall's side. "He's in the garage with Tom Sutton. What happened?"

Marshall looked at the older man and briefly recounted the incident that had taken place. "The saddest part is that Stewart really cared what his picture looked like," he concluded. "he just had the bad luck to pick out the same thing that Bert Grey was painting and he couldn't stand the comparison. I don't even know what I can say to make him feel better."

Mr. Olsen sighed. "I got to know Stewart pretty well when I had to take him on those weekly trips to the dentist last spring," he said. "Then he used to drop around and I would let him help out in the garage until they decided he needed constant supervision a few weeks ago. But we talked a lot. He really thinks he's a loser."

"He sure does," agreed Marshall. "Any suggestions?"

"You know," Mr. Olsen continued, shaking his head, "I been here a long time, and every once in a while we get a kid like Stewart. He doesn't believe in himself, so he doesn't try, then he gets mad at himself because he doesn't do anything. A lot of the kids are like that now and then, but nothing ever seems to go right for the ones like Stewart. I don't know what to tell you except that he needs a friend. A kid like that just feels like everything he touches turns to shit. Somehow, you've got to find a way to help him or else he won't make it."

(Supplementary discussion questions, page 303)

3.2 THE DEBUT

Bob Winters grinned as he gave out the last roll of crepe paper to the boys who were hanging streamers across the gym. The dance was scheduled for tonight and he was pleased with the enthusiastic way his group was working together on the decorations. As he scanned the room, he noticed that Kevin Edwards was standing alone beside a pile of mats.

"Anything wrong, Kevin?" he asked, walking over to join him.

"Mr. Winters, could you do me a favor?" the boy asked. "Could you put my name on the Refreshment Committee for the dance? Would you ask Mr. Shore in Cottage 3 if it's O.K.?"

Bob shook his head. "We talked about this when we were planning it, remember? It was decided then that each cottage would be one committee, with no trading back and forth. Our guys wanted decorations and we got it, so that's that."

"Won't you try?" urged Kevin.

"What's the matter?" asked Bob, looking amused. "Afraid you won't get enough to eat? Come on, once they get the stereo hooked up to those loudspeakers and the girls get here, you'll forget about food!"

"Please, Mr. Winters, at least ask."

Sensing there was more than just a job assignment on the boy's mind, Bob looked at him for a moment. "What's really bothering you, Kevin?" he asked.

"Nothin'—it's just that I . . . oh shit," Kevin blurted, "ever since we started getting ready for this dance all the guys have talked about is how they can score with girls. Like, even if you get together for two minutes, some guy starts talking about some great technique he's got and it's beginning to get me. That's why I don't want to have nothin' to do with that dancing and stuff. I thought if I served refreshments, I'd be busy and nobody would notice."

"Oh, well," Bob said slowly, "you know how guys brag . . ."

"No, you don't understand!" Kevin broke in. "I'm fifteen years old and I've never held a girl's hand. I don't even know how to talk to one! Come on," the boy pleaded, "help me!"

(Supplementary discussion questions, page 303)

3.3 FOR LOVE OR MONEY?

Wayne Albright, the cottage life supervisor, sat down and opened the meeting. "I think you all know why I asked you to come," he said. "Let's go over the facts together, though, before we decide what to do."

"I got to the cottage around four o'clock yesterday afternoon," replied Tom Wrens, a child care worker in Cottage 5, "and I changed into some old clothes to play touch football with the boys. I had cashed a check earlier, so I know there was a ten dollar bill and five fives in my wallet in the pocket of my trousers. I hung them up in the cottage office when I changed. After the game, I took out the wallet so I could pay Larry the ten dollars I owed him and I found that the money was missing." Larry Neilson was Tom's partner in Cottage 5. "About two dollars in change was gone, too. I didn't tell you about it, Wayne, until almost an hour later, after I had looked through my other pockets, around the office, and in the car. You suggested that I keep my eyes and ears open but not to mention it to the boys until later, in case something turned up. I thought that was the last I'd see of the money, and it was really my own fault for being so careless. But I know those kids pretty well, and they usually stay out of the office when there are no adults around. Besides, I guess I didn't think any of them would do something like this to me. This is the first time I've had anything stolen."

"We can never be sure," replied Wayne. "We have almost 200 youngsters here, and they have all kinds of problems. We never know how they're going to act out. I really thought that was the end of the money, too, Tom, until Carol came to me this morning." He gestured for her to tell them about it.

Carol, the nurse, was frowning as she told her story. "I was making a regular cottage checkup in Tom's cottage this morning and thinking about this incident. You had just mentioned it at the daily briefing meeting. In Terry Evans' room I noticed what looked like the corner of a dollar bill sticking out of a book that was partly buried under some other things on top of his clothes cabinet. Of course, it seemed all too simple. Anyone who had the nerve to take money from a staff member would probably hide it more carefully than that. But I looked anyway, and there it was. A ten and five fives. I hesitated, but I finally decided to take the book and the money, and I gave them to Larry outside the cottage. Tom was off duty. I guess Larry brought them to Wayne, and that's about it."

"A few of the boys asked me why Carol had taken Terry's book," said Larry, "but I told them it was a personal matter concerning Terry. Terry was in the cottage at the time, but he didn't say anything about it before he left for school. I don't know if he saw Carol take the book or not."

"Terry wasn't playing football with us yesterday," commented Tom. "He and two or three of the other boys said they would rather stay in the cottage, and we were playing right out front, so I let them. Terry usually seems afraid to participate with the other boys. He sits around the cottage a lot, as if he's thinking. He's likable and the others don't taunt him, but he is pretty isolated, even considering that he has only been here about a month. I can't imagine what he would be planning to do with the money. Now that I think about it, though, I guess we really haven't been giving him enough encouragement. It's so easy to forget about the kids who don't force you to pay attention to them. About the only thing he shows any enthusiasm about is mealtime. He's one of the few kids here who seems to like the food."

"Our meals are probably better than what he usually gets at home," said Anne Marks, Terry's social worker, as one or two of the others tried to hide a grimace. "This may be the first time he has ever had the security of knowing that he would be getting regular meals. His mother is a waitress and a part-time prostitute, I understand. No one knows who his father is, and the kids have pretty much had to shift for themselves. There are five of them. Apparently Terry was sent here because his mother wouldn't assure the court that she would stop his habitual truancy. I think she wanted him out of her way. Except for the truancy, there isn't much delinquency in his record. I think he was afraid to go to school. He's a bright youngster, but his achievement never reflected his ability. I understand he's beginning to make some progress in school here, though."

"Well," said Tom, frowning, "it's clear that we're going to have to try to do more for Terry. For a start, how do you think we should handle the money thing?"

"Remember, it hasn't been mentioned to Terry at all yet," Wayne said, "although he probably knows by now that Carol took his book, since some of the boys apparently saw it. We don't even know for sure that he's the one who took the money. What would you suggest?"

(Supplementary discussion questions, page 304)

3.4 THE REFORMER

"I guess you managed to get Ted calmed down," said John, the cottage relief worker, as the regular worker joined him in the cottage living room. "At least he's quiet."

"I think he's settled for the moment, anyway," Emil replied, "but it's no answer for the long run. Boy, was he steamed!"

John nodded. "Yeah, the way Chuck teased him before breakfast about wetting his bed last night was really bad."

"I know," agreed Emil. "It happens every time Ted has an accident. I really can't blame him too much for taking a poke at Chuck. Just between us, I guess Chuck had it coming to him!"

"Look," responded John thoughtfully, "Ted's only been here a few weeks. He probably doesn't know that way back when Chuck first arrived, he was a bedwetter, too. Do you think it might help if we told him?"

"I'd be afraid of that," replied Emil, shaking his head. "I wouldn't want to do anything that might start Chuck wetting his bed again, and bringing it up might just do it. Whatever else he's doing, you have to admit he's had that problem under control for a long time. That's a real accomplishment for a kid who used to soak his bed as much as he did."

"That's a point," replied John, "but you've got to get him off Ted's back somehow, don't you?"

"No question about that," Emil agreed. "As long as this goes on, I don't see how he can even begin to work on that bedwetting problem. I'll talk to Chuck," he continued. "You were in on the latest incident, so why don't you stay?"

John nodded, and Emil went to get Chuck. When he returned and they were seated, the boy looked at the two workers somewhat apprehensively.

"I guess you want to talk to me about what happened this morning," he said.

"From what I hear," Emil replied, "you were pretty cruel to Ted."

"Aw, I was only kidding," smiled Chuck.

"You know better than that, Chuck," said Emil firmly. "There isn't anything funny about insulting someone. Did it make you happy to see Ted throw a tantrum?"

"Listen," replied Chuck, "that kid's just a big baby and he won't even try to change. All I told him was the truth and you know it. What's wrong with that? Besides, if you're talking about me punching him, remember, he hit me first!"

"Maybe he did," conceded Emil. "but you keep needling him. Don't you remember what it felt like when you had the same problem? You did a good job with it, but I don't know if you could have made it if people kept riding you all the time. Besides, what business is it of yours if Ted wets his bed?"

Chuck bristled. "It's my business because I have to live with that lousy smell. I stopped! Why can't he?"

(Supplementary discussion questions, page 304)

3.5 "WOULD I LIE TO YOU?"

"Anything wrong, Donald?" asked Zeke Freeman. "You're muttering to yourself."

Donald Sanders looked up at his co-worker. "Oh, was I? It's just this report on Richard Brino. You know, that kid tells some unbelievable stories. I don't know what makes him think he's going to get away with them. They're such obvious lies that he's got to get caught."

"What else does it say?"

"Well, they seem to think he's one of those kids who has a lot of guilt feelings about something or other and tells lies so he'll get caught and punished. And probably he feels better when he's punished."

Zeke laughed. "It's always nice to know the latest from Freud and Company," he said, "but I've got to get over to the activities building. I have a program to run."

Donald glanced at his watch and nodded. "Yeah, and I better put this stuff away, too. The kids'll be back from school in a few minutes."

Half an hour later, all the boys had checked into the cottage and some were leaving for after-school clubs and outdoor play. Noticing Richard Brino among those headed for the door, Donald called him back. "Hold on, Richard," he said, "you know you're still on cottage restriction. You're grounded until tomorrow."

The boy turned toward the child care worker. "Whaddya mean?" he cried. "I got permission from Mr. Freeman this morning before you got here. We made a deal. Barney's in the infirmary and I did all his chores, so Mr. Freeman lifted my restriction one day early."

Donald looked puzzled. It was true that Barney, who had morning chores this week, had been sent to the infirmary yesterday with a sore throat, and it was also true that the boys were sometimes permitted to work off certain punishments, such as being restricted to the cottage. Taking advantage of Donald's hesitation, Richard pressed. "Come on, let me go. The guys are going to play football and we don't have much time. It gets dark early now."

"You can go," replied Donald, "if you're sure that story is true. I'll check with Mr. Freeman when he gets back."

After the boy had sped out of the cottage, Donald was still feeling uncertain. He didn't want to interrupt Zeke by calling him, but he did step into the office to check the daily log. Running his finger down the morning entries, he read and reread a few lines intently before slamming the book closed. Zeke had written that, due to Barney's absence, his chores had been handled by two other boys in his dorm, Juan and Alfred. Richard's name was not mentioned nor was there any indication that his restriction had been lifted. After cursing himself for being so gullible, Donald decided to wait until Richard came back to the cottage before confronting him.

When the boys returned shortly before dinner, Donald called Richard into the office and read the morning log entries aloud to him. Richard grinned and shook his head. "You're my friend, man," he said. "Would I lie to you?"

Donald saw red. "Listen, Richard," he said tightly, "you do this all the time and it only buys you trouble. Don't you know by now that you can't get away with it?"

"O.K., Mr. Sanders, O.K.," replied Richard, motioning with his hands as if to calm troubled waters, "let's cool it. Punish me if you want. But you'd be surprised how many times I do get away with it, and the way I figure, it's worth the chance."

(Supplementary discussion questions, page 305)

3.6 TRIAL BY FURY

Most of the boys and the other child care worker had left for dinner and Ron Edwards was preparing to follow when Ward Lester stormed into the child care office. "That bastard, Mike, took my record albums, Ron," he shouted, his voice trembling.

Ron paused for a split second before he replied. He had talked with his supervisor that morning about Ward's temper tantrums. They had become worse in the last few weeks, and Ward's roommate, Mike Dana, was often the target. "Did you check your locker and your closet, Ward?" Ron asked calmly, trying to lighten some of the anger he saw in the boy's face.

"Hell, yes!" snapped Ward. "Come up and look yourself. They're gone."

"Show me where they were," Ron said, following the boy out of the office and up to his room.

"See?" Ward said angrily when they had finished looking through the closet. "They were right on that shelf, and now they ain't here or in my locker. That bastard's got them."

Before Ron could reply, Mike, who had returned to the cottage, walked into the room and Ward rushed toward him. "You fuck!" he screamed. "You stole my records!"

"What the hell are you talking about?" yelled Mike. "What records?"

Ward ran over to Mike's locker, threw the door open, and pulled three albums from the top shelf. "These records!" he said triumphantly. "These are the ones you stole."

Mike looked at the albums in Ward's hand. "Man, you know I had those records," he said, shaking his head. "They're mine."

Ward exploded. "You heard him, he lied!" the boy shouted. "These records are going back where they belong!" With that, Ward quickly shoved the records into his own locker and slammed the door.

"Just a minute, Mr. Lester," complained Mike, "he can't do that. Those records are mine!"

Ron walked over to Ward's locker and opened the door. "I'll hold the records until you guys calm down and we find out whose they are," he said firmly. "Let's go downstairs and . . ."

Ward pushed himself between Ron and the locker. "Keep your fucking hands off my records," he screamed, his fist taut under Ron's nose, "or I'll smash your shitty face in!"

As Ron began to grapple with him, he realized that the boy was in a frenzied rage and out of control.

(Supplementary discussion questions, page 306)

3.7 OFF AND RUNNING

Tom Brady could feel the tension as he walked back to the cottage with his group after lunch. He had intervened twice during the meal to protect George Hardy from the other boys. Suddenly, as they climbed the steps, someone elbowed George, who dove at his tormenter, screaming.

"Get the fuck away from me!" he yelled.

Tom hesitated momentarily, and the other boys grabbed George and held him. "Let me go!" he shouted. "I'll kill him."

"Let him go," said Tom, approaching George. "I'll take care of him." Tom held the boy as gently as he could, trying to calm him. "Take it easy, George," he said reassuringly. "Let's go inside and work this out."

The other boys were taunting George in the background. "Let them fight, Mr. Brady," said one.

As George seemed to relax, Tom loosened his grip. Suddenly the boy pulled away from him and, crying, ran down the steps of the cottage and toward the rear entrance of the institutional grounds. Tom followed a few moments later, but George was about half a block ahead.

George was a fast runner and maintained about the same distance from Tom as they ran out the dirt road that led several miles to town. Winded, Tom finally slowed to a brisk walk and noticed that George, who was looking back at him every few seconds, also slowed down and still kept the distance between them about the same.

Thinking that this might mean the boy wanted to be caught without losing face, Tom slowly increased his speed and began to close the gap. When George noticed, however, he again broke into a run.

"Stay away from me," he shouted. "Go back and leave me alone."

"I just want to talk to you," Tom called to him. "Just for a minute."

"That's a trick!" responded George. "If you catch me, you'll take me back."

"They won't hurt you," Tom said, but he realized it was futile since the boy, who had slowed down momentarily, had again started to run.

Tom continued to walk and, after a few seconds, the boy also slowed down to a walk again. On a hunch, Tom sat down a few minutes later, at the side of the road. George noticed almost immediately and stopped. After eying Tom carefully and looking around, he sat down, too. The distance between them had hardly changed.

"You better get back to the cottage," George called out after a few minutes of silence. "You can't catch me anyway."

Tom thought he probably could catch the boy if he really tried, but he wondered if that would be the best thing to do.

"Do we have to yell like this?" he asked loudly. "I'd like to talk with you."

"Well, I don't want to talk to you," came the response.

"They'll just pick you up in town and bring you back anyway," warned Tom.

"I can cut through the woods to the highway," responded George. "Then I can hitch and get home."

"You've done that before, too," Tom reminded him, "and where did it get you? The court will just send you back here."

"You don't understand," George shouted, real panic in his voice. "I can't stand it any more! I'll just keep running away until you give up!"

(Supplementary discussion questions, page 306)

3.8 GRACIOUS LIVING

The two child care workers were smiling as they left the conference room. "The case conferences about Wally Smith are almost fun, aren't they?" asked Bill Brown.

"You just like the glory," laughed Andy Santo, his colleague.

"Well," responded Bill, "the least they could do is give us the Nobel Prize for child care work!"

"I must admit," agreed Andy, "that it's great to work with a kid who seems to respond to what we're trying to do for him. Do you remember what a breakthrough it was the first time Wally used a knife and fork all the way through a meal?"

Bill chuckled at the recollection. "Wally knew all about knives," he said. "It was just using them at the dinner table that was a mystery to him. Say," he added in a more serious tone, "remember the time you had to take a knife away from him by force?"

"I don't know which of us was more frightened, him or me,"

answered Andy. "It's hard to believe he didn't even know about sheets when he came, isn't it?" Without waiting for an answer, he continued. "I know almost none of our boys have had any of the luxuries of life, but kids like Wally haven't even had the things we think of as bare necessities."

They were silent for a moment, recalling some of the early incidents with Wally.

"Bill," asked Andy suddenly, "do you remember how bad Wally's language was when he first came?"

Bill groaned. "Do I?" he asked. "He couldn't say 'hello' without scorching your ears. It's amazing how that's changed. You hardly hear it from him any more."

As Bill and Andy emerged from the administration building, they met Ted Littleford, who had been the institution's chef longer than most people could remember. "Hi, Ted," said Bill. "We just came from a case conference about Wally Smith. It was good to hear Mr. Sibley report that he's doing so well with you in the kitchen. Do you remember what that kid was like when he came?"

Ted looked at them thoughtfully before he replied. "Wally's come a long way," he finally agreed, nodding.

"Mr. Sibley said he was going to try to get Wally into a work-study program in cooking when he leaves," added Andy. "How does that sound to you?"

Ted hesitated again before he spoke. "You know," he said, "I been thinking about Wally. I just hope you guys understand one thing."

"What's wrong, Ted?" asked Bill, noticing Ted's expression. "Isn't he really doing a good job?"

"That's not it," replied Ted. "You people around here get his head all filled with a lot of big notions, teach him all those fancy manners, then the bottom's going to drop out. You see," he continued, "he'll be out of here in a year or so—and right back into that miserable jungle he came from. How's he going to get along?"

(Supplementary discussion questions, page 306)

3.9 DADDY?

Soon after the mail had been distributed, Fred Goodrich noticed a group of the boys talking intently in one corner of the cottage recreation room.

"Why can't she have an abortion?" he overheard as he approached. "That's what my sister did when it happened to . . ." Al's voice trailed off as he saw that the child care worker was nearby.

"Anything wrong?" Fred asked pleasantly.

The boys all looked at Al Nolan, who was shaking his head grimly.

"I just got a letter from my girl," Al said. "She's gonna have a *baby*, Mr. Goodrich. It must've happened when I was home on that pass a couple months ago. I thought we were careful, but . . . anyway, I was just talkin' to the guys about what to do. I'm scared, Mr. Goodrich."

"Don't sweat it, Al," said one of the older boys. "It happens all the time."

"Shouldn't he get her an abortion, Mr. Goodrich?" asked the boy whom Fred had overheard before. "I can get him the name of the guy that helped my sister."

"Look," said someone else quickly, "it's not Al's problem. If she was dumb enough to get herself knocked up, that's her business. She can't prove it was Al, anyway. He should just say he didn't do it, that's all. How does he know it happened when he was home?"

Al winced. "She wouldn't do that with anybody else," he said earnestly. "I guess I really should marry her, but I can't do that in here."

"Do you *want* to marry her?" another boy asked.

"Maybe some day," replied Al, "but not now. We were just havin' a good time, that's all. I'll sure be more careful from now on. They can't do anything to me for this, can they, Mr. Goodrich? What should I do?" The boys all turned and looked at Fred.

(Supplementary discussion questions, page 307)

3.10 TOO GOOD?

"Maybe we should let well enough alone, Steve," said John Bauer, his co-worker. The two were talking about Kenny Grant, a fifteen-year old who was in their cottage. "After all, he seems to be happy enough, and the other guys accept him for what he is."

"It sure looks that way," Steve replied, "but I can't help wondering. What's he doing here, anyway, if he has so few problems?"

"You know the record, Steve. Learning problems and truancy. Apparently he's never been a behavior problem beyond that, either at home or at school. No police record, either. So it's not really surprising that he's so easy to handle."

"I felt that way when he first came, too," responded Steve. "Like everybody else, I thought, 'I don't know why he's here, but it's good to have at least one kid in the cottage who's not a hassle.' Then I began to think he should be released, that it wasn't fair to keep him here. He does what he's supposed to, no arguments, no crap, yet he's not too straight for the other guys, either."

"Maybe he should be released, then," suggested John, "if he could go home. I don't know how things stand there at the moment."

"No, John, that's not what I mean," Steve replied intently. "I'm beginning to think that this kid is up to here with a lot of anger that might break loose any time. He just doesn't assert himself enough, but I think he's been changing recently. Did you notice how he set up that fight between Billy and Chris in the cottage last night? Maybe if he could work out whatever it is that's blocking him, he'd have more energy left for handling his school work. He's not a dumb kid!"

"You're talking like a therapist, Steve," said John, smiling good-naturedly. "But maybe it is worth talking over with Kenny's caseworker. It seems to me that therapy is the place for him to let out his excess anger, if he has any."

"I'd like us to talk to his caseworker," agreed Steve, "but let's ask the cottage life director to be there, too. I think we need to work out a way to help Kenny in the cottage."

"What are you getting at?" John asked, with some surprise in his voice. "You don't think we should encourage him to act out in the cottage, do you?"

(Supplementary discussion questions, page 308)

4. RELATING TO OTHER YOUNGSTERS

In this chapter the emphasis is on difficulties that emerge in youngsters' relationships with others in the group, rather than problems that appear in the behavior of the individuals alone. Although this distinction is not always a clear one in practice, it seems useful to separate the cases in this way so the child care worker can begin to distinguish situations in which his efforts should be focused on an individual from those in which it might be better to focus on more than one youngster. Opportunities for effective work in this area often arise from relatively extreme relationship patterns, whether too close (and perhaps homosexual), antagonistic (resulting in overt conflict), overbearing (the bully), or instances of rejection (the scapegoat).

TABLE OF CASES

4.1 HOW CLOSE IS TOO CLOSE?

Gail and Marsha were fourteen years old when they became best friends. Both lonely youngsters, they met when Gail arrived at the institution a few weeks after Marsha did. They quickly became very close and one night, after Marsha had defended Gail in a cottage argument with the other girls, they pledged eternal friendship.

Mr. and Mrs. Arden, the cottage parents, had noticed the girls' developing relationship. "I'm glad those two girls are so close," Grace Arden remarked to her husband. "It's the first time either of them has shown any real feelings about anyone here."

"They sure were a couple of sad sacks when they came," Mack replied. "I think they were two of the loneliest girls we've ever had. They both ran away from home, didn't they?"

In the weeks that followed the Ardens began to wonder if the closeness between Gail and Marsha was as healthy as they had thought at first. Alternately, they would try to reassure each other that such relationships were perfectly normal among teenagers. "I don't know, Grace," Mack said one day. "It seems to me it's one thing to be friends, but to be so exclusive about it, that's another thing."

"Now come on, Mack, don't go worrying over nothing," his wife replied. "It's just an adolescent stage. You see how happy they've been. It's good for them to be friends. Besides they'll probably get over it soon."

A few days later, however, Grace approached her husband. "You know, Mack," she said, "I wonder what Gail and Marsha were doing in that room with the door closed. Maybe it's not healthy for those two to be so close all the time."

"You know what Marsha's social worker said when we told her about this a few weeks ago," Mack reminded her. "It's normal for teenagers to engage in some sex play, especially in an institution, and it's just a stage that should pass as soon as they get interested in boys or just tired of each other. Maybe it's an important stepping stone for them."

Nevertheless the Ardens soon became seriously concerned. It was Grace who mentioned it again one evening. "Mack, I really don't like the way Gail has been moping around whenever Marsha goes off to do something else. You can't even talk to her about it without almost getting your head snapped off."

Mack nodded slowly. "It's becoming something different than it seemed to be at first and I don't like it, either. Should I ask for a meeting and see if we can get a cottage transfer for one of them?"

"Let's try it," said Grace. "I hope they don't keep telling us that it's just normal sex play!"

The meeting was held a few days later and included each girl's social worker, the clinical director, the cottage life supervisor, and the Ardens. It was generally agreed that the relationship between Gail and Marsha had become an unhealthy one for both girls, and that they should be separated so that each would have a better opportunity to progress on her own. It was also agreed that Marsha should be the one to leave the cottage, since she seemed to be slightly stronger and better able to handle the stress. The two girls were to be restricted from visiting with each other temporarily, "until they've had a chance to make some new friends," as the cottage life supervisor put it.

Gail and Marsha were furious when they heard the news.

"You have no right to say who we can be friends with and who we can't," Marsha screamed. "Can we help it if you all have dirty minds?"

Gail was sobbing. "You two are just like everyone else after all," she said between gasps, as she turned toward the Ardens. "You're trying to take away the one person I care about here. Well, if you think we're not going to see each other, you're crazy." She tore out of the room with Marsha close behind.

"They'll get over it in a few days," Grace thought hopefully.

By the time Marsha's transfer to Cottage 8 was completed, the girls' initial anger had become somewhat cool and cynical. Things seemed to settle down in the days that followed but the Ardens were aware of rumors that Gail and Marsha were meeting secretly. Mack found them together only once.

"You've been told to stop seeing each other," he warned. "It's not good for you, and you both know why. Go back to your cottage, Marsha, and Gail, you come with me. I don't want to find you two together again." The girls smiled at each other as Mack led Gail away.

"Give them time," Grace cautioned her husband later. "You can't expect them to stop seeing each other at once. We have to get Gail more involved in other things."

"But it's almost a month already," replied Mack, "and Gail hasn't made the least effort to make friends with other girls. I hear that they're having the same problem with Marsha, too. We've got to show them we mean business."

A few nights later, Grace was making a routine bed check and found that Gail was missing. She quickly ran to Mack and told him. "We'd better call Cottage 8 so they can check on Marsha," she concluded.

"Just a minute," Mack replied, picking up the telephone. "I have an idea." After reporting Gail's absence to the duty officer and suggesting that he check with Cottage 8 before starting a search and calling the police, Mack made a request. "I have hunch, Chuck. Can you hold off for fifteen minutes to let me check it out?" A pause. "Thanks a lot. I'll get back to you."

"What do you have in mind?" Grace asked him.

"Do you remember the spot in the woods where they used to go together—down by the stream? Let's give it a try. It's only a few minutes' walk."

They stopped briefly at the cottage next door to theirs, explained the situation, and arranged for someone to keep an eye on the other girls, then they continued into the woods. There they found Gail and Marsha lying in each other's arms in the moonlight, fast asleep.

(Supplementary discussion questions, page 308)

4.2 THE FINK

As he approached the cottage through the blowing snow to report for work, Jack Hewitt could see his co-counselor, Greg Hilary, trying to carry several heavy pieces of wood up the icy steps.

"Why are you bringing lumber to work with you?" asked Jack, taking some of the boards. "Did I miss some news about a special project or something?"

"It's a special project, all right," said Greg dryly, managing to open the door so they could enter the cottage. "Did you notice the north side of the building as you drove up?"

"Oh, no!" groaned Jack. "Are those rec room windows smashed again?"

"They are," replied Greg, "and in about fifteen minutes the boys will be here from school. So, first, we board up the broken windows. . ."

"Then we hold a cottage meeting!" finished Jack, with some heat.

Greg called for order, and the boys fell silent. "All right," he started, "everybody's here now and I think we should get right to the point. Who broke the three windows in the rec room? It's clear that they were broken from the inside, so it had to be someone in this cottage."

"I didn't," said Al O'Kane promptly, rising to leave the room.

"Al, sit down!" ordered Jack. "If you didn't do it, you probably know who did. We'll start the questioning with you."

Looking highly offended, Al drew back. "The questioning?" he echoed. "Hey, what the hell do you think I am? A fink?" There was a general murmur of agreement that no one should be expected to be an informer.

"Look," said Greg, "this cottage is your home while you're here, and someone who is probably in this room has destroyed part of it. We tried to board the windows up, but the rec room's still going to be cold until we can get them fixed. Now if someone busts up my home, I'm not going to protect him. That just doesn't make sense."

The boys whispered among themselves for a few moments until Jack broke in. "Listen," he said, "this is a cottage problem. Until we know who broke those windows, everyone in the cottage is restricted except for meals and school."

One or two voices could be heard over the general clamor in the room.

"Does that mean everything, even special programs?" shouted one boy.

"How about off grounds trips?"

"What about varsity practice?"

Jack nodded, and Greg interrupted the chorus of questions. "We're not solving anything here," he said firmly. "This meeting is over until you guys decide you want to do something."

The two child care workers had been sitting in the cottage office for about fifteen minutes when they heard a soft tap at the door. Greg opened it to admit Kyle Donath, who stepped inside and quickly closed it behind him.

The boy looked at the two counselors for a moment or two before he started to speak. "I know who broke the windows," he began. "But if I tell you, then they'll get me." Jack began to say something, but Kyle shook his head. "No," he continued, "don't try to tell me they won't."

(Supplementary discussion questions, page 309)

4.3 "REALITY THERAPY"

Mark Grayson had worked with difficult youngsters for years and figured he could handle just about any kid who came his way. Even when everyone else gave up, Mark was usually able to find some redeeming quality and build on it to form a relationship. There had been aggressive delinquents, scapegoats, bizarre kids, even some whom his colleagues thought were totally obnoxious. But Sheldon Philbert seemed to be an exception. Although Sheldon had been in the group for only a few weeks, Mark felt completely frustrated already.

"I really don't know what I'm going to do," he groaned to Gene Chesney, another child care worker, one evening. "I never met such a kid. He's going to be the biggest scapegoat we've ever had, and you know what? He deserves every bit of it. He can't open his mouth without asking for it. I may just have to retire after another month with him."

Gene laughed. "Oh, come on, Mark, he can't be all that bad. You've had kids like him before. You'll find something to like in him."

"Oh, you think so?"

"You always do," said Gene, reassuringly.

"Well, you've never met a kid like this one. You come around a few days and then you tell me what you think of him."

Mark seemed angrier and more upset than Gene could remember ever having seen him. "Give it some time, Mark," he said. "You'll get to liking him yet."

"I don't know," Mark answered, shrugging. "I just don't know."

If anything, things got worse in the days that followed. The harder he tried to get close to Sheldon, the more he found that he disliked him. And he was not alone. Without exception, the other boys in the cottage had singled Sheldon out as their favorite target. Mark did his best to protect him, but he knew that a lot was going on behind his back. Maybe that's what he needs, Mark thought once or twice. If someone would really tell that kid off one of these days, it might set him straight.

Gene was concerned, too. "Try to take it easy, Mark," he said one day when they were talking about Sheldon. "You'll think of something when you calm down a little. You always do. You're letting him unnerve you."

It was true. That morning, Mark had addressed a special note to the cottage life director to emphasize his feelings of frustration and to ask for further help or advice. But he had thrown it away instead of submitting it because it embarrassed him. He resolved to try to follow Gene's advice.

That evening Mark was on duty in the cottage and suddenly became aware of loud angry shouts coming from Tony Bowman's room. Mark thought he recognized Sheldon's whining voice, barely audible above the din. He strode quickly down the hall and stopped outside the door.

"Well, it's about time someone told you off, you little punk." That was Tony. "Just who the hell do you think you are, reading my magazine? I never met such an ass in my whole life. And in case you didn't know it, this is the last warning you're getting. You just better shape up, or you'll be sorry you ever came here."

Another voice picked up the attack. "And if you don't believe it, just find out what happened to the last kid who came here and tried to play big shot with us." Loud, raucous laughter.

Mark could hear Sheldon whimpering. "You better leave me alone," he whined between sobs, "or you'll be sorry. I bet if Mr. Grayson knew the things you said to me, you'd all get shipped or something."

"You think so?" Tony replied triumphantly. "Well listen to this report he started to write about you. Coco and I found it crumpled up in the trash can when we emptied it this morning. He says, 'I really don't blame the boys too much for the way they gang up on Sheldon. I hate to admit it, but I really can't stand him myself.' What do you think of that, tough boy?"

In the hall Mark winced as he heard the taunts begin anew.

(Supplementary discussion questions, page 310)

4.4 HELPING THE SCAPEGOAT

"O.K., you guys, that's enough, knock it off," Chet Aronson said tightly. Then he turned to face Bruce Lang, a chubby fifteen-year old with carrot red hair and an overabundance of freckles. "Let's go downstairs, Bruce. What do you say?" The boy bobbed his head in reply, afraid to trust his voice. "And the rest of you guys get back to work," Chet added, turning back to the group.

As he began to walk away with Bruce, Chet could hear the boys behind them muttering under their breaths. "Jesus Christ, what a sissy!" one of them said.

Chet wheeled around. "I said to knock it off, or don't you guys understand English?"

"Yeah, we understand English," volunteered JoJo, "but, hell, we were just trying to teach him the facts of life. He better learn to fight back or he ain't gonna live too long when he gets back on the streets, and that's the truth."

"It's time you did some listening, JoJo," retorted Chet. "I'll do the teaching around here. You guys have enough problems of your own without worrying your heads about someone else's. Now get back to your jobs, all of you." The boys were silent this time and Chet and Bruce headed down the steps.

Chet was still feeling perturbed when he saw JoJo in the main building about an hour later. "Where are you supposed to be?" he asked, a little sharply.

"Hey, come on, man," JoJo replied, "Don't get sore at me again. I was just going down to the shop. See, I got a pass."

Chet eyed the pass and softened a little. "O.K. JoJo, I guess I was still mad from before. You guys shouldn't pick on Bruce all the time like that. That's not helping him any."

"Maybe not," JoJo replied, "but hell, Mr. Aronson, you sticking up for him all the time ain't helping him either. The guys don't like it. And we never really hurt the kid any, you know that. We were just kidding him a little. A guy's got to learn how to take some kidding without going all to pieces, don't he?"

"A little kidding is one thing, JoJo," said Chet, "but you guys don't let him breathe. Try to help him out sometime, instead of making it hard for him. He might surprise you."

JoJo was noncommital. "I have to get to the shop, Mr. Aronson," he said. "See you at the cottage."

That evening, Chet overheard one of the boys in the cottage ask where JoJo was, and someone replied that he had taken Bruce out for a little private conversation in the back yard. "You know what that means," someone else added, and the group snickered.

Annoyed, Chet turned and walked toward the back of the cottage. As he approached the door through the darkened kitchen, he could see it standing open and could hear the boys' voices from outside. JoJo was speaking, "Bruce," he said, "you gotta believe me when I tell you that you ain't gonna get nowhere in this place until you shape up. You gotta take your lumps!"

Chet had to strain slightly to hear the boy's response. "I can't," Bruce said tremulously. "They'll keep picking on me, and I can't fight all of you. I gotta have someone like Mr. Aronson on my side. He's the only one who can protect me from the guys. I have to keep going to him for help."

"Crap!" said JoJo in exasperation. "If you stand up on your own two feet and yell back when somebody's yellin' at you, you'll help yourself more than Aronson ever can."

"But what if I get hit?" asked Bruce.

"Hit 'em back," was JoJo's prompt reply. "Anyway, seein' you yelling back instead of blubbering is gonna shake them up so much, chances are they'll lay off."

"No, JoJo," protested Bruce, "I don't know how to fight, and if I start yelling around here I'll get killed. See? I just gotta keep going to Mr. Aronson!"

"O.K., kid," said JoJo in disgust. "You can't say I didn't try. But you better believe me, crying to a counselor every five minutes in a place like this is the kiss of death. And it's a damn shame you and Aronson are too stupid to see it."

JoJo then stomped through the kitchen, seemingly without noticing Chet standing there in the dark, and into the common room. Chet heard the boys ask him about Bruce as he entered, and he could hear Bruce sobbing just outside the door.

(Supplementary discussion questions, page 310)

4.5 THE LACKEY

"Eddie seems to be doing much better these days, doesn't he?" asked Maynard Ross as he waited with George Miller for the boys to return from school.

"I don't know," replied George. "It's true that he doesn't get picked on so much any more, but I have the feeling that he's Joe Mell's stooge. Joe arrived, sized everybody up, and traded his 'protection' for the services of a lackey. I don't like it."

"Well, it's a step up, anyway," laughed Maynard. "Eddie'll find a way to get out of Joe's clutches and stand on his own," he added more seriously.

"I'm not so sure," said George. "Joe has a lot of power in the cottage and he likes having an errand boy too much to let go easily."

"I still think we're ahead, George," replied Maynard. "At least we don't have to worry about Eddie being picked on all the time."

Realizing that George had a good point, Maynard smiled ruefully to himself that evening as he stood at the door of the recreation room and watched Eddie, Joe, and two other boys playing ping-pong. It certainly was a peaceful contrast to the typical scene of a month before when, until an adult stopped it, the boys often seemed to take turns baiting Eddie to see who could make him cry first, and loudest.

A little later, Maynard noticed what appeared to be a furtive conversation between Eddie and Joe. It looked as if Joe were giving Eddie detailed instructions about something. Eddie looked somewhat frightened, and both boys quickly turned toward the television set when they noticed that Maynard was watching.

"Well, let's see what happens if I give poor Eddie enough rope," thought Maynard as he said, clearly enough to be heard over the sound of the television, "O.K., boys, when this program ends, it'll be curfew."

Maynard then walked into the child care office across the hall and began to straighten up the papers scattered on the desk. In a few minutes he saw Eddie emerge from the recreation room and walk toward the front door of the cottage. Maynard followed quietly as Eddie continued out the door and around to an old tool shed at one end of the building. Within a few seconds Eddie practically walked into Maynard's arms on his way back to the cottage. "Hand it over, Eddie," said Maynard, noticing that the boy was carrying something. "Come on, what do you have there?"

Mutely, Eddie shook his head and tried to hide the package he was carrying. Reaching out, Maynard pulled it away from him and tore off the bag. "Oh, no," he groaned, "A bottle of wine. How in hell did Joe ever get a bottle of wine up here?"

"It's not his wine!" Eddie yelped, breaking his silence. "It's mine! I got it. It has nothing to do with Joe. It's mine!"

"Knock it off, Eddie," commanded Maynard, recalling his conversation with George Miller earlier in the day. "You and I both know that Joe just told you to get this wine back to him—and now it seems he also told you to take the blame if you got caught. Isn't that how it happened?"

"No, it isn't," screamed Eddie, "and don't try to get me in trouble because you want to pin something on Joe!"

(Supplementary discussion questions, page 311)

4.6 "I CAN'T GO BACK!"

The boy shook his head vehemently as he looked up at the faces around the infirmary examining table. The doctor had just finished stitching up a cut on his scalp a few minutes before, his right eye was swollen and almost completely shut, and the thin adhesive bandages covering the cuts on his face gave him a curious, patterned look.

"No," he said firmly, "I didn't recognize any of the guys who hit me."

"Come on, Ralph," said Bob Mays, his child care worker. "You've already told us you were beaten up by three boys right in back of the cottage. You must have some idea who did it."

Wincing slightly, Ralph shook his head again.

"Maybe we should give him his aspirin and let him get to bed," suggested Ann Frazer, the nurse. "He'll be feeling better in the morning, and you can talk to him then. He may even be able to leave the infirmary tomorrow."

Ralph winced again and the unit administrator, John Ryan, who had been standing silently at the foot of the examining table, spoke. "We can only help you if you tell us who was involved and why there was a fight, Ralph. Otherwise we'll have to take the time to find out for ourselves. Give it some thought, O.K.?"

"Forget it," gasped Ralph painfully, as he began to inch his way off the table. "Just forget the whole thing."

After helping the boy into bed, the two men stopped in the infirmary office so Bob could call the cottage. Learning that everything there was quiet, they accepted Ann's offer of coffee.

"Where do we go from here?" asked Bob. "If Ralph goes back to the cottage as scared as he is now, we're practically begging for more trouble."

John shook his head grimly and closed the door before he spoke. "Whatever we do, I want it made damn clear that behavior like that won't be tolerated and it better not happen again. That message might help Ralph relax a little, too, so we can bring him back into the cottage in a better way. Maybe we should also make an example of the kids who attacked him when we find out who they are."

"I can pretty much guess who they are," replied Bob. "Jack, Marty, and Kurt. They've been throwing their weight around lately, and this looks like something they'd do. But if the others think Ralph told us the names, it might make it worse for him. You know how they feel about 'ratting.' He might be isolated by everybody else in the cottage. Wouldn't it be better if he tries to work this out on his own when he comes back? Of course, we'll be there to help if he needs it."

John thought a moment before replying. "That's often a good technique, Bob," he said finally, "but it seems to me that things have gone too far for that here. We're the responsible adults and we have to let the boys know where we stand."

"Yes," agreed Bob, "but I'd like to find a way to do it without putting Ralph in an even weaker position. Maybe I should talk to him in the morning before we decide."

"Good," replied John. "See what he tells you then, when he's a little less upset."

The next morning, Ralph was sitting up in bed when Bob arrived. He seemed to be feeling better but still refused to name his attackers.

"I can understand why you'd rather not tell," Bob said, "but do you think you can work it out on your own when you get back to the cottage?"

Ralph looked at him briefly, then slumped against the pillow and, almost in tears, turned his face toward the wall. "Look," he said, his voice muffled, "those bastards beat me up because one of them found out I'm scheduled for a home leave. His girl friend lives in my neighborhood and he was just warning me what would happen if I talked to her. I don't even know the girl," Ralph continued, "but they don't believe that and nothing you can say will convince them. I'm not going back to that cottage. Never! I can't, don't you see?"

"Will it help if we promise that no one will hurt you again?" Bob asked.

Turning his head, Ralph looked at him desperately. "They'll find a way to get at me if I'm there," he said. "Can't I be moved to another cottage?"

"What will that solve?" asked Bob. "Will it stop them from getting at you if they really want to and if we don't even know who should be watched? And it won't help if they think you're running away from them, will it?"

Ralph looked more miserable than before. "I don't know, Mr. Mays," he finally said. "I'm scared stiff and I don't know what to do. I just don't want to get beat up again. Let me think about it for a while, O.K.? I don't have to leave here now, do I?"

Bob nodded reassuringly. "You'll be able to stay here until we have a plan. I'll remind the nurse on my way out. See you this afternoon."

Leaving the infirmary, Bob headed for the administration building to talk with John. "What am I going to suggest?" he thought. "How are we going to get this kid back so the other boys won't reject him before he even has a chance?"

(Supplementary discussion questions, page 311)

5. LIVING IN GROUPS

Older children and adolescents usually rely heavily on groups of their peers not only for social companionship, but also for mutual reassurance and at least some of their behavior standards. Partly for this reason, the behavior of youngsters in groups often appears to be different from and more complex than the behavior of the individual youngsters involved. These tendencies may be even greater in institutional settings because the youngsters live so closely together and share almost all parts of their lives, and because other influences are usually more remote. Therefore it is important that child care workers be able to work effectively with groups and to support the individuality of the group members while maintaining group morale and the institution's behavioral requirements.

TABLE OF CASES

114

5.1 PEER CULTURE

Realizing that a fight had developed, Barry Evans ran out of the office and down the steps to the cottage play room.

"Damn you, take that!" he heard, followed by a pained grunt as the victim fell against some chairs.

"Knock it off, you guys," Barry shouted as he reached the door. "That's enough!" Most of the boys were standing around watching as Tony and Greg went at each other again. "I said that's enough!" he continued, pulling them apart. Tony's nose was bleeding, and both were almost trembling with rage.

"Let them fight, Mr. Evans," said one of the onlookers. "They'll just finish it later on when you're not around anyway."

"That's enough out of you, too," replied Barry. "I've had it up to here with you guys fighting."

Bill White, Barry's co-worker in the cottage, entered the room. "What's going on here?" he asked.

"Another fight," Barry said. "Will you see if Greg's all right while I go up with Tony to stop that nosebleed?" Bill nodded and they left the room.

Things went smoothly for the rest of the afternoon, but Barry and Bill were disturbed about the fighting in the group. It seemed that there was at least one fight a day, and usually more.

"It's not that long since I was a teenager," Barry said, "and I think I remember what it was like. But I sure don't recall any of the guys fighting all the time like this. I guess there were fights after school once in a while, and once or twice there was some trouble after a football game, but these kids are at each other's throats."

"Of course, we weren't in institutions," replied Bill. "These are the most difficult kids of all."

"I know that," said Barry, "but there were some pretty tough kids in my high school, too. They got into all kinds of trouble—stealing, drugs, suspended from school, even picked up by the police and taken to court. I don't think they were any better than most of the kids here. But there was never this constant fighting, even among them, and most of them seemed to straighten out after high school. These kids are really trying to hurt each other. The whole feeling is different."

"I guess you're right about that," Bill responded. "What do you think we can do about it?"

"Maybe we should have a cottage meeting to discuss it with the boys. We always talk about it when the crisis erupts, but I'd like to try it in a calmer atmosphere, like before bedtime."

"I think that's a good idea," said Bill. "If nothing else breaks out today, let's do it tonight."

Barry and Bill were both on duty that evening and they gathered the boys together in one of the dormitories just before lights out.

"We've been concerned about all the fighting among you guys," Barry began, "and we wish we knew why there always seems to be a fight brewing around here. You're one of the best groups in the place—we know that—but it seems like there's an explosion every day. Can anybody tell us why? Or how to stop it?"

There were a few snickers and coughs, and one of the boys whispered behind his hand to another, but no one offered to respond.

"Could we all hear what you just whispered to Al?" asked Bill, looking at Frank Evans. "We really want to know what you think and how we can help stop the fighting."

"We just play around a little," Frank said, shrugging. "Why does it bother you so much?"

"It just seems to us that life is hard enough," said Bill, "especially for boys living away from home and in an institution, without wasting all this effort fighting among yourselves. When I was your age, the guys around our way didn't fight all the time, so I can't help feeling that you don't have to either. You know, you're not so different from the way we were at your age."

"Excuse me, Bill," interrupted Barry. "Some of the boys are shaking their heads. Can't we work on this and stop some of the fighting?" he asked, turning to the boys.

"Do you really want to know?" asked Frank, a little annoyed. "O.K., let me tell you how it is, 'cause you don't understand. Where we come from, you have to be able to fight or you'll get killed in the street. You guys never would've made it there if you didn't fight. That's how we know who's in charge here, too. The toughest guys run the cottage."

Barry and Bill glanced at each other to see who would reply.

(Supplementary discussion questions, page 312)

5.2 ON THEIR OWN

"Wait a minute," said Barney Holt to the boys in the cottage. "Let's forget about doing the Saturday cleanup detail for now." The boys relaxed a little, waiting to see what was coming next. "I'd just like someone to tell me why things usually go so well all week and then we fall apart on Saturday morning when it comes time to scrub this place. There must be a reason. I don't think you guys want to live in a pigpen any more than I do. Doesn't anybody have any ideas on what we can do about it?"

The boys looked uncomfortable, but no one spoke. Finally, Barney continued in a somewhat sterner tone. "I want to be completely clear about one thing," he said. "This cottage is going to be clean. There are health laws that require it, the institution insists on it, and I'm going to see that it happens, even if we have to stay in here all weekend. But I'd rather that we could find an easier way," he added a little more softly. "The whole job should only take about an hour."

The boys looked at each other and, after a few moments, Rocco Brown began to speak. Rocco was the acknowledged leader of the cottage. "Look man," he said, "don't go makin' a Federal case out of this. If it's so important to you, I'll see that the cottage gets clean. Just let me take care of it starting next week, O.K.?"

"Sounds good to me," Barney responded. "Let's give it a try. But this place has to be clean today, too."

"No problem," said Rocco, grabbing a broom and beginning to

sweep. The boys and Barney worked together and the job was completed quickly.

The following Saturday, Barney called Rocco aside before breakfast to remind the boy that he would be responsible for the weekly cleanup detail that day.

"Don't worry," Rocco said. "Just stay downstairs in the office, and I'll call you when the place is ready."

Sure enough, within an hour after breakfast Rocco told Barney that he could inspect the cottage, and Barney found all in good order.

"You really did a good job," Barney told the boys.

"We had a little static at first," Rocco explained, "but once we got organized and got everybody straightened out, we really got cracking."

"Well, it looks great," replied Barney, hoping it would continue. "Keep it up."

Things went well again the next week, and Barney began to think about giving the boys more responsibility in other areas as well. By the following Thursday, however, Barney sensed that the group was unusually tense and irritable, but he could not get anyone to open up about what was troubling them. That night one of the smaller boys in the cottage approached him just after lights out.

"Mr. Holt," said Victor, "I don't feel good. My stomach hurts real bad. Can I go to the infirmary tonight and tomorrow night?"

Puzzled, Barney looked closely at the youngster. "I can call the nurse and she'll see you if you don't feel well," he said, "but how on earth could any of us know how long you'll need to stay?" Victor just shrugged, and Barney picked up the telephone and called the infirmary.

About half an hour later, the nurse, Mrs. Fowler, called Barney. "I think I'll just let Victor sleep here tonight," she said. "I can't find anything specific that's wrong with him, but he might develop something more in the way of symptoms by morning. By the way," she added, "Vic seems to have some sort of strange idea about his 'sickness.' He keeps insisting that he has the 'two-day flu' and can't possibly leave here until Saturday afternoon. He was almost in tears trying to make me understand that he wouldn't be well enough to go back to the cottage before then. Does that make any sense to you, Barney?"

"I think it might, Mrs. Fowler," replied Barney, as the truth about the Saturday cleanup detail dawned on him. "I'll get to work on it and call you in the morning."

(Supplementary discussion questions, page 312)

5.3 THE CRUDE AWAKENING

Stan Jacobson smiled to himself as he completed the weekly report form for his cottage. He had worked at the institution only a short time, but everything seemed to be going smoothly.

As Stan stood up from the desk, Fred Sullivan, one of the boys in his cottage, slipped into the office through the partially open door and quickly closed it behind him. He took a deep breath and started to speak but, apparently changing his mind, suddenly shook his head and turned away. "Never mind, Mr. Jacobson," he said. "Sorry I bothered you."

"Oh, come on," urged Stan, "you didn't come all the way up here just to look at me. It must be something. What's the problem?"

"Nothing," the boy gulped, "but I'll have a *big* problem if I don't get out now."

"Look," said Stan firmly, noting that Fred was not making much effort to go, "you'll be in bigger trouble if you leave here without telling me what's on your mind."

"OK," Fred began in a rush of words, "it's this. Me and two other guys matched pennies and I lost so I had to be the one to tell. Mackie runs this cottage and it's getting worse and worse. We figure it's 'cause you're new and don't know about it. Anyway, we were only supposed to give them our seconds on desert and stuff like that, but now they're grabbing everything we got and they say if we open our mouths they'll beat the shit out of us."

Stan looked at the boy. "Wait a minute," he said, "let me get this straight. You mean Philip Mackie has a gang and they blackmail the rest of the kids? How long has this been going on?"

"I don't know," replied Fred. "It was set up like this when I got here. Another kid was in charge then, but Mackie took over when he left. I don't care about that," the boy added impatiently, "it's just that it's worse now. Can you fix it—at least back the way it used to be?"

"Did Mr. Lenox know about Mackie?" asked Stan, naming the child care worker he had replaced.

"I guess so," said Fred, shrugging. "It was O.K. then. I mean, like we gave those guys any extras we got and did some of their work jobs and stuff like that. And they fixed it so nobody from the other cottages messed around with us, and there wasn't no stealin' or nothing in our cottage even, because everybody was too scared of Mackie. But since Lenox left, it's terrible. They steal our money and everything. Look," he said, glancing at the clock on the wall, "I better get back. If they think I'm telling you about it, I'm dead."

Thinking, Stan looked at the boy for a second before he spoke. "Oh, OK, Fred," he finally said. "You go back now and I'll talk to you later."

Stan sat and thought for a long time before going out to watch the boys in the recreation room, where he hoped he would spot something to shed more light on Fred's story. He did not see Philip Mackie and some of his friends, so Stan went out into the hall, where he noticed that the door to the TV room was closed. As he approached, he heard Philip's voice from inside.

"Don't worry just cause some crybaby blabbed to Jacobson," Philip said. "Even if he believes the kid, there's nothing he can do about it. Business as usual!"

(Supplementary discussion questions, page 313)

5.4 EVERYBODY GETS HIGH
ON SOMETHING

Del Corbett was cutting across the grounds on his way to the junior cottage when he noticed that the door to the storage shed was ajar. Knowing the strict rule about keeping all unsupervised buildings locked, he stopped to investigate. Just as he was about to pull the door open, he heard familiar voices from inside.

"Hey, Charley, you're gonna get into big trouble!" said Juan.

"Shhh, keep your voice down," was the reply.

"Yeah, shut up," said a boy Del thought he recognized as Flip. "Charley knows what he's doing."

"And if you know what's smart, you'll get in on this deal," said Charley, "we're really gonna make us some money."

Del shook his head as he listened. Charley was a negative leader who seemed to have almost a magical power to influence and control the other boys in the group, and Del had been struggling with the problem for a long time.

"How'd you get all this grass, Charley?" asked Flip.

"Never mind. I got it. And remember, Juan, the only reason you're in on this is because you saw us before we could get the door closed. I got some acid here, too."

"Where you gonna take the stuff now?" asked Juan. "They'll be back here with the tractor pretty soon."

"That's why I need you guys," replied Charley. "We gotta get this divvied up, so we can hide it better."

"When can we have some, Charley?" Juan asked.

"Take it easy, kid," answered Charley. "There'll be plenty for us, but most of it, we sell! There's more where this came from."

"Jeeze," Flip said, "you really are smart, Charley. We get to keep some to get high on, and we sell the rest and make some money. I gotta hand it to you."

Abruptly throwing open the door, Del walked inside. "Yes, Charley," he echoed, "you're really smart, aren't you?"

"I got nothin' to say," replied the boy, deciding to brazen it out.

Del ignored him and turned to Juan. "Would you like to explain just how smart Charley was to get this stuff?" he asked.

"It's not my fault, Mr. Corbett," murmured Juan, looking frightened. "I just happened to be walking by when . . ."

Ignoring Juan's excuses, Del turned to Flip. "O.K. Flip, you tell me."

Excited, Flip began with a rush of words, "Well, Charley got it and was telling us how we could keep some and sell . . ." Uncertainly, his voice trailed off, as he realized he had said too much.

Del stepped back and looked at all of them. "And that's smart, is it?" he asked.

"Here comes the fancy speech!" sneered Charley.

Del paused, then allowed the anger to show in his voice when he spoke. "O.K., before we leave here for Mr. Farrell's office, there are a few things I want to tell you about being 'smart' as you call it. No big speech. But you better listen carefully—and try to remember while you still have a memory."

Flip's curiosity overcame his fear. "What do you mean, while we still have a memory?" he asked.

"Just what I said," answered Del evenly. "If you plan on using acid, you'd better remember that some people flip out after a bad trip. Drugs can mess up brain tissue, and that's where the old memory bank is stored, buddy. Not to mention what it can do to the rest of your body. And your children. Right now, though, all I want to tell you is about being 'smart' like your so-called friend here, Charley."

"Get off my back," Charley muttered sullenly. "I didn't invent the stuff."

"I know," agreed Del. "Way back when I was in school, I knew another 'smart' boy who figured all the angles, too. He would have thought what you guys were planning on doing is kid stuff. He started out smoking pot, but it wasn't long before he was trying whatever he could get his hands on. One day when he was mainlining H, he got an overdose—and nobody found him in time." Del paused a moment, then added, "End of story and end of 'smart' boy. He wasn't quite thirteen!"

Wide-eyed, Flip looked up at Del. "Wow!" he said.

Charley's composure was slightly shaken, but he still managed to sound contemptuous. "Crap! You adults make me sick! Everybody gets high one way or another. Listen, you have Saturday off and I see you comin' back here Sunday morning with your eyes plenty red, and they don't get that way from watchin' TV, neither. They get that way from you boozin' it up on Saturday night! Why can't we have a little fun, too?"

(Supplementary discussion questions, page 313)

5.5 HELP!

Lew Coyle was watching his boys seat themselves with their dinner trays when he noticed that Bud Campbell, the newest youngster in the cottage, seemed to be trying to stall at the end of the cafeteria line. From that distance, Bud scanned the group carefully for several seconds. Only after he seemed satisfied that everyone else was seated did he sidle over to sit down himself, obviously choosing a place as far away from one group of the other boys as he could. Glancing around, Lew noticed that Rudy, one of the older boys, and his small clique of followers were watching Bud closely. One of Rudy's cronies was speaking in a stage whisper.

"Hey, Rudy," he said, "I don't think little Buddy-boy wants to sit near us."

"Yeah," agreed Rudy. "I do believe he's shy. We'll just have to teach him to be more friendly." The others snickered, clearly enjoying the discomfort visible on Bud's face as he stared at his plate, picking at his food.

Several hours later, after a hectic evening in the cottage, Lew was slumped at the desk in the cottage office working on the daily log. Not quite sure how to report his observation at dinner, he glared at the hotplate on the corner of the desk, wondering why it always took so long for the water to boil when he wanted coffee so badly.

Rudy and his friends were suspected of a great deal of sexual acting out and Lew was convinced that they had been eyeing Bud in the hope of involving him in their sexual activities. Still, he hesitated to report what was really only conjecture. "Whatever is happening," he mused, "there's no doubt that Bud is scared stiff." Lew shook his head as he recalled the fear in the boy's eyes at dinner and, frowning at the hotplate again, decided that he'd better check that everything was in order with the youngsters. He picked up his flashlight, unplugged the hotplate, and left the office.

Halfway down the hall, on the floor above, Lew stopped in his tracks. He had heard a muffled cry coming from one of the rooms. Stepping quickly to the door, he strained to hear what was being said inside. After a moment's silence, he could hear Rudy talking in a soft, almost cajoling voice. "You might as well enjoy it," he said. "Everyone gets a turn."

Flinging the door open, Lew saw Bud stripped and pinned to the floor, held there by three of the boys. Rudy, who was also naked, was straddling him and stroking his body.

(Supplementary discussion questions, page 314)

5.6 INTERGROUP RELATIONS

Frank Hartley looked up from the magazine he was reading. "What do you want, Tim?" he asked the youngster standing in the doorway. "It's after curfew."

"Uh, Mr. Hartley," the boy began nervously, "don't tell I told, but there's something going on in that supply room upstairs. It's bad, I think."

"What is it?" asked Frank. "Kids fighting?"

"The guys up there are calling each other 'nigger' and 'white bastard' and things like that," replied Tim. "It sounds like there's gonna be a race riot or something."

"I doubt that," replied Frank, getting to his feet. "You go back to bed and I'll check it out."

"O.K.," agreed the boy, somewhat uncertainly, "but remember, I was the one who warned you. I'm not like some of those other black kids. I'm not looking for trouble!"

Dismissing the boy with a nod, Frank started down the hall. "What's this 'black kids' business?" he wondered. "There never has been any particular racial problem in the cottage. Although," he corrected himself, "it wasn't until the past three or four months that we've had more than a couple of black kids at a time."

Still mulling this over, Frank stopped as he reached the partly opened supply room door on the floor above. Stan Pierce, a white youngster, one of the oldest and most influential boys in the cottage, was speaking in muffled tones. "I warned you before, kid," he said. "Keep your voice down. You'll make it even worse for yourself if Hartley hears you. Any nigger gets me in trouble, I'll beat the shit out of him. Personally!"

After a moment, Frank heard a sneering voice in reply. "Whitey's gettin' scared, ain't he, boys? What you going to do about it, Pierce?"

"Look," replied Stan, "all I want is the stuff you stole from Boyd. It's that simple. And no more stealing from my boys around here!"

"Fuck you!" came the answer. "You guys blame us whenever anything is missing. Man, that jive don't go no more, and you better believe it!"

"I think these chicken-shit black bastards need a little lesson in who's boss," said Stan. "They don't seem to know."

Without waiting any longer, Frank bolted into the room. "O.K., that's all," he said. "You guys belong in bed. You've been warned about messing around after curfew. We'll deal with this tomorrow. Now get moving!"

The three white youngsters looked warily at Frank and began to move toward the door. The Negro boys, however, whispered together for a few seconds and then seemed to freeze into place.

"Come on," barked Frank. "We'll get this settled in the morning. All of it! But you guys get to bed now. Move!"

"No chance," said Leroy. "We're sick and tired of being treated like dirt around here. We have our rights and we ain't movin' one inch 'til this is settled!"

"Suits me fine!" said Stan menacingly as he walked toward Leroy.

"You're crowding me man," responded Leroy, pushing Stan backwards over a bundle of laundry on the floor.

(Supplementary discussion questions, page 314)

5.7 FOILED FROM ABOVE!

"That's great, Cliff," said Leon Brown to his fellow child care worker as they looked at the budding vegetable garden of Cottage 4. "I wish we had thought of it, too, but it's too late to plant a garden now. We could sure use a project to bring our guys together."

"The kids have done this one pretty much on their own," responded Cliff McGinnis. "I think it's doing all of us a lot of good, not to mention the fresh tomatoes and carrots we'll be eating soon. We might even decide to learn something about sharing," he added with a grin, "and give some to Cottage 3."

"Well, we'd be glad to help out," smiled Leon in response. "Any time you want to share, just give a yell and we'll make it easy for you."

"I just hope some of the kids in the other cottages don't decide to mess things up," said Cliff, more serious now. "The boys would find it hard to take, and I can't say I'd blame them. It's the one thing that worries me about this project. We can't guard it all the time."

"I don't think it's likely," replied Leon reassuringly. "You put it in a good spot here, between your cottage and the woods. Someone would really have to be looking for trouble, because almost no one comes by here."

"I hope so. That's why we chose this spot."

"Good luck, anyway," said Leon as he turned to go. "Mr. Fowler will be pleased when he comes back from his vacation, too, and that can't hurt you, you know. Let me know if you think of any cottage projects that I might be able to use."

Later that day, Cliff heard a small bulldozer outside the cottage and wondered vaguely what the latest new construction on grounds would be. He thought little of it, however, until he heard shrieks from two of the boys who had just returned from school. "Mr. McGinnis," they yelled, running up the cottage steps, "look what old man Hull just did. He wrecked our garden!"

Cliff ran outside and saw the beginnings of a ditch where the garden had been. Mr. Hull was on the bulldozer behind the cottage, continuing to dig.

Quickly recovering from his shock, Cliff realized that the boys were gathering as they arrived back at the cottage and preparing to confront Mr. Hull. "Get inside the cottage, all of you," he ordered. "I'll talk to Mr. Hull."

After the boys were inside, where they gathered at the cottage windows to watch and listen, Cliff walked quickly toward the bulldozer and signaled to Mr. Hull to stop. "What the hell happened to our garden?" he asked angrily.

"Look," Mr. Hull began, "all I know is that I got my orders from the office. This here slip," he said, pulling a work order out of his shirt pocket, "says they want this ditch dug for the new sewage line before Mr. Fowler gets back from his vacation. He'll be back in a couple of weeks, and then they want to get started laying pipe to where they're building the new treatment plant. They're going to get bids so it can be built this fall."

"This fall?" echoed Cliff indignantly. "By then the boys would have had a chance to see everything grow, and the garden would have been . . ."

"I don't know nothin' about that," Mr. Hull interrupted testily, "but to tell you the truth, as hard as it's been for me to try and run a mower around that garden, I ain't sorry . . ."

At this point a yell cut across the yard, causing both men to turn toward the cottage.

"Oh, yeah?" bellowed Frankie, leaning out one of the windows. "You'll be sorry, you old bastard! Just wait and see, Mr. Hull, we'll fix you!"

Abruptly, Mr. Hull turned and started up the bulldozer, drowning out the shouts of the other boys, and went back to his work. Cliff continued to stand there for a moment, indecisively, before turning to walk back toward the cottage.

(Supplementary discussion questions, page 315)

5.8 A THIEF AMONG US

Hank Lee and his supervisor were discussing the problem of stealing in Hank's cottage. "So," Hank concluded, "the kids are angry because they think someone's taking their things, but some of them may not be losing as much as they say they are."

"Does everyone seem agreed that it's happening within the cottage and not coming from outside?" asked Mr. Thomas.

"Yes," Hank replied. "The cottage is always locked when we go out, and the kids seem to be convinced that it's an 'inside job,' as it were. Everyone claims to have lost something or other, but they think that the thief is making up stories about that as a cover. In fact, that's partly why I think they're exaggerating. Anyone who didn't say that he had something stolen would be suspected by the others."

Mr. Thomas shook his head. "Stealing is always a problem in places where people are gathered together," he said, "whether it's lockers that get rifled in public schools or whatever. And it seems to appear in waves—in a few months, it might develop in a different cottage. Would you like to try a new approach?"

"What's that?" asked Hank.

"Something I heard suggested once, but I never tried it. Suppose you suggested that the kids set up their own insurance company."

Hank was perplexed. "What do you mean?" he asked.

"The idea works like this," Mr. Thomas replied. "Each kid puts in so much a week from the money he earns on grounds or his office credit—say fifty cents. Then anyone who has something stolen can make a claim."

"But wouldn't most of them claim as much as they could?" Hank asked. "The fund wouldn't last two days."

"Making a claim doesn't mean you get paid that amount," responded Mr. Thomas. "The kids could investigate each claim, and they would have a stake in finding out whose claims were true and who was doing the stealing. It would put the problem back on the group rather than your always being in the position of judge and jury. In a way, it might even get you off the spot and help them solve the problem at the same time. Anyway, that's the general idea."

"I don't know," said Hank slowly. "It seems to me that there might be some problems, but maybe it's worth a try."

"It's just an idea, Hank," Mr. Thomas replied, "and it's your decision. I've never seen it tried and I don't know whether it would work, although it sounded interesting when I heard about it. What do you think?"

(Supplementary discussion questions, page 316)

6. RELATIONSHIPS BETWEEN YOUNGSTERS AND ADULTS

The relationships between adult staff members and youngsters comprise what is probably the most important element contributing to the success or failure of an institutional program. Child care workers usually relate more closely to institutionalized youngsters on a day-to-day basis than do any other adults. Their relationships with youngsters are fundamental both in cottage management and in promoting favorable changes in behavior.

TABLE OF CASES

6.1 CHALLENGING AUTHORITY

Bill sighed to himself as he walked toward the dining hall with the boys. Although his group was reputed to be one of the toughest on grounds, his first week as a child care worker had generally gone smoothly and he felt he was doing pretty well. There had been some of the testing the director had warned him to expect, however, and Bill was glad he had taken pains to be strict. He planned to ease up later, when the boys had gotten used to him and knew who was boss.

When he reached the dining hall, Bill realized that the boys had already disappeared inside. Hurrying, he arrived just as they were seating themselves. Sunday dinner was served family style, a pleasant change from the cafeteria lines Bill had come to expect. He quickly reviewed the serving procedures he had learned from the manual: one boy gets the food, the counselor serves, another boy clears.

As Bill approached the table, Ted, a tall hefty boy, was ordering Sam to get the food. Bill was not pleased with the way this was being done but because he had arrived late and not seen the beginning of the incident, he decided to wait to see what would happen before saying anything. He knew that Ted was the informal leader of the group and often bullied the smaller boys. In fact, he had talked with Ted about it and Ted had seemed to understand.

Sam struggled to the table under the burden of the heavy tray, depositing the food in front of Ted.

"I'll have that here," Bill said forcefully, looking straight at Ted.

"Mind your own business," retorted Ted. "This is the way we do things in this cottage and you might as well start learning now."

Bill felt himself flush. The boys were looking at him expectantly. He glanced around quickly. A hush had fallen over the dining hall and all eyes seemed to be focused on him.

(Supplementary discussion questions, page 316)

6.2 "IF YOU DO THIS FOR ME . . ."

It was late when Jeff LaBonte rushed into the administration building to pick up the day's mail for his cottage.

"Hey, Jeff," called Gary Bott. "How are things going in the Senior Cottage?"

"Better," replied Jeff with a grin, "of course, for the first few days things were so low there wasn't any place to go but up!"

"Are the older kids much harder to handle than our junior boys?" asked Gary, who had been Jeff's co-worker prior to his transfer.

"They are that!" replied Jeff as they turned to leave the reception room. "Somehow, a seventeen-year old doesn't seem to care like a nine-year old does when you tell him he's going to get a big green demerit if he doesn't keep his clothes picked up."

"Doesn't he know," asked Gary, grinning widely, "that four green demerits equal one red demerit and that means no canteen for candy on Saturday?"

"No," laughed Jeff. "As a matter of fact, he's quite explicit about telling you what you can do with your demerits—red and green!"

"That figures!" called Gary as they separated on the way to their respective cottages.

Jeff grinned in response and started across the grounds thinking about how different it was to work with the older boys and how hard it had been at the beginning, particularly when it came to discipline and getting the boys to perform their assigned cottage tasks. However, he felt that he had hit on a technique that seemed to be working. He thought that if the older boys could be made to see the value of performing in a positive way, they might begin to respond. Therefore he had carefully started distributing extra recreation passes and other special privileges to those youngsters who complied with the rules. Gradually life in the cottage had improved to the point where Jeff felt he could almost relax. Today, though, the special shopping trip he had taken the boys on ran much later than he had anticipated and here he was in the middle of the afternoon with none of the weekly cottage chores done. Well, he thought hopefully, maybe the kids have taken some initiative in getting started so we can be finished by dinnertime.

Entering the cottage, Jeff was encouraged at the sight of several boys busily cleaning the day room and mopping the hall floor. When he checked the kitchen, however, he found Ben working alone, with the other boy assigned to kitchen duty nowhere in sight.

"Hey, Mr. LaBonte," called Ben when he saw Jeff at the door, "I can't clean all this up alone in time for those other guys to start supper."

"Where's Eddie?" asked Jeff.

"I don't know. Goofing off outside, I think. Just remember, I warned you," he added, glaring at the cluttered room.

Jeff opened the back door of the cottage and walked down the steps. Eddie was stretched out on the ground, holding a transistor radio in one hand while he turned the pages of a comic book with the other.

"Come on, Eddie," said Jeff, "the other guys are working, and I want to see you get busy in that kitchen now, too."

"Can I get a grounds pass to go to the canteen after dinner if I do my job?" asked the boy.

Jeff frowned down at him and replied, "You know one thing doesn't have any bearing on the other. You're supposed to do your job—period. We don't make 'deals' about it."

At this point Jeff glanced at the cottage and saw that Ben had stopped working and was standing at the open door. A few of the other youngsters were watching and listening from the windows. "No deals," he repeated a little more firmly. "Just get to the kitchen."

Eddie, who was slowly getting to his feet, started to laugh. "Listen, man," he sneered, "all these guys have your number. The only way you ever get us to do anything is by bribing us. That's what the trip today and all those extra privileges are all about. So don't try to hand me that jive about no deals!"

(Supplementary discussion questions, page 317)

6.3 "PLEASE, MR. CAMPBELL, PLEASE . . ."

"Couldn't you please go in to Cooper and ask him to change his mind? Please?" Jackson's voice was pleading, and Elliott Campbell had to turn briefly to gaze out the window before he could reply.

"Look, Jackson," Elliott began, "we've been through this before. Every time we get a program worked out for you, you manage to do something to foul it up and everybody ends up in a mess. First, you decide you're through with school and you get your therapist to convince Mr. Cooper to put you on the work detail. We beat the bushes to find you a job here you'll really like. So Mr. Bowman takes you on as his apprentice and tries to teach you about mechanical maintenance. Then you decide working isn't for you, and you tell Mr. Bowman he's driving you crazy and you can't work. Because of that, Mr. Bowman doesn't want to have boys working with him any more, and it makes the people who got you the job look bad, too. Now you decide that what you really want is to get back into school and you want me to go in and plead your case with Mr. Cooper and the school!"

Jackson leaned across the desk, begging earnestly. "Mr. Campbell, if Mr. Cooper won't let me back in school, I'm dead. You know I gotta be in a program to stay here. I got no parents and I'm not old enough for the army yet, so I got no place else to go. Please fix it up for me to get back in school. I'll be O.K. then. Besides," he added defensively, "that Mr. Bowman lied, anyway. I never said he was driving me crazy. He said I was crazy, and I got mad and left. Honest!"

Elliott got to his feet slowly, sighing, "All right, Jackson, I'll go in and talk to Mr. Cooper. I really don't know if it will do any good, but I'll try."

The following morning, Elliott Campbell made the unit bulletin board his first stop. He noted with approval that Mr. Cooper had indeed put Jackson's name on the school list. Their conversation about the boy yesterday had not been an easy one, and Elliott had really gone out on a limb by promising that the boy would repay this vote of confidence by trying to do his best in school so that Mr. Cooper would not regret the decision. Thinking now about how alone Jackson really was in the world, despite his air of bravado, Elliott was pleased that he had been able to help him.

As Elliott entered the cottage and walked toward the common room, he heard Dino, Jackson's closest friend, talking dramatically to the group. "Jackson is bee-u-tee-ful!" he said. "He can get anything he wants in this place. The payoff came this morning. He got his name back on that school list just like he said he would. He's got them in the palm of his hand!"

"Dino, you gotta do something in my honor this time," Jackson said.

"Sure," replied Dino. "Let me name a dinner after you. Chile *Con* Carne. Do you guys get it? *Con*!"

The room echoed with the boy's laughter, and Elliott could hear Jackson laughing loudest of all.

(Supplementary discussion questions, page 317)

6.4 YOUNGSTERS OR ADULTS— WHO'S IN CHARGE?

The assistant director was summarizing the results of the case conference. "We all seem to agree with Jim, then, that Billy needs to learn that the adults are in charge here. We can control him, and we will. He's a bright kid with a lot of charm, and most of us have been taken in by him at one time or another. But it must be frightening for him to think that he can't be controlled, that he can talk his way out of anything. We'll all work through Jim, so Billy can't play us off against each other. Any requests he makes should be referred back to Jim, and I think the rest of us should even discourage long conversations with him until the line of authority is clearly established. And refer him to me in an emergency if Jim is unavailable. How do you feel about taking this on, Jim?"

Jim had been on the staff for only a few weeks, but he had had experience in the child care field elsewhere. It was he who had focused attention on Billy's problem, since Billy had managed to make "deals" for himself with enough of his previous child care workers to stay out of the limelight most of the time. In effect, Billy had traded off "good behavior" for favors. Jim had resisted such arrangements, Billy had begun to incite the other youngsters, and the cottage had become generally difficult to control as a result. The file suggested that Billy had been a successful manipulator for years and had somehow rarely been called to account. "I think it has to be done if we want to help Billy," said Jim. "And I think it makes sense for a child care worker to be the main person in this, since he's always there, so I'll give it a try."

"Jim, we have a great deal of confidence in you or we wouldn't have suggested it," said Dr. Blair, the psychiatrist, "but I don't want you to underestimate how hard it's going to be. Billy will fight you tooth and nail. In effect, he's made himself a contract with the people around here, and you're going to be trying to change the terms. We'll help you all we can, but most of it will be up to you. It will start when you tell him we decided not to give him the cottage transfer he wants."

"That seems to be a big issue for Billy," interjected his caseworker. "He told me he'd sooner be shipped to maximum security than stay in Jim's cottage. I still wonder if that isn't too big a handicap for Jim to overcome."

"I'm really reluctant to let Billy continue calling the shots," responded the psychiatrist. "We have to begin learning to say 'No' to him, and I think now is the time. I know he's angry at Jim, but that's going to happen no matter who's involved and Jim understands the situation already." The others nodded. "Besides, if we can't help him here, we might just as well find that out now and give the bed to someone else."

"Well," Jim said, "I'll certainly do my best."

"Good luck, and keep me posted," said the assistant director. "Of course, we're all available whenever you think we might be able to help."

Jim left the building and started across the campus toward his cottage. He had not gone far when Billy caught up to him.

"Hey, Jim," Billy asked, "when do I change cottages?"

"You belong in school, Billy," Jim replied. "What are you doing here?"

"I was too excited to go to school, knowing that you guys were meeting about me. You can understand, can't you? When do I move?"

"Look, Billy," said Jim, firmly, "just get back to school. I want to talk to you later about the meeting and about skipping school, too."

"Wait a minute," the boy responded, apparently making an effort to control his growing anger, "I'm not staying at this place if I don't get into another cottage. You told me yourself that the director said I'd be shipped for good if I went AWOL again. So if you want me to stay here, you better get me that cottage transfer. Otherwise I'll get them to ship me or I'll just take off. Nobody else is going to run my life!"

"Billy," said Jim letting his own annoyance show, "you're not going to be transferred to another cottage and you're not going to be shipped, so you might just as well begin to learn how we can live together in the cottage. The first thing for you to do is to get back to school, then we can talk it over this afternoon. I'm not going to talk with you about it until you calm down a little, anyway." They were at the door of the cottage by this time, and Jim walked inside.

"You son of a bitch!" Billy yelled through the door, and he turned and walked away.

"He'll cool off," thought Jim, "but this isn't going to be easy." He sat down to work on some reports, but his mind was on the meeting and his conversation with Billy. Finally, he called the school and asked if Billy had arrived.

"He was here this morning," responded the school secretary, "but he didn't come back after lunch and we've been looking for him. We called the cottage but there was no answer."

"I got back from a case conference about Billy not too long ago," Jim said, "and no one else was here. I saw him on my way across the campus and told him to get back to school, but I guess he never made it. I'll see if I can find him."

Jim opened the cottage door and saw Billy approaching with one of the maintenance men. "I just went AWOL into the village," Billy said, "and I have a witness. Mr. Jenkins saw me at the station and gave me a lift back. Remember what the dirctor said—one more AWOL and I'm shipped! Are you bigger than he is, wise guy?"

(Supplementary discussion questions, page 318)

6.5 TABLE TENNIS, ANYONE?

"Has anyone seen Joel?" Terry Mead asked a group of youngsters in the recreation room. "He doesn't seem to be around." Someone recalled that Joel had received a letter after school but no one had seen him since, and Terry decided to search the cottage before calling the officer of the day. He had started as a child care worker only a few weeks before, and this was his first experience with a missing boy.

He was almost ready to give up when he stepped into the shower room for a last look and, turning the light on, he noticed that the canvas curtain on the farthest stall was partly closed. Walking back and pulling the curtain to one side, Terry looked down and saw Joel, fully clothed, sitting on the floor. He was hunched over and looked like he was trying to hide. "Hey, buddy," asked Terry, not quite sure what was going on, "what are you doing here?"

"Nothin'," replied Joel. "Just go away and leave me alone."

"What's the matter?" asked Terry.

"Everything," was Joel's quiet, almost tearful response. "I'm scheduled for a trial home visit this weekend and, like a stupid ass, I wrote this girl I used to go with and told her. I also told her I loved her," he added in a whisper after a moment's pause.

"So? What's wrong with that?" Terry asked, consciously trying to maintain a casual tone.

"Nothing," said Joel bitterly, "except today I got a letter from my brother and he says she's been showing my letter to everybody, and they all got a big laugh out of it."

"Oh, well," began Terry in a placating voice, "you . . ."

"Hell," interrupted the boy despairingly, "I feel like walking right outta here and jumping off a bridge."

"Come on, Joel," said Terry briskly, trying to ease the tension, "let's go downstairs with the other kids." He reached out to help the boy to his feet.

Joel stood up and gave Terry an anguished look. "Honest to God," he said, "I feel like I want to kill myself! What can I do?"

Feeling very uncomfortable, Terry cast about for a way to change the subject. "Joel," he said finally with a forced cheerfulness, "why don't we go down for a quick ping-pong match, best two out of three. I'll spot you five points each game!"

Later, when the recreation period was almost over, Terry overheard Joel talking to some of the other boys. "You can have that guy Mead! He's a real loser. I try to tell him how bad it's gonna be for me at home this weekend and he says, 'Let's play ping-pong!' I thought those guys were supposed to know how to help us."

(Supplementary discussion questions, page 318)

6.6 "DO AS I SAY . . ."

As Keith pulled his car into the parking lot he was still fuming with rage. "Imagine," he growled to himself, "being stopped for driving a few lousy miles an hour over the limit—and in this county a speeding ticket means at least twenty-five dollars!" He was still muttering as he approached the cottage, and he wondered glumly why the police were not out catching "real" criminals instead of persecuting innocent citizens. Breaking into his dour train of thought was the sight of Eric, one of the smaller boys in the dorm, flinging the front door open for him and yelling, "Hiya, Keith, how's it going?"

Grinning in spite of himself at the boy's exuberance, Keith replied, "Fine! What's new?"

Eric stepped aside to let Keith enter as he responded. "I think we're getting ready for a cottage meeting about . . ."

"I'll take over, Eric," interrupted Phil Greene, not unpleasantly. Phil was Keith's co-worker and had stepped out of the common room to join them in the hall. "We'll see you in a few minutes."

"O.K., O.K.," growled Eric with mock severity as he turned to go.

"Why has a cottage meeting been called?" asked Keith. "Did something happen?"

"Yes," answered Phil, lowering his voice. "When I got to work this morning, the night watch reported that sometime after eleven last night he caught six of our boys who had somehow slipped outside."

"I see what you mean," agreed Keith soberly. After talking briefly about how they would handle it, they met the boys in the common room.

About half an hour later, after they had brought the meeting to a close and the last youngster had filed from the room, Phil shook his head. "That wasn't one of our bigger successes, was it?" he said slowly.

"No, it wasn't," replied Keith. "But rule-breaking is always a tough subject. These kids get pretty hot when we have to remind them there are limits."

"That's true," said Phil. "Some of the boys seem to feel that obeying rules is for the other guy and that we're just being picky when we talk about the importance of . . ."

"Hold on!" interjected Keith, looking at his watch. "If I'm going to pick up those supplies over at the commissary, I'd better get moving. It's getting late."

"I forgot about the time," Phil replied. "Why don't you take along a couple of the boys to help? It'll be faster."

On his way out the door, Keith saw Eric talking to Gary, one of the boys involved in last night's episode. "You two want to drive over to the main area and help me load some supplies to bring back to the cottage?" he asked.

"Sure," replied Eric quickly. Gary merely shrugged, but both boys followed Keith down the path to the parking lot.

As they got into the car, a small piece of brightly colored paper blew off the dashboard and fell into Gary's lap. As he began to replace it, he glanced at it casually, then, more intently, looked at it again. "Hey, Eric," he finally yelped excitedly, "Guess what? The big shot here got a speeding ticket today, and then he had the guts to walk right into that meeting and preach about rule-breaking! What do you say to that, Mr. Law and Order?"

(Supplementary discussion questions, page 319)

6.7 THE DIFFERENCE

Nick groaned as he turned away from the cottage common room windows where he had been looking out at the rain. "Christ, how I hate this weather," he said. "There's nothing to do."

"We got all the luck," Herb added sarcastically. He was slouched in an armchair, halfheartedly turning the pages of an old magazine. "Everybody in the cottage but us guys is off grounds on a special rec trip and we get stuck on Saturday with the rain and a busted TV set."

"Ain't we ever gonna get the TV fixed, Mr. McQuaide?" asked Nick, turning to the child care worker who had just entered the room.

"Of course it'll be fixed, Nick," replied Tom McQuaide. "It's been broken less than a week and you know repairs take time. They'll get to us soon. Listen," he suggested, "why don't we go downstairs and play a couple of games of ping-pong?"

"Because there's nothing to play with," said Herb. "There's no more balls, and the paddles are busted anyway. Boy," he added, "talk about lousy breaks." Tom decided it was not the time to talk to them about taking better care of the equipment.

At this point, Stan Keith, who had been seated in a corner of the room hunting for pieces of an old jigsaw puzzle to put together, suddenly looked up. "Hey, aren't the junior basketball team tryouts in the gym today?" he asked.

"Yeah," someone said. "So what?"

"That's better than nothing, I guess." Stan turned to Tom. "Can I go over and watch them play for a while?"

"Sure," said Tom. "I'll write you a grounds pass."

Taking the pass, Stan got as far as the door of the room when he turned and asked, "Anybody else want to come?"

Herb and Nick both shook their heads disgustedly. "It's just those little kids trying to show that they can reach the basket," Nick said. "There ain't gonna be nothing worth watching."

"OK," said Stan as he walked out the door. "But it'll beat sitting around here all afternoon."

After a few minutes, Herb stood up. "Come on, Nick, Stan's right," he said. "Anything beats sitting around here."

Yawning, Nick nodded in agreement as Herb walked over to where Tom was sitting. "Guess we'll go watch the babies play basketball, too," Herb said disgustedly. "Can we have a couple of passes?"

"Wait a minute, Herb," replied Tom. "You know you're grounded for the week."

"Oh, come on man," groaned Herb. "Stan had a fight, too, and you let him go."

"There's a difference," Tom explained. "Stan was being picked on and he was just trying to defend himself."

"Oh, shit," Herb exploded, throwing the magazine he was still holding to the floor.

Surprised at the sudden outburst, Tom looked at him. "What's eating you?" he asked.

"That's not the difference," Herb replied. "Stan's white and I'm black. That's the real difference, you racist bastard!"

(Supplementary discussion questions, page 319)

6.8 ARE YOU A FAG?

The path leading toward the cottages was filled with youngsters on their way from lunch. As Vince Lundy hurried to catch up to his boys, he noticed two of them, Jimmy and Mal, lagging behind the rest. "Hey, what's up?" asked Vince, a tallish man, as he stepped between the two thirteen-year-olds and draped his arms over their shoulders. "This is Tuesday, and that means chocolate pudding for dessert tonight. So why are you looking so grumpy?"

Jimmy smiled, but Mal flashed an unpleasant glance as the child care worker and pulled away from his grasp. "Come on," he said, "chocolate pudding doesn't make up for the rest of the garbage we get to eat."

Vince looked at the boy understandingly. He knew Mal was edgy as he awaited the outcome of today's administrative meeting, which would determine whether the boy would be allowed to leave the institution on a trial placement basis. Thinking that a little personal comforting and attention might ease Mal's anxiety, Vince threw his arm around the youngster again. "If you'll stop being so bitter," he said cheerfully, "maybe I can check and see if we have time to get some mats out before the afternoon classes start."

"Hey, Mr. Lundy," replied Jimmy excitedly, "would you really? Could you show us some wrestling holds? We got almost twenty minutes!"

Vince, who had won a letter for wrestling in school and enjoyed teaching various techniques of the sport to the boys, nodded as he pulled the youngsters along toward the cottage. "Sure! Who wants to go first?"

"Not me," responded Mal coolly, pulling away again. "I'll watch you and Jimmy."

Later that afternoon, shortly before dinner, Vince anticipated trouble as he waited in the cottage for Mal to return from the administration building. Vince had gathered earlier, when Mr. Baxter called to ask that Mal be sent to his office, that the boy's trial placement had been postponed. When he looked out the small window next to the door and saw Mal rushing headlong toward the cottage, he knew they were in for a bad night. The boy flung open the door and ran up to Vince with tears in his eyes. "Those bastards!" he blazed. "They lied to me. They promised I could leave and . . ."

"Wait a minute," began Vince, reaching out to grasp the boy's shoulder reassuringly. "Tell me . . ."

The youngster recoiled and turned on him. "Yeach," he said with disgust, "take your hands off me! Always touching us. What are you, a fag or something?"

(Supplementary discussion questions, page 320)

6.9 INDIVIDUALIZATION OR FAVORITISM?

"You seem to have a good relationship with him," concluded Mr. Porter, "and I think you're the best one to handle it. Just try to talk to him when he's calm instead of in the middle of a crisis."

Al Borden nodded. "Thanks," he said, as he stood up to leave his supervisor's office. "I'll try to find a way to talk with him tonight."

Al had come to Mr. Porter to discuss the problem he was having with Barry Johnson, a small fourteen-year old, in the dining hall. Barry had a bad temper, but he generally seemed to be manageable except at mealtimes, when he repeatedly became the center of angry disputes. He often responded by throwing food at the other boys until he was sent away from the table.

That evening, Al made it a point to play a game of ping-pong with Barry. Dinner had gone smoothly and it seemed to be a good time. After the game, Barry asked Al to help him with a model airplane he was building, and Al broached the subject of the mealtime problem as they were working.

"Barry," he said, "I'm concerned about the trouble you've been having in the dining hall, and I'd like us to decide what can be done about it. I feel badly when I have to send you out, but we can't have all that fighting and throwing of food at the table. It's not fair to expect the rest of us to eat with that going on."

"I know, Al," replied Barry. "I just lose my temper sometimes, and then I can't stop myself."

"Isn't there any way you can tell me what's happening before you really blow up?" asked Al. "You know, when you start getting upset? If you could, I'd let you go eat outside the dining hall until you calm down. Then you could tell me when you're ready to come back in."

"Oh, you mean like when I think I'm getting in trouble in the cottage and I tell you and you find something else for me to do?"

"Yes, like that," said Al. "Should we give it a try?"

"Maybe I can do it," Barry said. "I sure don't like it when I miss a meal."

"Good," responded Al. "Now where are you on this model?"

Nothing more was said about the problem for the next few days, and Barry seemed fine in the dining hall.

On Thursday the boys played football after school and were particularly hungry for dinner. "They better have something good tonight," one of them said on the way to the dining hall. "I could eat a bear!"

Steve was the tallest boy in the group and the only one who could look into the dining hall windows from outside. "Oh crap," he groaned, "it's liver!" The other boys echoed his disgust. "Al," continued Steve, "let me sit out here tonight. I'll throw up if I have to sit and smell that stuff."

"It's not all that bad," replied Al. "If you try it, you might even like it. Besides, there are other things there, and you must be hungry after that game."

"I was hungry until I saw that liver," Steve said, with the others nodding their agreement. "But I never ate liver and I'm not about to start here!"

"Well, you'll just have to sit and look at it, then," replied Al, firmly. "Nobody gets excused because they don't like to look at the food."

Grumbling, the boys entered the dining hall and sat down. Most began to eat, but Steve sat in sullen silence across from Barry Johnson. "Stop kicking me," Barry said to Steve after a few minutes.

"Sorry," replied Steve, offhandedly.

A minute or two later, Barry spoke to Steve again. "I said cut it out!" he said, his voice rising slightly. Al noticed the change in Barry's tone and was alert for possible trouble.

"I said I was sorry," Steve said.

"You're still doing it," persisted Barry. Then he looked at Al. "Can I go outside?" he asked earnestly. "He keeps kicking me, and if I don't get out of here I'll kick him back, and you know what'll happen then!"

Al nodded. "O.K., Barry. You can take your plate with you if you want to."

"No, I'll just go out for a few minutes," replied Barry as he got up from his seat. "I can't stand liver anyway."

Furious, Steve jumped to his feet. "What's that for?" he yelled at Al.

"Barry don't like liver and you're letting him go out. Why not me? He's your little pet. Or do I have to throw a tantrum to get away from this crap?"

(Supplementary discussion questions, page 320)

6.10 "IF I GIVE MY HEART TO YOU . . ."

"I enjoy working with the kids," said Frank Voit to his supervisor, "and I just thought it might be helpful if I stayed through the evening."

"I'm sure it was," Mr. Ecks replied, "but working too many extra hours usually causes problems over the long pull. Child care work is very difficult, and you need your time off to relax and get back to the outside world. Otherwise, it'll catch up with you. You won't have the same patience with the kids. Things like that. Remember, these kids really haven't had the attention and affection kids need from adults, so their demands are unrealistic and insatiable. We have to draw the line, or we'll just be snowed under."

"I'll watch myself," responded Frank. "Sometimes it's hard to leave, though, when it seems like something important is happening."

"That's true," Mr. Ecks agreed, "but one of the things kids have to learn is to deal with separation. Of course, there are emergency situations, but as a rule it's best to try to handle all you can during your regular work week."

As he approached the cottage after the conference had ended, Frank saw one of his boys, John Lyons, smashing a rake into the hedge that surrounded the small yard in front of the cottage. John was a lonely boy, and Frank had made a special effort to get close to him, partly by helping the boy with his schoolwork. A relationship seemed to be developing, but John often had wild, destructive tantrums. "What's going on here, John?" called Frank.

"Leave me alone," the boy replied sullenly, turning from the hedge to face Frank. "I'm just trying to do my lousy work chore with this crappy rake."

"Give me the rake," said Frank, firmly.

"Sure," John replied, as he threw the rake to the ground, turned, and walked toward the cottage door.

"Just a minute, John," said Frank. The boy paused and Frank continued. "What happened? Why were you trying to mess up that hedge?"

"I didn't hurt nothin'," replied the boy, looking back over his shoulder at the child care worker. "I got mad 'cause that stinkin' rake is half shot and I couldn't work with it."

Frank looked at the youngster for a moment before speaking. "I checked all the yard equipment myself, John. You know you're not telling the truth."

The boy turned his head to avoid meeting Frank's gaze. "So what?" he asked in a bored voice.

Shaking his head in puzzlement, Frank said, "John, I don't understand. Everything seems to have been going well recently. All that studying we've been doing together seems to be paying off, and I noticed that Mr. Stevens recommended that you have a regular rec pass. That's a big step. Why are you starting to act up now?"

John turned and looked at Frank defiantly. "What's the difference if I rake that yard or not?" he asked. "Who the hell cares what the outside of this dump looks like, anyway?"

Frank grinned in spite of himself. "You're really in great form today, aren't you?" he said. "In the first place, this isn't a dump. It's where we live and I care what it looks like, even if you don't. We've been through all this before, John. Now, please just get outside and clean up the mess you made and finish the rest of the yard."

"I suppose I get grounded if I don't?" asked the youngster.

Frank nodded. "That's right. No weekend rec program, and I don't want to see that happen any more than you do."

"Bullshit!" John exploded. "Why would you care?"

Frank was stunned for a split second by the boy's attack. "Johnny," he said quietly, "I can't make you believe I care, but why do you think I don't?"

"I'll tell you why!" the boy shot back angrily. "Because when you're in the cottage you're always after me to study and do good in school, but now it's your turn to have the weekend off and you don't care what happens to me."

"What are you talking about?" Frank asked, shaking his head.

"We're gonna have a science test on Monday and I really need extra help this weekend to keep from failing. But you don't care because you're gonna be in your real home. It doesn't matter to you that the guy who'll be working in the cottage doesn't understand science and wouldn't help if he could. That shows you don't really care about us—you only care when you get paid to care!"

(Supplementary discussion questions, page 321)

7. AUTHORITY, LIMITS, AND DISCIPLINE

The word "discipline" has, unfortunately, become closely associated with the idea of punishment. Its use in this book, and particularly in this chapter, refers also to the important process of maintaining clear limits on one's own behavior. Although punishment is one way of trying to enforce behavioral limits, the development of self-control or self-discipline is usually more effective as well as more constructive in terms of the youngsters' subsequent growth.

TABLE OF CASES

7.1 THE ROAD TO AUTONOMY

"So the real challenge," concluded the director, Mr. Packard, "is to let these kids discipline themselves as much as possible without letting them get beyond their depth. If they can't learn it here where their lives are so structured, there's not much chance that they'll be able to handle the extra freedom they'll have when they get out."

"How can we tell in advance when something's likely to be too much for them?" asked Norm Franklin, one of the child care workers at the meeting.

"Experience helps some," Mr. Packard answered, "but it's always partly a guess. Try to move into it gradually. When it starts to overwhelm the kids, their behavior will let you know. And don't be afraid to let them fail once in a while, either. We learn more from our failures than from success, and the kids do too."

"But if a kid fails and it's too painful," asked another worker, "won't he stop trying?"

"Yes, he might," Mr. Packard agreed. "That's why a lot of these kids are here. But they'll never get their confidence back if they don't have the chance to try, and that means they're going to make mistakes. We just have to make sure the mistakes aren't too serious from our point of view or theirs."

On his way back to the cottage Norm thought about what Mr. Packard had said. Although he agreed in principle, he was not quite sure how to implement it in the cottage. He finally decided to discuss it with his supervisor at their scheduled conference a few days later.

The next afternoon several of the boys approached him when they returned from school. "Hey, Mr. Franklin," said Mike Bauer, "why didn't you tell us about the new policy that the kids can decide things like when we can leave this place?"

Norm was taken aback for a moment but recovered quickly. "I don't think that's quite the way I heard it," he said, "but we do want to give you as much freedom as we can to handle the things that concern you. If you don't learn how to control yourselves and make decisions here, you won't be ready to live outside. I was going to bring it up at our cottage meeting next week."

"Let's talk about it now," countered Mike, and he was quickly supported by the others.

"Well, I guess they made their own decision," Norm thought, smiling to himself, as he agreed to meet with them. When they had all gathered in the cottage common room, he explained what Mr. Packard had said.

"Then why can't we decide about getting out of here?" someone asked. "Some of the guys in the other cottages said that's the new rule."

"Look," Norm replied firmly, "don't believe everything you hear. First of all, most of you are here on court commitments, and when you leave is up to the court. But even more important, I'm not sure you really know when you're ready to leave. If you leave too soon, you might end up in even worse trouble, and it's our job to protect you from that until you're ready to handle it for yourselves. But the decisions you make and what you do while you're here do have an effect."

"What about home visits?" suggested Mike. "Could we decide when we're ready for things like that?"

"Same problem," Norm said, a little less sure of himself this time. "We need to have some feeling that you can handle the responsibility involved."

"But you said we have to try some of these things, and we can even learn from our mistakes," someone else said. "What can we practice on, then?"

Norm was groping for an answer when another youngster spoke. "Adults always do this," he said. "You tell us to act grown up, but you don't let us make our own decisions. Who decides if you can smoke? You do. But I can't decide if I can smoke around here. The same goes for drinking, gambling, and almost everything else."

"Wait a minute," said Norm, trying to keep up with the conversation, "in the first place, home visits are decided in case conferences. I couldn't let you make the decision on that even if I wanted to. Let's start with cottage rules and routines and see how much you guys can really handle. We'll let you go as far on this as you show us you're ready for."

Mike, who had been thinking quietly since he initiated the

conversation, finally spoke. "Look, Mr. Franklin," he said, "you have a vote in those case conferences. Would you agree to vote for home visits and try your best to get them approved for anyone who decided he was ready, as long as he wasn't being punished or anything? That's the least you could do!"

(Supplementary discussion questions, page 322)

7.2 STICK WITH ME!

"Hey, Mr. Bryan," said Corey Dawson disappointedly, "there's nobody here! Isn't there a meeting today?"

"There should be. It's Thursday," Larry Bryan replied, puzzled. He had walked over to the school building with Corey on his way to the gym, where he was scheduled to lead the tumbling club. Larry looked into the empty room, then saw a small note taped to the door frame and read it aloud. "No model making club meeting this week. Report to the gym."

"I guess Mr. Wallace isn't here today," he continued. "You'll find something to do in the gym. Jimmy, Van, and Bobby are in the model club, too, so they'll be there and maybe you can get up a basketball game."

The other three boys were not in the gym, however. After explaining the situation to the recreation director, who had not seen the boys either, and asking him to keep an eye on the tumblers, Larry left Corey in the gym and headed back to the cottage. He searched the first and second floors of the cottage without success and was on his way to the staff office to call the duty officer when, on a hunch, he decided to check the basement. Larry opened the basement door as quietly as possible and kept his hand away from the light switch as he crouched in the dim light. He heard the boys' whispered voices and gradually was able to see them seated in a circle on the floor. They appeared to be passing around a small paper bag, and each boy was bending forward, placing his face in the bag, and inhaling before passing it on.

"Come on, Van, take a deep breath," Jimmy urged. "No, not like that. Here, let me show you." Jimmy took the bag and breathed deeply before continuing. "See? Like that. Here, try it," he concluded, handing the bag back to Van, who put it over his face.

Pulling his head away from the bag a few seconds later, Van exclaimed, "Hey, it's like I'm floating! See?"

Turning toward him, Bobby asked, "Do you really feel like you're floating, Van? I don't feel anything."

"Neither does he," Jimmy said scornfully. "He's fakin' it. You gotta do it a couple of more times before it hits you. Here, Bobby, try it again."

"Just think," Van said dreamily, "we've been wasting all this good glue on models. . . ."

"Sure you were," agreed Jimmy. "I figured it out the first time I went to that stupid model making club. Those jerks don't even lock up the cabinets! Of course, we were really lucky today, with no meeting."

"Hey!" yelped Bobby excitedly, "I feel woozy. Jim, this is great. You're . . ."

"Shh!" said Jim. "Keep your voice down!"

Feeling that he'd heard more than enough by now, Larry braced himself and walked quickly down the steps.

(Supplementary discussion questions, page 323)

7.3 PROMISES

Jim could not help smiling as he looked at Craig Evans, whose tall, lanky frame was spread out over his bed. Craig had only been in the institution for a month or two, but Jim felt that they had become very close. "You know," he said to Craig, "for a smart kid you do some pretty stupid things."

"Yeah, I know," Craig replied. "But hell, I've been on cottage restriction for over a week now and I'm going nuts."

"Well, if you'd start behaving like you wanted to get off restriction, you might make it one of these days," Jim suggested. "Smoking that cigarette in the bathroom Tuesday night wasn't the brightest thing you've ever done."

"Shit, man, you'd go nuts, too, if you were cooped up as long as I've been." Then Craig lowered his voice. "Say, Jim" he went on, "if I tell you something that's just between us will you promise not to tell?"

"What's the big secret?" replied Jim noncommittally.

Craig's voice dropped to a whisper. "Well, last night when just the night man was on, Mark and I snuck out the back door and went for a long walk. He had a joint he got somewhere and he shared it with me. I just had to get out of this place. Then we snuck back in and the old guy didn't even notice."

"Didn't you think you'd get caught?" Jim asked, not quite knowing what else to say.

"Well, I figure you gotta take some risks. Besides he hardly ever checks after the first hour or two. Pretty slick, huh?" Jim was feeling more than a bit uncomfortable and it must have shown on his face. "Now you promised you wouldn't tell anyone, right?" said Craig, looking straight at him.

(Supplementary discussion questions, page 323)

7.4 "CARDINAL SINS"

Tom Goodwin knew that, whether written or unwritten, every institution has its list of "cardinal sins," offenses that lead immediately and without question to severe penalties. Such things as attacking staff members physically and selling drugs are usually included. But maybe, thought Tom, cigarette smoking should be in a different category. He had just received a memo addressed to all staff spelling out a new and more rigid antismoking policy.

Although smoking had been forbidden before with a standard one dollar fine for each offense, there was a tacit understanding that the older boys would not be punished for smoking as long as it was done unobtrusively and did not involve the younger ones. Some of the therapists had even been permitting younger boys to smoke in their offices. Recently, however, the smoking problem had seemed to escalate and many of the younger boys were boasting about smoking. It seemed that they were virtually asking the adults to stop them.

It was against this background that the new policy had been developed. Although Tom and many of the other child care workers felt that the older boys should be permitted to decide for themselves whether to smoke, there was a great deal of concern about the younger boys who were being drawn into it.

Under the new policy, boys would be subject to a one dollar fine for the first offense, a one-week cottage restriction for the second, and reassignment to the discipline cottage for the third. When the new regulations were being developed, Tom and others had expressed the feeling that the penalties were out of proportion to the seriousness of the infraction, but they had been overruled.

During the next few days, a number of boys were caught smoking and fined. Although they had been informed of the change, some had assumed that discreet violations would continue to be overlooked.

"You know, the kids are bound to test this out," said Tom to another child care worker at the change of shifts one evening just after the boys had gone to bed. "And the administration is probably going to want to set an example so the kids will know they mean business. How can you let kids go along smoking and develop a habit and one day just go 'zap' and expect them to stop?"

Irv looked sympathetic. "You're worried about Oliver, aren't you?" he said.

Tom was surprised at Irv's insight. "You're right," he replied. "He was caught today for the second time, and now he's restricted to the cottage for a week. I'm not sure he'll be able to take it, and if he gets caught again, he'll be sent to the discipline cottage. You know how much progress he's been making here, I've been trying to talk some sense into him, but who knows? He's thick sometimes."

"I know how hard you've been working with him, and he's come a long way since he's been here," replied Irv, "but this smoking thing needs to be handled, too. It's also important that Oliver learn to face the fact that breaking rules has certain consequences."

"Agreed," said Tom. "I think he's learning. But it's still a struggle for him, and the whole thing might go down the drain if he's sent to the discipline cottage. I just hope it doesn't happen."

"I hope not, too," Irv said, getting up to go. "I hope he makes it. I've got to get home now, but I'll see you tomorrow. Take it easy."

"Good night, Irv," Tom said, walking him to the door. I'll try."

Tom sat down at the desk, from where he could see both corridors. Except for an occasional trip to the bathroom or the water fountain, things seemed quiet. After a few minutes, Oliver looked quickly into the hall and disappeared into the bathroom. "He probably didn't see me with the desk light out," Tom thought. Oliver soon returned to his room, then almost immediately went back to the bathroom. Five minutes, then ten minutes passed and he did not come out. "I'll bet he's smoking," Tom thought as he stood up. "What do I do now?"

(Supplementary discussion questions, page 324)

7.5 WELCOME MAT?

Harry scanned the almost empty sidewalks as he cruised slowly through the streets. The snow was beginning to fall and a big storm was expected. The boys had been gone for a good half hour before anyone had noticed that they were missing and Harry was beginning to get worried. He decided to try the railroad and bus stations again, but the boys were not there and no trains or buses had left since he had last checked. Tired and discouraged, he got back into the car and headed back to the institution.

The other boys were in bed and Gil Norris, Harry's co-worker, was waiting for him at the cottage. "No luck, Gil," said Harry. "And it's getting bad out there. Do you know if they were dressed warmly?"

Gil ignored his question. "Did you check the airport?" he asked.

"The airport? They'd never have enough money to fly anywhere."

"They might," Gil replied. "While you were gone, I questioned the other boys. Raymond slipped and mentioned the airport. It seems that Mike told him he had somehow stolen fifty dollars last weekend, and that he and Billy planned to fly somewhere. I've already notified the police, but I think I'll drive out there myself and take a look around. It's a long way to hitch and they might not even have gotten there yet. That is, if that was where they were going."

"I guess it's worth a try," said Harry. "We haven't got anything else. Just be careful with the driving in this weather."

Gil had been gone less than ten minutes when the phone rang, and Harry picked it up expectantly. A local police officer identified himself. "We found your two boys," he said. "They were hitch-hiking on the road out to the airport. Michael Owens and Billy Smith."

"That's them," Harry said, feeling relieved. "Can you drop them off here? Cottage 4, first one on the left."

It was a good half hour before the patrol car stopped in front of the cottage. The boys slumped out into the snow, obviously tired, but working hard to maintain their air of triumph. "It's good to see you guys again," Harry said. "We were worried about you. You could freeze out there on a night like this."

When they were inside the cottage, Harry realized that the boys were soaked through and still shivering. "Get into your pajamas and slippers quickly," he said, "and come back down for a hot drink."

They were all in the kitchen having hot chocolate and cookies when Gil returned, cold, wet, and tired. He was relieved to find the boys were back, but he called Harry out of the kitchen. "What's going on?" he asked. "What are you doing?"

"Doing?" Harry echoed. "What do you mean?"

"Do you really think we should be serving those kids snacks when they just came back from running away and maybe even stole fifty bucks. It seems too much like a reward."

"Actually, I didn't think of it that way. I was worried about them and just glad to see them back, I guess. And they did look half frozen. I guess I thought we could handle the rest of it in the morning."

"I was just as worried about them as you were," said Gil firmly. "But fill them up with hot chocolate and cookies now, then punish them in the morning? Doesn't that sound a little inconsistent?"

"I guess I just did what seemed right at the time," replied Harry, shrugging his shoulders. "How would you have handled it?"

(Supplementary discussion questions, page 324)

7.6 "GIVE US A BREAK!"

Ed Conklin shook his head and smiled as he watched the boys quietly plugging away at their homework. Amazing, he thought, what a tight major league pennant race can do. Three teams were tied for the lead with less than a week to go, and the institution had given permission for a curfew extension so the boys could see the game on television. Ed had told his group that he would only let them watch it when they had finished their homework, and he had never seen them working so quietly and so well.

The boys were finished and in their pajamas in time for the telecast. When the set was turned on, the boys all groaned as they learned that the game would be delayed because of rain. Ed assured them that even if the game ran later than usual as a result, he would let them stay up to watch all of it.

The game finally started, but the rains came again in the second inning and, after another delay, it was postponed. "Sorry, boys," said Ed, turning off the set. "Maybe we'll have better luck next time. We'll get our snack, then it's time for bed."

"Hey, Mr. C," called out one of the boys, "can't we watch a movie or something instead?"

"No," replied Ed. "It's half an hour past regular curfew, and tomorrow's a school day. We'll arrange for you to watch another game one night."

"That's not fair!" complained another boy. "You said it would be at least 11 P.M. before we had to go to bed."

"Come on, now," said Ed firmly. "You know that late curfew was set for the baseball game. Let's get going now."

Still grumbling, the boys had their snack and went to bed. After seeing that they were settled for the night, Ed walked to the duty office to drop off his log book and check out with the nightwatch, Sam Kelly. "Were you waiting to see the game, too?" asked Sam.

Ed nodded. "When it was rained out," he said, "I sent the kids to bed. They weren't too pleased about it."

"Looks like some of the cottages are staying up until 11 P.M. anyway," replied Sam, looking out the window at the buildings. "But everything seems to be pretty quiet."

A few minutes later, as Ed was unlocking the door of his car, he glanced back toward the cottage. Then, looking more closely, he saw a dim light from the television room. "Damn," he breathed aloud. "Those kids are downstairs watching TV again."

(Supplementary discussion questions, page 325)

7.7 PAVED WITH GOOD INTENTIONS

Albert Tate checked the list one more time before handing it to the office cashier. "That's it, Mrs. Dunn," he said. "Six boys on the honor roll skating trip this month."

Mrs. Dunn nodded as she gave Albert the money. "That's thirty five cents for each boy for refreshments," she said. "Just let me check the accounts to be sure they each have that much credit."

"It must be quite a job to keep track of all these small items," commented Albert, watching her scan the pages of the loose-leaf account book.

"It wasn't too bad until they made that new rule that the kids can't keep any cash in the cottage," she replied. "Before that, it was just their work earnings, an occasional withdrawal, and paying them the balance when they left. They usually had pocket money when they needed it. Now we have to record every dime."

"I guess it has managed to cut into the drug traffic around here, though," said Albert. "And the kids seem to be less concerned about who has how much money, knowing they can't get it so easily."

"That sounds logical," agreed Mrs. Dunn, "but it's still a lot more work. Your list is fine," she continued, looking up from the desk. "Just sign this receipt for me and you can go."

Later, the boys chattered noisily as they returned their skates to the desk. Scotty, who had had trouble staying on his feet all day, tried to change the subject. He grabbed his stomach dramatically and began to complain loudly of acute starvation. "Hey, Mr. Tate," he gasped, "did you see that big pizza place we passed on the way here? If we hurry, I think we could get there in time to save my life!"

"Do you really think so?" Albert asked, grinning. The trip had gone well, he was in a good mood, and he was tempted to go ahead and treat them.

"Yeah," another boy yelled. "Make it sausage."

Struck by a sudden thought, Albert quickly checked his pockets. "Sorry, boys," he announced. "You've already spent your refreshment money and I forgot that I had to buy a tankful of gas for the wagon on the way over here. My worldly goods," he added, looking down sadly at the coins in his hand, "consist of thirty-eight cents. Maybe next time."

Amid the groans that followed, Albert saw Ronald, one of the shyer boys in the cottage, take a five dollar bill out of his pocket. "Let's go," Ronald said with a bashful grin, "the treat's on me. I've had this five dollars hidden since my birthday. We might as well use it now! You don't mind, do you, Mr. Tate?" he added quietly, looking at Albert.

(Supplementary discussion questions, page 326)

7.8 WHO SHOULD BE PUNISHED?

Ted Schaeffer should not have been sleeping on night duty, but he was. He had taken the job as a child care worker to supplement the income from his graduate school fellowship, and the institution had asked him to take a great deal of overtime work lately because of a staff shortage. He had been dozing in the chair for perhaps an hour when he was startled into consciousness by a hand on his shoulder and an excited voice. It was Mike Ryan, one of the boys in the group.

"Hey, Mr. Schaeffer, you better get up. Brian fell off the roof. I think maybe he broke his arm."

Ted shook his head and tried to collect his wits. "Where is he now?" he asked.

"He's lying on the ground outside," Mike replied. "The rest of the boys were afraid they'd get in trouble for being on the roof if they told you. Does that mean I'll get punished for being up there?"

"We'll talk about that later," Ted replied, as he ran outside. There he saw Brian on the ground, alone, writhing in pain and holding his arm. "Try to take it easy, Brian," he said. "I'll call the nurse and be right back."

By the time Ted had called the nurse, the other boys were coming down the steps. Apparently Mike, who was still very excited, had called them. Ted looked at them briefly. It was difficult to tell who had actually been sleeping and who had not. "Who was up there with Brian?" he asked. No one answered. "All right everybody, go back to bed," he continued. "Brian will be O.K. It looks like it might be a broken bone, but it could have been much more serious. We'll straighten it all out in the morning." The boys filed silently back upstairs to their rooms.

Ted discussed the incident with George Fraser, the unit supervisor, the next morning. "So the only ones I know for sure were involved are Brian and Michael," he said. "I tried to find out who else was up there, but I couldn't. Where do we go from here? It seems to me that this is too serious to ignore, but how can we punish the whole group? I'm sure that not all twenty were involved."

"But," interrupted George, "all twenty know who was involved."

"Sure," Ted agreed, "but you know they won't 'fink' on a buddy. Besides, Brian has probably been punished enough already, with a broken arm, and Mike was the only one with the guts and decency to come and tell me. I'd hate to punish him for that!"

"Well," George said, "this still seems to be a group problem. How do you want to handle it?"

(Supplementary discussion questions, page 327)

7.9 SETUP

Fred Jason walked from room to room talking to the boys and hoping that someone would confess. "They all look so innocent," he thought, "except maybe Steve. Steve could be the one who did it. It would be just like him—breaking into Dominick's locker and tearing up his stamp collection. "That's all the poor kid had. But how can I prove it? You can't punish a boy just because he looks guilty."

After questioning all the boys without success, he sat in the cottage office and tried to decide what to do. After a few minutes, Jack Austin, another child care worker, came in and Fred told him the story. "I've questioned everyone and I've come up with a big zero," he said, "but I think we have to do something. If we ignore this, we're just asking for more of the same. And poor Dominick. Whoever did it must have known how much it would hurt that kid. He's enough of a scapegoat as it is, but we have to show him as well as the others that we take it seriously. Any ideas, Jack?"

"Maybe the whole group should be kept back from the game this afternoon. I hate to punish a whole group like that, but I don't know what else to suggest."

"I don't like it either, but I think it's the best we can do under the circumstances. They're really looking forward to that game. But do you see any reason why Dominick should be punished, too?"

"No, I don't think so," replied Jack. "He could go with another group."

Fred called the boys together and told them how seriously he regarded the incident and how the group would be punished.

"And," he continued sternly, "you are to stay in your rooms all afternoon and I don't want to hear a word out of you. No radios or record players either. If you have to leave your room, get my permission first." There were a lot of disgruntled faces. "I'm sorry to have to punish the whole group for the behavior of one or two of you, but we want to make it clear that these things are not funny and we will not tolerate them." He paused briefly. "O.K. Now back to your rooms and stay there until dinner time."

The boys filed out silently, glaring at Dominick as they left.

"You big baby," Lester muttered. "Can't even take a little joke. Got to get us all in trouble."

Dominick looked a little smug and, when he came back from the game, he lost little time in telling the other boys what a good time he had had. They ignored him and, after a short while, he sidled over to Fred and told him about it in a voice that reverberated down the hall.

Club activities were scheduled that evening, and Fred spent the time with his woodworking group. Toward the end of the club period, one of the new child care workers ran in and called Fred aside.

"You'd better get back to the cottage on the double, Fred," he said. "Somebody threw red paint all over Dominick's room. Clothes, ceiling, walls, bed. It looks like blood. Then they stuck a knife through the blanket, with paint splattered all over it. I thought Dominick was really going to flip out. Jack Austin came in to help and is holding him in the office, but he could probably use more help. I didn't know who did it, so I told all the boys to go to their rooms until you came back. I just didn't know what else to do. I can keep an eye on things here."

Fred looked grim as he turned to go.

(Supplementary discussion questions, page 327)

7.10 SHOW NO SCARS

Doug Daniels stood on the small back portch of the cottage shaking his head as he looked at the brimming garbage cans lined up against the railing.

"Jim," he called out loudly, turning toward the screen door. "Jim Watson! Get out here!"

"You want me, Mr. Daniels?" asked the tall boy as he stepped out onto the porch.

Doug nodded. "Did you forget?" he asked. "Today is Thursday—garbage day. You'd better take these out to the curb before the truck comes by."

"Get somebody else," replied Jim. "I told you last time, that's not my kind of job."

"Come on, Jim," said Doug mildly. "Don't be so hard to get along with. It's your job this week and you know it."

"I'll trade jobs with Sam or Richie," offered Jim. "I just won't cart garbage and that's that."

Doug looked at the boy for a moment before replying. He did not want to get caught in a battle of wills with Jim, and that was what usually seemed to happen when the boy refused to do his job. This time, Doug decided to try to shame the boy into it.

"No, Jim," he said firmly. "I won't rework the schedule and stick Sam or Richie with your work. I always thought you were reasonable and appreciated people being fair, but I guess I was wrong about you. I'll take it out myself." Jim simply shrugged and walked back into the cottage.

Doug had just finished carrying the last of the garbage cans to the curb when Will Jefferson, the child care worker from the next cottage, strolled over to join him.

"Another run-in with Jim Watson?" asked Will. Doug nodded and started to recount the incident, when Will interrupted him. "Yeah, I was out in the yard and heard part of it. You know," he continued, "if you'd just let him know who's boss once and for all, there wouldn't be any problem."

"Sure, sure," Doug said wearily, "here we go again. You're going to tell me that I can let him know who's boss by hitting him, aren't you? In the first place, I'm bigger than he is, so what the hell would it prove?"

"It would prove you're in charge," said Will, "and sometimes that's what these kids have to know. He's just asking for it, don't you see? Even the boss wouldn't object, as long as you have enough provocation."

"Look, I don't believe hitting helps, anyway," said Doug. "Maybe it's better to make Jim feel guilty about something like this, so he'll think about it. Anyway, shouldn't the punishment be related to what the kid has done?"

Will raised his hands as if to stop Doug's flow of words. "Will you cut out that middle class bullshit!" he groaned. "You keep talkin' about 'psychological punishment' and the kids' 'superegos' but where does it get you? All I know is that my mother and father would strap me good if I did something wrong when I was a kid. I don't hate them for what they did. I'm glad they raised me right. You talk good, Doug, but my way works and these kids respect me!"

(Supplementary discussion questions, page 328)

7.11 CONFINEMENT

Hank Osborne was furious. He clenched his fists to keep them at his sides as he stared at the boy in front of him. "Look, Ernie," he began, biting off each word, "get inside that cottage. Right now!"

The boy boldly returned the child care worker's stare. "You can't scare me," he sneered.

Hank's voice rose as he replied. "You heard me! Inside. Now!"

"Try and make me," Ernie taunted, unflinching.

Hank hesitated. He had not worked at the institution very long and this was the first time he had felt so angry or quite so unsure of what he ought to do. He finally decided that he had to follow through. "If that's the way you want it, O.K.!" he said grimly, grasping Ernie's arm. He tried to turn the boy around, but Ernie spun toward him, throwing them both off balance and causing them to fall together in a tangle on the cement walk.

Hank quickly jumped up and he yanked Ernie roughly to his feet. Wordlessly, he began to walk the boy away from the cottage. "Where are we going?" asked Ernie, no longer resisting. "Mr. Goddard's office?"

Hank shook his head. "No, you're headed for the confinement cottage."

"You bastard," spat Ernie, "that's not fair! You're not supposed to stick me in there because of a little fight."

"We'll see how you feel about 'a little fight' by the time you get out, buddy," replied Hank, still fuming.

At the confinement cottage, Tom Bascomb assigned Ernie to a room, and the boy was locked inside. "How long do you want him to stay here?" asked Tom. "I have to give an estimate when I report his admission."

"Just say indefinite," Hank replied. "I'll be back to get him when he's had some time to think it over."

Less than half an hour after Hank had returned to his cottage, he saw Mr. Goddard, the group care director, heading up the steps. When Hank opened the door, Mr. Goddard walked in and called him aside.

"What happened?" asked Mr. Goddard. "Why is Ernie Miles in confinement?"

"He was being very difficult about doing his house chores," explained Hank, "and when I pressed him, he walked out. He refused to come back, so I tried to take him inside forcibly and we ended up in a scuffle. I thought it was an appropriate time to isolate him for a while."

Mr. Goddard nodded. "Did Ernie try to hit you during all this?" he asked.

"No," responded Hank, with some heat, "but he might as well have. He threw himself against me and we both ended up on the ground."

Mr. Goddard looked at Hank for a moment and then glanced at his watch. "O.K., I understand Ernie went in about one o'clock. I'd like you to go over and release him by 2 P.M."

"But that's only an hour, Mr. Goddard," protested Hank. "How can I let him out so soon? He'll laugh me out of this place."

"Wait a minute," Mr. Goddard replied firmly. "What were you trying to accomplish when you put him in there? What do you think the confinement cottage is for, anyway?"

(Supplementary discussion questions, page 329)

7.12 A JURY OF HIS PEERS?

The first thing Al Monroe noticed when he entered the cottage was that the cottage floor had not been cleaned. The second was Jimmy Carter stretched out on the couch, reading a comic book.

"Jimmy!" called Al. "Why aren't you mopping the floor?"

"I ain't gonna do the whole thing," replied Jimmy. "Get Lou Robinson to do his part."

"Lou Robinson?" asked Al. "What's he got to do with this? Bill Green has floors today. Where is he?"

"No, Mr. Monroe," Jimmy continued, "some of the guys were playin' cards again last night and Lou lost, so Bill made him promise to do his job."

"Wow," thought Al as he tried to keep up, "maybe I should go out and try coming in again. I thought we had that gambling thing licked."

"Jimmy," he finally said, "you start on the floor. I'll get someone to help."

As Al walked toward the television room, Jimmy slowly stood up and went to get the broom.

Both Bill and Lou were among the boys watching television. "Bill," said Al, loud enough for the others to hear, "aren't you supposed to be cleaning the floor?"

"Lou said he'd do that for me," Bill replied.

"Lou, is that true?" Al asked.

Lou looked at the other boys before he answered. "Yes, I guess so," he finally said, reluctantly getting to his feet.

"What makes you so generous?" Al asked him quietly as they walked out into the hall.

"Oh, he's my friend, that's all," Lou replied.

"You're sure it's got nothing to do with a gambling debt?" persisted Al.

Lou looked at him. "Who told you?" The words had slipped out, and he quickly tried to cover up. "It was just something left over from before," he said. "We quit that since you spoke to us."

"O.K.," replied Al, "we'll get to that. Next time I want to see you start your job on time."

"You'll get yours later, you little rat," Lou mumbled to Jimmy as they passed him in the hall.

"Come on," protested Jimmy, "you didn't expect me to do the whole cottage myself, did you? You should have been here."

"I was coming," sneered Lou. "You could've gotten started in the meantime. Shouldn't he have started, Mr. Monroe?" Lou added, looking at Al.

Al decided that Jimmy was in enough trouble with Lou and the other boys already, so he avoided Lou's question. "Just get to work," he said, "both of you. There's too much talk and not enough action around here."

Shortly after lights out that night, as Al was thinking about the day's events, he heard voices from the second floor and crept quietly up the stairs to check. Bill was whispering, but Al could hear the words clearly as he stood in the hall.

"The court will now come to order. This is the case of the people versus Jimmy Carter. Carter is charged with getting Lou in trouble over sweeping a lousy floor and being a general crud . . . ."

Al listened as the mock trial continued for about fifteen minutes, complete with lawyers, witnesses, and a jury. Jimmy was found guilty, and Bill pronounced sentence. "You will give one dessert to each boy in the cottage. You'll help with all the cottage jobs for one week, or you'll get the shit beat out of you. And," he continued in a threatening tone, "from now on, keep your damn mouth shut. Court adjourned."

(Supplementary discussion questions, page 329)

UNIT THREE

LIFE IN THE INSTITUTION:
THE PROGRAM AS EDUCATION AND TREATMENT

8. THE DAILY ROUTINE

The major events in the daily cottage routine comprise much of the child care worker's job and often present significant opportunities as well as problems, partly because they may tend to remind youngsters of how different things were at home. The cases that follow portray some of the primary cottage routines as well as the kinds of changes in routines that may occur from time to time.

TABLE OF CASES

8.1 I REMEMBER MAMA

It was 7:15 A.M. and the dormitories in Bradley Cottage began to stir as most of the boys got up and started to dress. Murray Welk, the child care worker on duty that morning, stood at the top of the stairs and checked his watch again.

"Last call!" he announced loudly. "Everybody up! This means *you!*"

"O.K., sergeant," replied one of the boys in Dorm A good-naturedly as Murray entered the room to check. "What do you think this is, the army?"

Noting that everyone was up, Murray smiled. "No," he replied, "I just figure there's no reason you should be able to sleep if I have to be up. See you downstairs." Then he walked to the second dorm. "Everybody up in here?" he asked as he entered.

"All except sleeping beauty over there," replied Andy Stoll, one of the leaders in the group, jerking his thumb over his shoulder toward the one cot that was still occupied. "He's glued to that sack."

Murray shook his head. "Come on, Joseph," he said, walking toward the cot. "Let's go. It's time to get up." Incoherent mumblings issued from under the blanket. Leaning over the boy, Murray tapped his shoulder. "School's closed today, Joseph," he said, "and if you stall much longer, you'll miss the special rec trip."

Joseph threw the covers back and jumped up quickly. "Hell, I forgot it was a holiday!" he exclaimed. "I'll hurry up—O.K.?"

Murray nodded. "It'll be O.K. if you get moving," he said. "On the double!"

A little over an hour later, Murray and the boys were aboard a chartered bus and the trip was under way. "Whew!" exhaled Murray as he sat down. "Getting some of these kids off on an outing like this seems like a full day's work in itself."

"Anything special?" asked Alex Compton, a recreation worker who was seated beside him.

"No," laughed Murray, "just the usual problems involved in getting them to the right place at the right time. Especially when it means getting up early." He paused for a moment, then added thoughtfully,

"Except for Joseph Reid. Something dawned on me this morning. The only time I have to blast that kid out of bed is on school days."

"Sounds pretty normal to me," responded Alex.

"No, actually it's odd in Joseph's case," replied Murray. "The kid seemed to take a real interest in school from the time he got here early last month. He does his homework faithfully, he gets fairly good grades, and he's one of the few kids in the cottage who I honestly think could finish the academic program. Yet it's harder to get him out of bed on school days than anyone else in the cottage."

"Do you have any idea why?" asked Alex.

"I've tried to figure it out," Murray replied, "but I haven't got a clue. There's nothing in the case record that seems to help, either."

"Have you asked Joseph what it's all about?"

"I've tried," said Murray, "but he just shrugs it off. I really don't think he knows."

The following morning, Murray found himself again standing alongside Joseph's cot. All the other youngsters were up and dressed, but Joseph was still apparently asleep. "Come on, Joseph," Murray said, "you're going to be late for school. Get up! Now!"

"Lemme alone," muttered the boy.

"Hey, Joseph, just tell me one thing," asked Murray, almost casually. "How come you don't fight me about getting up, except on school days?"

Rolling over, Joseph grunted. "That bag, Mrs. Green, teaches the first class—she's a bitch," he mumbled. "Nags me all the time and never listens, just like my mother . . ." The boy stopped as his eyes focused on Murray, and he pulled up the blanket and rolled over again. "I must have been dreaming, Mr. Welk," he said softly. "Just leave me alone, huh?"

(Supplementary discussion questions, page 330)

8.2 WHY SHOULD THEY?

"Why the long face, Marv?" asked Danny White as he overtook his younger colleague on the way to the administration building.

Marv looked up in surprise. "I didn't think it showed," he said with a smile. Then, shaking his head grimly, he continued. "Danny, I just haven't been able to get these kids to clean up that cottage. It's a big hassle every morning, and it wrecks the whole day. How do you handle it?"

"You learn some tricks when you've been in this work as long as I have," Danny replied kindly. "Sometimes they work, sometimes they don't. Some places have a formal cottage inspection every morning and they give a prize to the cottage with the highest score at the end of the week."

"Why don't we have that here?" Marv asked.

"The child care workers suggest it every once in a while," responded Danny, "but the boss won't buy it. He says its too much competition for the kids. Hell, these kids are competing with each other all the time. Anyway, I have a setup in my cottage with daily inspection, and the guy who does his jobs best gets extra candy or some other treat at the end of the week. Like I said, it doesn't work all the time, but I think it helps."

By now they had reached the steps of the administration building, and it was time for Marv's supervisory conference. "Thanks, Danny," Marv said. "I have a conference now, but will you tell me more about your system later?"

"Sure, kid, any time," Danny replied as Marv continued up the steps and into the building.

When Mr. Oliver asked him how things were going, Marv told him about the cottage cleanup problems in detail and asked about setting up a formal inspection system to give the boys more incentive. "We've considered that from time to time," Mr. Oliver replied, "but we haven't done it for a number of reasons.

"In the first place," he continued, "it's phony, because it tells kids that having a clean cottage is important only to win a special treat. Not only that, but why put a premium on having the best? Remember, beyond a certain point neatness and cleanliness can be a fault."

"But isn't there some value in having a clear symbol, like a prize, that kids can understand?" responded Marv. "They really don't care much about keeping the cottage clean just to have a clean place to live. I guess that's how kids are, especially boys."

"There are other problems with competitive cleanups, too," Mr. Oliver replied, "but I guess what we're doing now isn't the answer, either. I'd be willing to see us try something new if you have an idea and can sell it to the staff, as long as it makes sense in terms of our goals for the kids, too."

The next morning, Marv found himself shouting at the youngsters again as he tried to get them to make their beds and clean the cottage. There's got to be a better way than this, he thought, shaking his head.

(Supplementary discussion questions, page 330)

8.3 COME AND GET IT!

"That's the smallest size we stock, Harry," said Mrs. Lockman, the institution's veteran housekeeping manager, as she looked at the label and handed the blue jeans back to the child care worker. "I'll send in a special order, but you'll have to make do with those in the meantime. What's Tommy been wearing?"

"I guess this size fit him O.K. when he came," Harry Miller replied. "He's lost quite a bit of weight in the few weeks I've been here, though, and we didn't notice how droopy his pants were getting until now." Harry paused for a moment. "You know," he continued, "we even had him at the infirmary. The doctor said nothing is wrong. He just wants him to eat more."

"How does he get along with the other boys in the cottage?" asked Mrs. Lockman.

"He's pretty shy, I guess," answered Harry. "The other boys don't dislike him, but he's not always part of what's going on, either. Why do you ask?"

"Sometimes the bigger kids don't give the shy ones a chance," Mrs. Lockman replied. "have you ever watched him closely in the dining hall?"

"Not really," said Harry. "The cottage uses two tables and Tommy usually sits at the other one. But I have eaten with him and don't recall any special problem. Do you think the other boys are taking his food?"

"Could be," responded Mrs. Lockman, "but there are other possibilities, too. He may just be a slow, picky eater who doesn't get a chance to finish when the rest of your crew digs in like there's a race going on. I think it might be worth checking, anyway."

"Thanks a lot, Mrs. Lockman," said Harry thoughtfully as he turned to go. "I'll talk to Tommy about it and see what he has to say."

After the boys had returned to the cottage from school, Harry asked Tommy to come into the cottage office. "Did I do anything wrong, Mr. Miller?" the boy asked as he sat down.

"No, Tommy," replied Harry. "Mrs. Lockman said she'll have to order new jeans for you, and they should be here in a few days. In the meantime, you'll have to wear the ones you have."

"Sure, Mr. Miller," said the boy. "Thanks. Is that all?"

"Well, I've just been wondering," continued Harry, "You've really lost a lot of weight. The doctor says there's nothing wrong with you, but he would like you to eat more. Is there any problem?"

The boy shook his head. "I never eat much anyway," he said. "My mother always said that when I was home, too. What's the big deal?"

"I just don't like to see you losing so much weight," Harry replied. "I'm not asking that you stuff yourself, but it might be a good idea for you to at least try to put back the weight you had when you came here. You were thin then, but now you're even thinner. Can't you make up your mind to eat a full meal each time you go into the dining hall?"

The boy groaned. "That dining hall!" he said. "It's like feeding time at the zoo! By the time we get into that hot, smelly barn and the cook throws the food at you and the rest of the guys yell and slobber all over the tray—it just makes me sick. I can't really eat in there, Mr. Miller."

(Supplementary discussion questions, page 331)

8.4 BEDLAM

"What do you want, Mr. Harrington?" asked the boy a little nervously as he entered the cottage office.

Mac Harrington returned the child's gaze for a moment before responding. "Close the door and sit down."

"I didn't do nothin'," Joey protested. "I ain't in no trouble, am I?"

"Sit down," Mac said again. "I want to talk to you about the problems we've been having around here at bedtime."

"Wait a minute!" the boy replied firmly. "Why talk to me? That's everybody, not just me."

"Take it easy," said Mac, holding up his hand. "Let me finish. Twice this week I've found you running through the hall after lights out and disturbing everyone else. Maybe most of the kids were sounding off and some were out of bed, but you were the only one out of your room."

"That don't mean nothin'," retorted Joey. "You just didn't catch the other guys."

Ignoring this, Mac continued. "I just read over the night duty log notes for the last few weeks. Do you know what I found out?"

Joey, looking very worried now, shook his head.

"It seems you're the only boy who's reported to be calling out or running up and down the hall night after night. Your name comes up several nights a week, sometimes more than once, when the night worker says that he had to speak to you or send you back to bed. Other names are mentioned now and then, but not all the time. What's with you?"

"Aw," said Joey, looking down and absently rolling a pencil back and forth against the edge of the desk, "that night guy gets everybody mixed up. He always thinks it's me."

"Joey," said Mac impatiently, "stop fooling around and tell me what's going on. You've been in this cottage over a month and there's been trouble almost every night since you came. We've talked about it before and you're not like that other times. What's wrong?"

The boy stopped rolling the pencil and looked at Mac. "Mr. Harrington," he said slowly, "I just can't get to sleep at night. At least when there's something going on, I don't have to just lie there and think. I can't stand it!"

(Supplementary discussion questions, page 332)

8.5 TIME'S UP!

Glancing at the wall clock in the recreation room, Will Talbert rapped again for quiet. "Let's go," he said, raising his voice. "We have something important to say and it concerns all of you."

"They're going to let us have beer in the cottage, aren't they?" asked Tim, the cottage clown.

The other boys roared and hooted their approval and, as the noise was subsiding, Will asked again for order. When they were quiet, he began to speak. "Boys," he said, "as you know, this cottage is still having trouble getting to bed on time. You all know the rules—lights out by 10 P.M. on nights before school days. Only you haven't been making it, and all our requests and reminders seem to be ignored. Therefore, we're going to begin having 'lights out' at 9:30 P.M. until you guys learn what it means. Starting tonight!" he concluded emphatically.

Most of the boys groaned, but Matt tried to take the offensive. "That's not fair," he said. "You just said the rules say ten."

"Forget it, Matt," said Fred Johnson, Will's co-worker in the cottage. "We'll try ten again next week if this cottage shows us it can make nine thirty. We've told you enough times that this would happen if things didn't get better, and last night was the worst yet."

Tim's shrill voice was heard above the grumbles. This time he was serious. "How about a compromise?" he asked earnestly. "Why not nine-thirty a couple of nights, then try ten again?"

Raising his voice, Will replied. "No negotiations! You were warned and you kept stalling around night after night. Anyway, it's time to get ready for dinner."

186/Critical Incidents in Child Care

"Remember," Fred added as the angry group began to disperse, "all cottage time schedules following dinner will be moved forward one half hour. We're calling it 'curfew savings time,' " he concluded with a grin.

"You're not funny," said Matt spitefully. "You stink!"

After dinner, the boys returned to the cottage to do their homework and finish their cottage jobs. Everything was going smoothly and, aside from denying a stream of requests that they reconsider the curfew decision, the two counselors began to relax. By eight-thirty or so, most of the boys had finished their work and drifted down to the recreation room. They were sitting around watching TV, having their evening snacks, and talking with Fred and Will. Somehow, the conversation got around to the problems that had brought the boys to the institution and what life would be like for them when they got out. The counselors were pleased to see that the group could talk so easily and openly with them and felt that, perhaps for the first time, they were "reaching" the youngsters on a basic level and were in a position to be genuinely helpful.

Everyone was absorbed in the conversation when Fred happened to glance at the wall clock and noticed that it was almost nine twenty and time for the boys to get ready for bed. Matt, who was in the middle of explaining why he felt that he would never be able to succeed outside, saw Fred looking at the clock. "Aw, come on," he said, almost pleading. "This is really getting to be interesting. Can't you give us a break?"

Fred and Will looked at each other, not quite knowing what to say.

(Supplementary discussion questions, page 332)

8.6 STUDY HOUR

A noisy cottage meeting was in progress and Luis Santiago, the child care worker, had to raise his voice to be heard. "O.K., you guys, that's enough!" he barked. "Quiet down so we can discuss it!"

"Sure, sure, Mr. Santiago," called a voice from the side of the room, "you don't have to be locked in this room with your lousy books for an hour every night. It's no skin off yours!"

Luis broke into the laughter that followed. "Look," he said, "What's the big deal? Listen to it again. The director is concerned about the guys who've been flunking in school, so he wants to try out a new schedule. Dinner will be half an hour earlier, and you'll have a study period in the evenings. Anyway, you're the ones who might get better grades, pass more subjects, and come out ahead."

Ron Green kicked at a nearby table in disgust. "Shit! I always get my studying done. Why the hell do we have to have this?" The boys quieted down and looked at the child care worker for a response.

Luis shook his head. "You guys are too much!" he said. "If you study anyway, what difference does it make?"

"It makes a lot of difference to us," grumbled the boy who had spoken before from the side of the room. "But there's no point sitting around talking about it. This place just tries to make things hard for us. Come on, you guys," he concluded, standing up, "let's watch some TV." Realizing that he was up against a stone wall for the moment at least, Luis made no comment as the boys began to file out of the room.

The next morning, Luis described the scene to his supervisor. "I don't know what to do, Mr. Donovan," he concluded. "I don't understand why they're so upset. It's not that much of a change."

"Maybe it's not just the study hour," Mr. Donovan replied. "Any change in routine is hard, especially for kids like these. Some of them never had stability in their lives before they came here. Suppose you look at their reaction in that light. Would you handle things any differently?"

(Supplementary discussion questions, page 333)

9. INTAKE AND DISCHARGE

A youngster entering an institution must make a major adjustment, and he must make another major adjustment when he leaves. The group must also adjust to significant changes as individuals come and go. Some of the important problems and opportunities often encountered in these areas are portrayed in the cases that follow.

TABLE OF CASES

9.1 NEW MAN IN TOWN

Phil, the night relief counselor, saw Ralph Barron enter the cottage and start to remove his coat. "What are you doing here so early?" asked Phil. "You're not on duty for another half hour. You a glutton for punishment or something?" he added with a grin.

"Not exactly," laughed Ralph. "We're expecting a new boy in the cottage today, and I want to be sure that everything's ready for him. You never know how early they may show up."

"I guess being ready is pretty important," responded Phil. "Some of the kids must be really scared when they get here."

"I think it's half the battle," Ralph agreed. "If we can help a new kid get off on the right foot, it makes a big difference."

The morning passed quickly and Ralph was satisfied that Kurt, the new boy, would have everything he needed. His room was ready, and Ralph had made a point of reminding Vince Roman, who was to act as Kurt's "big brother" during the first week, to return to the cottage promptly after school so the boys could meet.

It was shortly after 2 P.M. when Ralph saw a River County car stop in front of the cottage. The driver, whom Ralph assumed to be a county corrections officer, stepped out along with a frightened-looking youngster and the cottage life director, Tom Evans. Ralph met them at the door and, after introductions were made, Tom and the corrections officer left to complete the necessary paperwork at the administration building. Ralph took Kurt into the common room, where they sat down and talked about cottage routines and rules, and Ralph explained what the boy's general schedule would be during the next few days. As the conversation progressed, Ralph noticed that Kurt seemed to be more relaxed and by the time they were ready to tour the cottage his responses offered more than his initial "Yeah's" and "No's."

As they headed upstairs to the sleeping area, Vince entered the cottage. "I'm glad you're here, Vince," said Ralph. "Kurt, I'd like you to meet Vince, your big brother here at the cottage. Remember? I told you he'd be around to help you out this first week. Vince has been through it and done well, and he'll be leaving us soon."

"Hi," said Vince. "How's everything going?"

"O.K., I guess," replied Kurt. "Glad to meetcha."

"We were just going upstairs to show Kurt where he'll be sleeping," Ralph explained. "Why don't you come with us?"

Once the three of them were in the dormitory-type sleeping room, Vince began to explain where Kurt would bunk, which locker he was to use, what the shower schedules would be, and the like. However, it appeared to Ralph that Kurt was beginning to feel uncomfortable again. He wondered if it was because most of the other boys had returned from school by now and several had gathered outside the half-open door.

"Do you have any questions?" asked Vince, finally, apparently having covered everything he could think of. "Then we can go out and meet the rest of the guys."

Kurt nodded and gave the room a final, searching look before he answered. "Where do we change?"

Vince looked puzzled. "What do you mean?"

"Change clothes," Kurt explained, glancing at the doorway. "I'm not going to get undressed in front of all those guys."

Ralph saw Vince try to hide his grin as the boys in the hall began to snicker.

(Supplementary discussion questions, page 333)

9.2 WELCOME TO THE CLUB

Mort Long crossed the last item off of his inventory list before turning to the youngster standing next to him in the dormitory. "Well, Dean," he said pleasantly, "I think that does it. You are now officially a member of this institution. Welcome to the club!"

They shook hands and, with an uncertain grin, the boy replied, "Thanks, Mr. Long. What happens now?"

"It's almost time for lunch," said Mort, noting the boy's nervousness, "but let's talk for a few minutes before we go downstairs. You're probably anxious and a little scared about being here. All the boys go through this when they first arrive, but we'll do our best to make you feel at home. If you have any questions, just ask me or one of the other child care workers or one of the boys. O.K.?"

"Yeah, that sounds O.K.," said Dean, with a little more assurance in his voice.

Dean was the first new boy who had entered the cottage since Mort had started working there, and Mort had been warned that the initial period of adjustment was often difficult. It was with satisfaction, therefore, that he observed that afternoon and evening that the boys seemed to be accepting Dean into the group. Furthermore, Dean, a youngster who had seemed to Mort to be rather shy, appeared to be getting along well with the others. Mort reflected that maybe the secret was to try to make the new boy feel as comfortable and secure as you could and then perhaps he would have the confidence to meet and mingle with the others on a better basis.

Still turning these thoughts over in his mind, Mort stepped into the dorm office for some report forms. Turning to leave, he overheard a few of the boys talking outside the office door. "Man, tonight we'll really initiate little Dean," whispered Artie, one of the older boys, excitedly.

"Yeah," chimed in Chino, laughing, "we'll give him a blanket party. He'll get the works!"

Moving to open the door, Mort stopped as he heard Angelo, one of the younger boys, ask, "Hey! Won't the night watch stop us?"

"Forget that," Artie replied. "It's O.K. with them."

"Yeah," said Chino, "old man Jenkins has been here for ten years and he knows this happens to every new boy. He won't bother us as long as we don't hurt the kid too much."

(Supplementary discussion questions, page 334)

9.3 SUDDEN DEPARTURE

Ralph Smith had a lighted match half way to his pipe when he heard a loud knock at the cottage door. He quickly extinguished the match, pulled the unlit pipe from his mouth, and headed for the door. Pulling it open, he found himself standing face to face with Dick Heiser, one of the night security guards.

"This belong to you?" asked the older man gruffly, pushing a youngster in front of him into the open doorway.

"Yes, it does," sighed Ralph, stepping aside so the boy could enter. "Mike, what are you doing outside after curfew?" he asked, looking the boy full in the face. "Aren't you in enough trouble already?"

"Go to hell, you bastard," replied Michael, in a toneless voice.

"That's enough," said Ralph brusquely. "Get upstairs. I'll be there in a minute." The two men stood in silence as the boy slowly disappeared up the steps. Shaking his head, Ralph turned to the security guard and asked, "Where did you find him, Dick?"

"He was hiding in the bushes just inside the front gate. With this," he added, pulling a kitchen knife from his pocket. "And he tried to use it."

Ralph winced as he took the knife. "Did you get hurt?" he asked.

"No," answered Dick. "I've learned a few things in eighteen years around here, and how to take a knife away from a kid is one of them. But he did try."

"Well," said Ralph, shaking his head, "I'm afraid this'll be the end of the line for Michael. When this comes up at the meeting tomorrow, on top of everything else he's been doing, it'll be all over but the shouting."

"I know," said Dick thoughtfully, as he turned to leave, "but that's how it goes sometimes."

The meeting the next morning went just as Ralph had predicted. Michael Waner and the episode with the knife had been the main topic, with most of those present agreeing that Michael's behavior had been getting increasingly out of control. Somewhat reluctantly the staff had come to the conclusion that the boy would have to be sent to the prison farm, a more secure facility. The youngster had no family, he was not a candidate for a mental hospital, and it seemed apparent that the institution could not safely maintain him in such an open setting. Some hope was expressed that a few months at the prison farm might help Michael learn to control his behavior enough so that he could be returned to the institution.

Ralph had mixed feelings about the decision and did not look forward to telling Michael about it, although he knew that he was closest to the boy and the logical one to do it. That did not make it much easier, of course. Arriving back at the cottage, Ralph saw Michael sitting alone in the living room, apparently waiting for him.

"Well?" asked Michael glumly as Ralph sat down nearby.

"Michael," Ralph began, "what I have to say may be hard for you to understand, but we have decided that in view of your recent behavior here it would be best for you if you go to a prison farm for awhile . . ."

Not allowing Ralph to finish, Michael burst out shouting. "You fucks! You're sending me to jail instead of helping me. I know I have a temper, but I thought that's what you're here to help me with!" The boy's upper lip curled into a sneer as he finished. "And you like to think you're my friend. I never did trust you."

Ralph looked at the boy and shook his head. "Michael," he said, "whether you believe it or not, we do hope that after some time at the farm, you'll be able to return to us in a better way."

Michael stood up and moved toward Ralph. "Bullshit!" he screamed. "You can say any damn thing you want to make yourself feel better, but you're sending me to jail with a bunch of crooks, and you know as well as I do that that won't help me." The boy turned on his heels and began to walk toward the door.

(Supplementary discussion questions, page 334)

9.4 DOING TIME

"It seems like it's always the same three girls lately, Sue," said Helen Phillips to her friend. Both were child care workers at the institution and they often talked together about their problems on the job. "Yesterday they tried to hide in the back of a delivery truck so they could get into town. They're lucky the driver spotted them before he left the grounds. Mr. Pearsons put them on cottage restriction again."

"What do you think is bothering them?" Sue asked.

"I don't know," replied Helen. "It's really unusual behavior for them. They arrived around the same time, they've all done well here, and they're scheduled to leave at the end of the summer. I hope they don't mess it up for themselves."

"Do you think it's jitters about going home?"

"I thought so at first, but it seems like more than that. I'm going to have a talk with them when I get back to the cottage."

Later, Helen sat facing the three girls in the cottage office. "Look," she said, "you girls are scheduled for discharge when your court commitments terminate within the next two months. You all seem anxious to go home. I really don't understand why you're all starting to get into trouble when you're so close to leaving. What's going on?"

The girls looked at one another, shrugged, and said nothing.

"Are you afraid of leaving here?" she finally asked. "Is that the problem?"

All three girls giggled and began to whisper back and forth. After a few seconds, Joan responded. "Look, Miss Phillips," she said, "you've got it all wrong. We really want to go *now*. Everybody says we're ready but there's a stupid rule that says kids can only leave 'when their sentence is up.'"

"Don't you see?" chimed in Betty. "That's the problem. We have to cool our heels until the court says we can go. All we're doing is killing time and it's really getting to be a drag!"

(*Supplementary discussion questions, page 335*)

9.5 NO PLACE LIKE HOME

Hearing his name as he walked across the grounds, Larry Spencer stopped and looked around to see Joe Steiner, the shop teacher for most of the boys in Larry's cottage. "Larry," Joe called again, "wait a minute. I want to talk to you!"

"Hi," said Larry, as Joe headed toward him. "What's up?"

"What the hell is it with Rusty Woltz these days?" asked Joe. "I can't do a thing with him anymore. I thought maybe you could give me a clue."

"I don't know," answered Larry. "I know he's been acting up a little, but nothing serious. I figured it was a combination of spring fever and anxiety about leaving next month. He's been here three years, you know, and in other institutions and foster homes before that."

"Well, he deliberately broke the forming machine in shop today," replied Joe. "It's completely wrecked and . . ."

"Deliberately?" echoed Larry in a surprised voice. "Something must really be bothering him. That kind of thing is very unusual for Rusty."

"Maybe it used to be unusual," protested Joe, "but no more. He's been building up to this for almost a month. There's been nothing actually broken until today, but he's been disruptive in class, he doesn't do his assignments, and he's been a general problem. In fact, I've asked for a case conference. I can't keep him in the class if things don't get better."

"Hey, wait a minute!" said Larry. "Rusty is scheduled to finish the vocational program this spring and then graduate. After that he'll be released. If you drop him, that means he'll have to repeat the shop course and his release will be delayed. The kid might just give up if that happened."

"I know that, Larry," answered Joe quietly. "But we aren't using toys to work with in that shop. Those machines are real, and they're dangerous if they aren't handled properly. You can't have kids horsing around in that class, much less deliberately trying to do damage. You know that. It risks the safety of every boy in the room and I just can't permit it."

Larry nodded slowly. "I wish we had a little time to work on it," he said. "When is the meeting?"

"They're going to try to set it up within a day or two," replied Joe. "They have to check times with the various people. Look, I'm not trying to mess the kid up," he continued. "I'd like to see him make it. I just have to consider the others, too, and the safety angle."

"O.K.," said Larry, "I'll go back to the cottage now and talk to him. Maybe I can get some idea of why he started acting up like this. His behavior in the cottage hasn't been disruptive the way you describe. In fact, he's always been kind of a quiet kid. Almost depressed. I'll let you know what happens."

Ten minutes later Larry had found Rusty in the cottage kitchen, where the boy was finishing his assigned cottage chores.

"Are you almost done, Rusty?" he asked. "I'd like to talk to you."

"Sure, Mr. Spencer. Just let me put this pail and mop away, and I'll be there," the boy replied.

"Listen, Rusty," Larry began when they had seated themselves in the cottage office, "I just spoke with Mr. Steiner and you're in big trouble. Do you want to talk about it?"

Rusty looked down and shrugged. "Naw," he said, "there's no real trouble. I was just foolin' around and had an accident. It's no big deal."

"Oh, come on," said Larry, "you know better than that. Mr. Steiner was very upset about that forming machine and if you keep up the way you're going, you'll have to repeat the shop course."

"So what?" asked Rusty quietly.

"So you'll miss your scheduled release date, that's what," replied Larry, a little puzzled. "You know you're due to be discharged right after your graduation. This would hold it up."

Still looking at the floor, Rusty was silent for a moment. "Listen, Mr. Spencer," he finally said, "I'm going to level with you. This is the first time in my life I've had a roof over my head, three meals a day, and someone to talk to when I'm up tight. I know it's never going to be that good for me on the outside." Tears welling up in his eyes, he looked at Larry. "Don't you understand?" he asked pleadingly. "I don't want to go."

(Supplementary discussion questions, page 336)

9.6 THE VACANCY

Dennis Bowen marched into the cottage day room and turned off the television set. "That's it!" he said firmly. "No more TV tonight, and it'll stay off until the wise guy who took the channel selection knob returns it. What the hell is going on here, anyway?"

"I only took it to protect my rights," protested Richie Sterling. "It was my turn to pick the program and the other guys kept flipping to other stations. So I turned my show back on and then hid the knob. Come on, Mr. Bowen," he added in a pleading tone, "let me watch the rest of the show. Be fair!"

"I'm being fair," replied Dennis in a calmer tone of voice. "I warned all of you twice tonight to stop the commotion in here. You didn't listen, so no TV. This cottage has been in an uproar the last two weeks, and it's time things settled down." A chorus of complaints began, but Dennis remained firm.

As he walked back into the hall, Dennis met Eric Clark, his co-worker, who was just coming on duty. "What's up?" Eric asked. "You look grim."

"God, I don't know what's happened to those kids!" responded Dennis. "They've been acting like monsters and the cottage is a mess. I don't understand it. It seems like all we had going in this cottage just crumbled about a week ago, and now it's total chaos. What the hell's going on?"

Eric, who was several years older than Dennis and had been a child care worker for a long time, nodded. "Yeah, suddenly everything does seem out of whack," he agreed. "Frankly," he continued, "I trace it all back to the day Leon Whitney left."

"Leon?" asked Dennis. "But he was kind of a troublemaker. I thought the kids were a little scared of him."

"You're right," responded Eric, "but Leon was a strong leader, too. In his own way he kept the other kids in line." He paused for a moment, and then he smiled. "Did you ever shoot any geese?" he asked.

Dennis shook his head. "What are you driving at?"

"Well, if you ever do, try to pick off that lead bird. You know, the one that flies at the point of the V formation. You'll see all the rest of them flounder around all over the place until they get a new leader. Then they form a new V with him at the point."

"Oh," said Dennis slowly, "and you think that's what's happening with the kids?"

Eric nodded. "Yes, I really do. They have no leader and that's why there's so much confusion."

"But how long do we wait for things to straighten out?" Dennis asked. "And what should we be doing in the meantime?"

(Supplementary discussion questions, page 336)

10. SCHOOL, WORK, AND LEISURE TIME

Institutionalized youngsters divide most of their waking hours among three kinds of activities: school, work assignments, and formal or informal recreation. Although child care workers usually have relatively little direct involvement with the school program, they may frequently be called on to deal with school-related situations that are brought to their attention. The same is true of work details and formal recreation programs that may be supervised by maintenance personnel and athletic coaches, for example, although child care workers sometimes have greater direct responsibility in these areas. Informal recreation or "cottage time" is usually almost fully the province of the child care workers. The cases that follow illustrate the kinds of opportunities and problems that may arise in these several types of situations.

TABLE OF CASES

10.1 LEISURE IN THE COTTAGE

"What do you usually do when the kids come back to the cottage after school?" asked Leo Dunbar, the new child care worker.

"When it's cold out, they usually play in the rec room or watch TV," replied Tom Sanders, one of the more experienced men in the room. "Sometimes they go out and play near the cottage. I usually work in the cottage office except when something happens. You can tell after a while just by the tone of their voices when a fight or something is brewing."

"Tom and I argue about this all the time," interjected Sam Metcalf, who had also been a child care worker for many years. "I think the more we can be in there doing things with the kids, the better it is. That goes for playing ping-pong, pool, or whatever."

"You're wrong, Sam," said Tom. "These kids have had it up to here with adults. They've got to learn how to get along with other kids, and the more freedom we can give them to do it, the better. I figure that when the group doesn't need me any more, when they can handle themselves, then I've done my job."

"But Tom," responded Sam, "one of the reasons kids are here is because they've had trouble relating to adults. We can't begin to help them until we have a relationship with them, and we can't do that if we only see them when there's trouble brewing. We have to get in there and live with them—play, work, eat, whatever."

"Sam, you missed my point," said Tom. "What the kids want from us is privacy. We're outsiders. Where they come from, all adults are outsiders, even their own parents. We have no right to intrude ourselves on them, just like they have no business with us on our time off. You can't push yourself on them like that."

Leo broke into the conversation. "Thanks, you guys," he said, laughing at the wide difference in their opinions. "Now I know just what to do when I go on duty. I better get over to the cottage."

On the way to his cottage, Leo decided to start getting more involved with the boys in their leisure-time activities. He had stayed away from them before, but he thought he'd give Sam's idea a try.

Leo walked into the rec room, where he found some of the boys taking pool shots. He picked up a cue, missed a shot, and the boys laughed. Soon they were ready to play a game and began to make teams. "Count me in," said Leo.

"No offense, Mr. Dunbar," said one of the boys after a few moments of embarrassing silence, "but if you don't mind, we just want to have a little game among the guys."

Leo smiled and nodded. As he walked away, he wondered again how much he should try to involve himself in the boys' activities, and how to go about it.

(Supplementary discussion questions, page 337)

10.2 AS THE REAL WORLD TURNS

It was shortly before the boys were expected back from school and the two child care workers were sitting in the cottage office.

"The kids go to the gym tomorrow for the start of that new Saturday intramural basketball league, don't they?" asked Del. "It sounds like it might be a good idea."

"Could be," said Mark. "I can only foresee one problem. It's not going to be easy to pry some of our boys away from the TV set on Saturday mornings. Especially the nonathletic ones."

Del raised his eyebrows. "Well, being on the team isn't mandatory," he said, "but do you think we'll get that much static? It's only an hour."

"Want to bet?" asked Mark. "Between practices and games over the next few months, they'll be at the gym every Saturday morning. Besides," he continued, "some of our kids are so addicted to that stupid set that they have square eyeballs. They sit planted there, like a bunch of vegetables."

Del nodded slowly. "Do you think that's partly our fault?" he asked. "We do sometimes use TV watching as a bribe and a reward."

Mark shrugged. "Maybe that's some of it, but I think the kids often try to use it almost like a tranquilizer. No matter how hard we try to push other activities, there's always that group, like Earl, Hank, and Terry, who gravitate to the set whenever they get a chance."

"Like when they sit for hours on Saturday morning with all those dumb cartoons running on endlessly," agreed Del. "Maybe this basketball league is a good opportunity for us to change that."

"I'm with you," said Mark with conviction. "We'll make it clear at the cottage meeting that TV isn't an alternative."

That evening, halfway through the meeting, Mark and Del exchanged glances as Earl, Hank, and Terry, along with one or two others, declined to join the basketball team. Since none of them was particularly good at the game, there was little reaction from the group. When the meeting had ended, Mark and Del called together the boys who had refused.

"What do you mean, no TV for us while the others play basketball?" asked Hank hotly as Mark was explaining such alternatives as indoor games, model-making, and hikes and handball in good weather.

"That's right," said Mark. "There's too much TV watching in this cottage and not enough other activities. We need to . . ."

"What did we do wrong?" demanded Earl, interrupting him. "You guys only take the TV away when you're punishing us!"

"New rules, that's all," explained Mark. "We think you kids should unplug yourselves from that set more often and see what the real world is all about."

Terry, who had remained silent throughout the conversation, finally spoke. "Real world?" he echoed sarcastically. "You mean like all of us being put away in this crummy institution? You can shove the real world!"

(Supplementary discussion questions, page 337)

10.3 "WHERE IS IT WRITTEN?"

Andy Carr and Walt Rowe motioned for quiet in the recreation room where the boys were assembled for the weekly cottage meeting.

"Let's have a little order in here!" called Andy. "We have a lot to talk about."

"Hey, Mr. Carr," exclaimed Leo Moore, taking advantage of the momentary lull, "what's in that box you have beside you?"

"That's one of the things we're going to talk about this afternoon, Leo," replied Andy. "Next Sunday evening is our turn to conduct chapel services, you know. Those cartons have books and music sheets for us to use to get ready."

"Come on," Walt said as the moans and groans began, "you boys know that the services are led by one of the cottages on the first Sunday night each month. It's our turn, that's all, so let's settle down and get organized."

"Here are three sign-up sheets," Andy said when the noise subsided, indicating the papers on the table next to him. "I want everyone to write his name on at least one sheet. Each sheet is marked and you can choose whatever part of the service you're most interested in. You can start planning what you want to do, and we'll be around to help."

As the boys divided up to get started, Andy noticed that Hardy and Joe had disappeared. They were among the newer boys and generally held themselves aloof from the group, so Andy was not particularly surprised at their absence. Leaving Walt with the group, he left to check the cottage living room, where he found Hardy and Joe watching television.

"Have you two decided which part of the service you'd like to help with?" Andy asked.

"That's not for me," said Hardy. "Count me out."

"Me, too," echoed Joe.

"Look" said Andy, trying to be patient, "no one's going to force you to get up in the pulpit and preach, but we do expect everyone in the cottage to take part in our particular chapel service. You two can sing with the choir if you like."

Hardy looked at Andy coolly. "I don't believe in that mumbo

jumbo," he sneered. "So forget it. Besides," he continued without waiting for Andy to respond, "you don't have any right to make us take part in something like that, and we're not going to do it!"

(Supplementary discussion questions, page 338)

10.4 THE WORKING CLASS

"Boy, is this a lousy job," complained Nick, as he leaned against the wall and watched Ramon take a load of sheets out of the washing machine.

Ramon nodded as he threw the sheets into the dryer. "It wouldn't be so bad if you helped more," he added.

"You guys have to admit that a work detail in a nice warm laundry room beats shoveling snow and chipping ice off the sidewalks," chided Jay Morgan, their child care worker, who was folding the sheets from the previous load.

"Maybe," said Ramon grudgingly, looking up through the small window at a patch of bleak January sky.

"That's a lot of crap," exclaimed Nick. "A basement is a basement and work is work! It stinks to have to work on Saturday after they make you sit in school all week."

"Come on, Nick, get your ass in gear," said Ramon, indicating the bulging laundry bags on the floor. "We'll never get done at this rate."

Ignoring Ramon, Nick turned to Jay. "You know," he said, "I was thinking the other day—this place is run like a chain gang."

"A chain gang?" repeated Jay in surprise. "That's a new one! What makes you say that?"

"I saw a movie about it," replied Nick. "All these prisoners were forced to work on road gangs and clear out swamps and stuff. They were all chained together. It reminds me of this place."

"Tell us, when were you last in chains?" asked Jay dryly, looking at Nick. "Or a swamp? The only chores you have here are the kinds of things you'd probably be helping with in your own home. They have to be done and they might even help you learn to accept the responsibility of helping the place you live in to run properly."

"That sounds fine," countered Nick, "but boil it all down and it comes out forced labor—just like in the movie."

"Hey, man," interrupted Ramon, "are you gonna help sort out this stuff or not? I keep telling you—we ain't got all day!"

"Don't bother me," snapped Nick. "Can't you see I'm busy talking?"

"That's enough," said Jay, quietly. "Get to work, Nick. You've used up your debating time. Just stop stalling and start sorting that laundry."

"Sure," responded Nick sarcastically, "I'll start working, 'boss.' I'll make it easy for you. You won't admit it, but you'd be doing the dirty work if we didn't. That's the real reason you care if it gets done or not."

(Supplementary discussion questions, page 339)

10.5 PROGRAM FOR WHAT?

"Come on, Lillian," said Virginia, who was on her way to the auditorium to begin the drama club rehearsal, "you'll be late. I want to get started quickly."

"I can't come today, Miss King," replied the shy, teenaged girl sadly. "Miss Dixon told me to get right back to the cottage because I didn't finish making my bed and cleaning up."

After dinner that evening, Virginia stopped Ethel Dixon to talk with her.

"I'm sorry Lillian had to miss the rehearsal," said Ethel. "She's interested in the play, so I think she'll be more careful to get her cottage chores done in the morning after this."

"I hope so," replied Virginia. "I think this play just might help her break out of her shell, and I'd hate to see us miss the chance. But she'll get discouraged if she doesn't feel she's good enough, and she has to come to rehearsals regularly for that. Couldn't she finish her chores at night if she needs more time?"

"I agree that the play is a good thing for her," responded Ethel, "but she also has to meet her cottage obligations. I can't see the value of attaining one goal at the expense of another. The rules are clear about the kids' work schedules and if we let Lillian slide by, the other girls will get their backs up about favoritism. They might even take it out on her. And Lillian will figure she's blackmailed us into rule breaking. It's not worth it!"

"But Lillian doesn't know about blackmail," protested Virginia. "All she knows is that she has a small part in one of the drama club's plays, and she's thrilled about it. If she doesn't get to practice with the rest of the group, she'll feel too self-conscious about participating and drop out. Is that worth it?"

"Suppose I try to go over her lines with her," responded Ethel. "Would that help? I'm not trying to punish her or keep her out of the play. It's just that the chores have to be done, too."

"I think that would be great, Ethel," said Virginia enthusiastically.

The next day, Lillian was ready to leave the cottage for rehearsal when Ethel stopped her. "I'm sorry, Lillian, but your work isn't finished yet," said the child care worker.

"Please, Miss Dixon," pleaded the girl, "let me go. I'll finish my chores before dinner. Just let me go to the rehearsal."

"You know the rule," replied Ethel, not unkindly. "Would you like me to help you finish? Maybe you could get there before the end if we hurry."

Lillian was fighting to hold back the tears. "I'll do it, Miss Dixon," she said. "I'll be back in five minutes."

"Where are you going?" Ethel asked.

"I have to return my script to Miss King," the girl replied tearfully. "I can't be in the play any more. I won't know enough and I'll make a fool of myself."

(Supplementary discussion questions, page 339)

10.6 THE GOAL OF THE GAME

"But Mr. Moore," protested Paul Maxwell, "the coach called a special practice for tonight. He wants everybody there because we have a big game on Friday."

"I'm sorry, Paul," responded Tim Moore, the child care worker on duty, "but the cottage is grounded tonight and that's it!"

"But I'll make it up another night," pleaded Paul. "I have to be there."

"I'll talk to the coach and tell him you tried to go," Tim promised, "but that's the best I can do. It's time for dinner now and I don't want to talk about it any more."

On his way back to the cottage after the meal, Tim stopped at the gym to see Hank Lee, the physical education teacher and basketball coach. "Hank," he said, "Paul Maxwell won't be able to get to practice tonight and I promised him I'd tell you. He's very worried about it."

"What's wrong?" asked the coach. "Is he sick?"

"Oh, no," Tim explained. "It's just that the cottage raised too much hell after curfew again last night, so we decided to try grounding them for a day. Maybe they'll get the idea we mean it."

"That puts me in a real bind," responded Hank, shaking his head. "Paul's one of our best men, and it's hard to hold much of a practice without him."

"I know," said Tim, "and I'm sorry. He even asked if he could make it up another time, but he's been the ringleader of the trouble at night so I didn't see how I could do that. Really, he shouldn't be on the team, anyway."

"What do you mean?" asked Hank.

"Well," Tim replied, "he's a troublemaker from the word 'go.' I've got kids in that cottage who'd really appreciate playing on the team and really deserve the privilege, too."

"But Tim," Hank protested, "how could I run a varsity team like that? I choose the best players, the ones who can win the most games, and that's the only fair way to do it. The varsity is supposed to represent the best we've got, isn't it? Besides, it gives the kids a chance to see other places, mostly regular high schools, and it helps the spirit in the whole institution."

"I guess so," Tim agreed, "but the boys on the team do get special privileges, like off-grounds trips and excuses from other activities now and then. Not to mention the honor. It just seems to me that in a place like this, those things should be based on the way kids act instead of whether they're lucky enough to be able to play basketball better than someone else."

"Tim," Hank replied, "every kid here needs to feel he's special in something. You know that as well as I do. For some kids, it happens to be basketball, and maybe that's just the thing we can use to help them."

Tim shook his head. "I'm sure that's true in some cases, Hank," he said, "but why should a kid have to be a top basketball player just to get help? And what about the ones who use it because they think it makes them privileged characters?"

"Look, I work those kids hard for their privileges," argued Hank. "Any kid that doesn't work doesn't stay on the team. If we tried to do it your way, it wouldn't be a varsity team. It'd be something else. And how do you think the other kids would feel if we lost because a kid like Paul wasn't allowed to play?"

Later that evening, when Tim's co-worker came on duty, Tim told him about his conversation with the coach. "It's a real problem," he concluded. "How do you think a place like this should handle it?"

(Supplementary discussion questions, page 340)

10.7 THE ACID TEST

"Mr. Gordon, Mr. Gordon," called Terry Conner as he ran into the cottage. "I got it. I got the job."

"Congratulations," said John Gordon, the senior child care worker, smiling and shaking the boy's hand. "That's great news."

"My social worker got the letter today," the boy continued. "I'll be the assistant lifeguard at this swim club. I'll be watching the little kids in the wading pool."

"That means you'll be able to leave next month," said John, "instead of staying until school starts. You're lucky. Not many of the kids can get summer jobs, so they end up staying here until the fall."

"All I have to do is pass my life saving, and they're giving the course here starting next week when Mr. Shore comes." Ted Shore was the swimming instructor who would be joining the institution's staff for the summer. "The course takes two weeks, then I leave to take the job."

Terry had done nicely in the institution and John was glad to see things working out so well for him. The boy was not a strong swimmer, but he worked hard and enthusiastically during the next two weeks. John was not surprised, therefore, when Terry came to happily show him his life saving certificate. "Now I'll be able to go home next week, Mr. Gordon," he said. "The job starts a week from tomorrow."

"I'm really pleased," said John, beaming. "You have a right to be proud of yourself. That's a hard test, too," he continued, as the boy smiled his appreciation. "I could never make the endurance part of it. Four hundred yards, isn't it, using four strokes?"

Terry hung his head a little. "Actually, I didn't pass that part of the test," he said. "Mr. Shore said he didn't have time to give it to me again and as long as I knew the strokes, that's all he cared about. Besides," the boy continued after a slight pause, "I think he really wanted me to be able to take the job. I guess it doesn't matter, since I'll just be watching the little kids in the shallow water anyway."

(Supplementary discussion questions, page 341)

10.8 DETOUR

Rose Jackson came into the cottage to take the evening shift. "Anything new?" she asked Doris Heywood as she entered the office.

Doris nodded. "Karen came in reading a comic book," she said. "She wanted me to help her with a word. I bet it's the first time she's read anything voluntarily since she's been here. It's all they can do in school to get her to even open a book!"

"Sounds good," replied Rose. "Maybe we can get her some more."

"The one she has is called 'Young Love Comics,' " Doris explained. "I think that has something to do with it."

Rose thought for a minute. "It seems to me that my hairdresser's daughter reads those. She had some in the shop one day. If I tell her about Karen, maybe she'd give me some of the old ones for her."

Within a few days, Karen had several more comic books. Despite their shabby appearance, they were new to her, and she was thrilled in her own shy way. She read them avidly and guarded them closely.

Karen continued to ask the child care workers when she found new words she could not read. In the office one day, she read a whole story aloud, and Doris was surprised to see how well the youngster was doing.

"Why don't we arrange for you to read that story to the other girls before they go to bed tonight," Doris suggested. Although Karen was pleased, she was also hesitant and afraid, but she finally agreed to try.

The girls loved it. They gathered around Karen with their snacks and looked at the pictures while Karen read the captions with the appropriate dramatic inflections in her voice. The readings became a nightly ritual, and Doris and Rose began to notice changes in Karen and in the group. As Karen's reading improved, so did her self-confidence in other areas. She seemed more outgoing and more sure of herself, and even began to read books that had sat untouched on the common room shelves for months. As Karen gained status in the cottage, her weak smile came more quickly and spontaneously. And the group seemed more relaxed and cohesive as a result of the nightly "story hour."

One morning Karen asked Doris if it would be all right to take the comic books to school to read during free time.

"I think that would be O.K.," Doris responded, "as long as you read them only at free time."

Karen was engrossed in one of her favorites when Mrs. Cameron, her teacher, noticed. "What do you have there, Karen?" she asked coldly. "Comic books? Bring them here right now."

Karen lowered her head, close to tears.

"Only ignorant people read such things," Mrs. Cameron continued, walking toward Karen's desk, "and I'm sure you wouldn't want people to think you were ignorant. We have enough worthwhile books in our library without your having to read trash. Now give them to me!"

Trembling, Karen began to fumble in her desk. "But Miss Heywood said it would be all right to bring them," she whispered, trying to hold back the tears, "as long as I only read them during free time."

"You tell Miss Heywood that I'll take care of school business," Mrs. Cameron said tightly. "No wonder you girls never learn anything, if they encourage you to read that kind of junk in the cottage." Reaching into Karen's desk, she picked up the stack of comics. "I don't ever want to see you reading these things again," she added. "And I'm going to speak to Mr. Grant about your reading them in the cottage, too. Now find something else to do."

Mrs. Cameron turned and Karen slipped out of her seat and left the room. Walking slowly, Karen reached the cottage and quietly opened the door. Doris was sitting at her desk.

"Karen, what's the matter?" asked Doris. "Don't you feel well?"

The girl looked at her somberly. "I feel O.K. I just had to get away from Mrs. Cameron for awhile."

"What happened?" Doris asked.

"Oh, she blew up when she saw the comic books," replied Karen quietly. Then she started crying and sobbed out the rest of the story.

(Supplementary discussion questions, page 341)

10.9 STUPID AGAIN

"And one for you, Duane," concluded Al Wagner as he finished giving out the mail. As usual, he noted the boys who had not received anything and the expressions on their faces as the others read their letters.

About ten minutes later, Al noticed that Duane Cooper was still sitting in the same chair, holding his letter, and staring at the floor. "Anything wrong, Duane?" he asked.

"I got a letter from my folks," Duane replied with a forced laugh. "Like to see it?"

Al scanned the one-page note. After saying briefly that they had enjoyed seeing the boy on their visit to the institution the previous weekend, his parents went on to complain about how poorly he was doing in school. Duane's brother had graduated from high school and gone on to a technical school, and they could not understand why Duane had not followed in his footsteps. Al nodded understandingly as he handed the letter back to Duane. "You look discouraged," he said.

"Sort of," the boy agreed. "I've always had trouble in school. I try, but things always seem to get messed up for me. I began to cut and get in trouble 'cause I just couldn't stand it. That's how come I got sent here."

"You haven't been in trouble in school here have you?" Al asked.

"Not really. They're nice in school here. They know we got problems and they try to help. So I don't mind it that much, but I'm not doing so good. I'm just not as smart as my brother," he concluded. "That's all there is to it."

"What do your teachers say about your work?" Al asked, looking for a clue as to how he might be able to help. "Do they have any suggestions?"

"I guess they'd like me to study more," Duane replied. "Maybe it's worth a try. I have a test tomorrow," he continued, standing up. "I'll get my book and see what I can do."

Al was pleased to see that Duane was studying all afternoon and evening. The boy also asked for special permission to study in the common room after lights out, a privilege that was allowed before important tests, and Al noticed that he was still studying long after the other boys had gone to sleep.

Al came on duty the next afternoon shortly before the boys were scheduled to return to the cottage from school. Duane was a few minutes late and as soon as Al saw him, he knew things had gone badly. "You look like you had a rough day," he said as the boy approached.

"I stopped by to see if Mrs. Murdock had marked the papers yet," Duane replied, "and she told me I flunked again. I stay up half the night studying and I get a 47. I guess school just isn't for me, Mr. Wagner," he continued, shaking his head sadly. "I just can't do it."

(Supplementary discussion questions, page 341)

10.10 THE CIVICS LESSON

"Since things are going so well," continued Ed Larson, Bill's supervisor, "I'd like you to begin to think about involving the boys more actively in planning their cottage life and activities."

"We talked about that during orientation," replied Bill, "and I'm all for it, although I haven't done much about it yet."

Ed nodded understandingly. "Usually we get so busy with cottage routines and the daily problems that we don't take time for this kind of thing," he said, "but it can make all the difference in the world in kids' progress. Youngsters can't learn to run their own lives successfully if they don't have a chance to try. Luckily, we're in a position to let them take on responsibility for themselves gradually, and to let them learn from their mistakes, too."

"The way I see it," added Bill, "it's a question of democracy. They have to learn to make responsible decisions if they're going to be good citizens."

"You're right," Ed replied, "but remember that democracy is a difficult concept, particularly for kids who have lived by the law of the streets all their lives. You know—'might makes right' and all that. If you tell them about democracy, they may figure it means taking a vote. With everyone voting the way the leaders say they should, of course, and afraid not to. Or they may see it as a chance to gripe without offering any constructive proposals, or a license to do anything they want."

"What I have in mind is getting them involved in planning their program," Bill explained. "Maybe a special camping trip to begin with, or a cottage improvement project, or even a better way to handle daily cottage routines. The kinds of things that are suggested in the staff manual."

"That's really what we're here for, Bill," agreed Ed, "and your group is ready. Just remember that the whole idea is new to the kids and it may take a little while for them to be able to handle it."

The next day Bill called a cottage meeting shortly before lights out. "I'd like to see you boys play more of a part in deciding what the cottage should do," Bill began. "We might plan a camp out or some other kind of special project."

"Great!" said Henry Wood, one of the older boys. "Let's camp out this weekend." There were shouts of approval from most of the others, and a few of dissent.

"First, I think we should talk about where we want to go, and things like that," said Bill. "We don't even know if most of us like the idea."

"Let's take a vote!" suggested Henry, enthusiastically. "All those who want to go camping raise their hands." Bill noticed that three of the boys looked around warily before slowly raising their hands to make the vote unanimous. "Well," announced Henry, "We're going. The institution only lets us hike to two places—Sloane's Hill or Thatcher Woods. We went to Sloane's last month, so we'll go to Thatcher's this time. We can leave Friday and come back Sunday. Let's start packing." At that, the boys began getting up to head toward their dorms.

It took Bill some time to reconvene the group for another try. "The camping was just a suggestion," he said, "and there's no reason why we can't do it, but I really wanted to talk about something else and I'd like you to hear me out." The boys were silent, wondering what would come next. "I want you to begin to have more of a voice in everything we do around here, so we can run the cottage together in a way that seems best for all of us. I think you're mature enough to begin to make the kinds of decisions that adults make about themselves, at least within the limits of the overall program."

"What are you selling?" asked Henry, skeptically.

"A cottage government?" suggested Ralph.

"He means democracy!" explained Frank.

"What do you mean by democracy, Frank?" asked Bill, pleased with this response.

"Everyone does what he wants," was Frank's reply.

"We elect a cottage president to run things," volunteered Hal.

"No," disagreed Ralph, "it means we vote on everything, don't it, Bill?"

Bill paused, beginning to realize how far he had to go. "I'd prefer not to give it a fancy name," he finally said. "As you can see, everyone has his own meaning for it. Let's just talk together about what can be better here and how we can make it better. Any ideas?"

"The food is lousy." Everyone seemed to agree.

"They serve too much of that free surplus cheese."

"We can't go off grounds often enough."

"They make us get up too early on weekends."

"They read our mail."

The list of gripes seemed endless, and Bill finally interrupted. "Let's talk about some of these things," he said.

"What's to talk about?" asked Henry. "You wanted us to tell you what's wrong, and we're telling you. What are you going to do about it?"

"Let me explain what I had in mind," Bill said, deciding to try again. "I don't think I made it clear. The institution has certain rules and policies, and these create a kind of framework or boundaries within which all of us have to live. This doesn't mean we can't suggest changes, but it does mean that most of what we decide should be within those limits. It's a little like the U. S. Constitution, which provides the ground rules for running the country. So I think it's important to learn what we can and what we can't decide. I'll be happy to take your complaints to the people in charge, but I also want to see us working on the things we can do ourselves."

Bill could tell that Henry and some of the others took a dim view of his little speech, and no sooner had he stopped than Henry began to talk. "That's just a con job," he said, "because we have no real power to work with. You can still knock out or veto anything we decide if you don't like it. Why should we waste our time?"

Bill was a little annoyed as well as disappointed, and there was a slight edge to his voice when he replied. "No one'll knock out or veto anything as long as it's within your jurisdiction," he said.

"See? That's what I mean!" said Henry triumphantly. " 'Jurisdiction'—that's a good old establishment word! That means all we really get to do is decide big-deal things like whether to play ping-pong or pool and we do that already. But we're supposed to keep quiet about the things that really count. So don't try to pretend you're giving us any real power. Don't try to sell us that democracy crap!"

(Supplementary discussion questions, page 342)

11. THE CHILD CARE WORKER
AND FORMAL TREATMENT

In addition to the kinds of routines and activities explored in the previous chapters and any necessary medical care, most institutional programs include some form of psychosocial treatment services. Although this work is normally the function of psychiatrists, psychologists, social workers, and other mental health specialists from outside the child care field *per se,* it relates to the job of the child care worker in a variety of ways.

TABLE OF CASES

11.1 HOW MUCH THERAPY

Eileen Young was talking to her supervisor about Patty Wilson, a sixteen-year old who had arrived that morning and been assigned to Eileen's cottage.

"I've never seen such intense, piercing eyes," Eileen said. "What do you think of her, Betty?"

"It's hard to say," Betty replied. "Patty does seem to have a tense secretive air about her. Yet this is the first day. She'll probably loosen up later."

"I don't know," Eileen said slowly. "It seems different than the usual first-day shyness to me; but you may be right. I guess we'll just have to wait and see."

In the days that followed, Patty Wilson became a special challenge to Eileen. Patty had picked up the residence routine by the end of the first week and rarely needed to be reminded of what she had to do. She was agreeable and polite to the other girls and to the staff but there seemed to be something missing.

"There's nothing personal between Patty and any of the rest of us yet," Eileen remarked to Betty one night. "I stand there wondering what's going through her head. Even the other kids seem to sense it. They don't taunt her or anything, but they do stay away."

"Be patient," Betty warned. "We'll get to know her. Don't forget, building trust often takes a long time. Besides I think you two are beginning to develop a special relationship already." Betty also suggested that Eileen might want to talk with Patty's therapist, and Eileen made a mental note to do so.

Three weeks passed and Eileen felt more perplexed than ever. She did indeed seem to be developing a special closeness to Patty, although the girl still said very little and appeared to be as uncommunicative and aloof as ever. Patience, Eileen told herself, and she waited.

One evening Eileen passed Patty's room after lights out and peeked in. Patty was still awake, lying flat on her back, with her eyes wide open. "What's the matter, Patty, can't you sleep?" she asked softly. Patty turned toward Eileen and shook her head in silence, and Eileen noticed that there were tears in Patty's eyes. "Sometimes it helps to talk about things that are bothering us, Patty," she said. "Would you like to talk for a little while?" Patty made no reply but shifted her eyes to the ceiling again.

"I think that means yes," Eileen thought to herself, and she quietly sat down on the chair next to Patty's bed. Patty had already begun speaking very softly, and Eileen had to strain to hear her.

". . . and I just can't get it out of my head . . . every time I stop thinking it's there . . . and it's so clear and real to me . . ."

"What is?" Eileen asked gently.

"That day . . . when it happened . . . when it happened . . ." Her voice trailed off. A few minutes passed. Eileen began to feel uncomfortable.

"When what happened, Patty?" she asked. Patty was silent for a long while, and Eileen wondered if she had fallen asleep. Eileen got up slowly and as quietly as she could, and she was almost out of the door when Patty began to speak again.

"I've never told it to anyone before," she began, her voice barely a whisper. Eileen had to lean forward again to catch all the words. "The sun was very hot that day . . . walking in the woods . . ." Now Patty's voice was getting louder. "Heard voices and footsteps . . . and men talking . . . ran and ran . . . couldn't get away . . . threw me on the ground . . . threw me on the ground . . . threw me on the ground . . ."

Eileen could hear Patty sobbing as she sat there, stunned. This is important and I must try to say the right thing, she thought. But what to say? She didn't even know if Patty's story was true. She wished that she had read the case record more closely, that she had talked to Patty's therapist before this—anything! This must be what they meant when they warned us not to get involved in things that should be worked out in therapy, but what else could I have done? Patty was still sobbing as Eileen started to speak.

(Supplementary discussion questions, page 343)

11.2 "THANKS A LOT!"

Bert Carter glanced at his watch again, climbed the stairs, and rapped briskly at the closed dormitory door. Hearing no response, he opened the door and looked inside. Sprawled on his bunk was Jim Lucas, fully dressed and wide awake, staring at the ceiling. "Hey, I thought you were missing," said Bert. "Isn't it time for you to see your social worker?"

"I'm not going to see that idiot," replied Jim. "It's the same old crap all the time. We never talk about anything that makes any sense, and now that I'm getting out of here soon, the whole scene is really a waste of time."

Bert sat down on the cot beside Jim's and looked at him. "Come on now," he said, "you're not leaving yet, and if you hadn't been seeing Mr. Parks all this time you probably wouldn't even be this far along. Besides, part of what it means to be here is that you have to see your social worker and talk with him about the things that are bothering you."

"Big deal," responded Jim a little disgustedly. "Nothing's bothering me."

Bert shook his head. "That's not so, Jim. Didn't you come back from your first trial home visit last week a day early and tell me that you'd had it with your mother and you didn't want to see her any more?"

"Oh, that was just a little hassle," Jim replied. "I didn't really mean it."

"Maybe you didn't," replied Bert, "but those are the kinds of things you should discuss with Mr. Parks. He can help you understand what's going on so things like that won't keep happening." Bert stood up and put his hand on Jim's shoulder. "Come on, give it a try," he said. "It can't hurt."

Jim sat up and shrugged, "Well, I still think it's stupid," he said, "but I'll see Parks if you want me to." Bert thought about saying something to remind Jim that he should be doing this for himself, but he decided to leave well enough alone, and Jim left to go to Mr. Parks' office.

About a half an hour later, Jim came running back into the cottage, slammed the door behind him, and rushed up to Bert. "Thanks a lot, you louse!" he snarled sarcastically. "Mr. Parks told me that I shouldn't be going home until he has a lot more time to talk about it with me. He even took away my trial visits! Now I'll probably never get out of this place, thanks to you. Oh Jesus, why did you make me go?"

(Supplementary discussion questions, page 343)

11.3 CONNING THE THERAPIST

"Hey, Mr. Palmer, look at my new model," Alex called as he came into the cottage. Mr. Palmer and the other boys gathered around to look.

"Did you make that one in therapy, too?" asked Don.

"Yep!" Alex was one of the leaders in the cottage and spoke with a casual authority. "I really got that guy all wrapped up. I never have to talk to him when I go to therapy. He just lets me make models."

"That's nothing, so does mine," said Lennie. "I don't have to talk about problems or anything. Once she told me I could only work on my model half the time, the other half we had to talk. That lasted about two weeks. I just sat and stared at her for the talking part. She couldn't stand it, I guess, so now she lets me do the model the whole time. I give her a few stories now and then just to keep her thinking she's helping me." The boys laughed.

"Hey, I ought to try that," said Randy. "Give her the old silent treatment for a while. Then maybe she'll let me have some fun." There was a chorus of agreement from the rest of the group.

Mr. Palmer noticed that Jimmy, who had a real attachment to his therapist, looked disturbed but was not about to say anything. "Don't you guys think it's a waste of time to make models in therapy?" Mr. Palmer said.

"So what?" countered Alex. "If he don't care, why should I? Besides we have to go to our caseworkers—we don't have a choice, do we? So why not make the most of it?" Mr. Palmer looked at Alex intently and then at the rest of the boys. On the basis of his long experience in child care work, he sensed that the boys were more concerned about therapy than they admitted, and few of them would have openly differed with Alex in any case.

Mr. Palmer also knew that the caseworkers working with Alex and Lenny were new and inexperienced, and he wondered if they were having the same difficulty that he had had when he had first started as a child care worker—wanting the boys to like him so much that he would do just about anything to win their favor and acceptance. "Perhaps I ought to talk with them," he thought, "although child care workers rarely got involved with therapy matters in this way. But then again," he concluded to himself, "they probably know what they're doing and besides what could I say to them?"

These thoughts were interrupted as Mr. Palmer realized that the boys were drifting away and exchanging ideas on how to "con" their therapists. He knew that if he were going to say anything about it to the boys as a group, he'd better do it now, before he lost their attention completely.

(Supplementary discussion questions, page 344)

11.4 HOW MUCH IS TOO MUCH?

The two child care workers were the first to arrive for the case conference on Tony Brooks. "Sometimes I think if we have to wrestle that kid through one more day in the cottage, I'll cut my throat," muttered Gus Long, lowering his voice as he saw the clinical director, Dr. Benson, enter the room.

"Or Tony's," murmured Burt Conner wryly in reply.

A few minutes later Dr. Benson opened the conference. "As you know," he began, "we're here today to talk about Tony Brooks. Tony's new and seems to be a particularly difficult youngster, and I'd like us to discuss his treatment plan as fully as possible. Would you review Tony's case for us, Sue?" he asked, turning to the social worker.

"Sure," Sue Chandler replied. "Originally there was some question about whether this was the place for Tony, and there was a meeting with the court officials before we decided to give it a try. Although he's only fourteen, Tony's record and his behavior since his arrival suggest that he may be the most severely acting-out boy we've had here." The group looked at the two child care workers and responded with chuckles to Burt's grim nod.

"It's not completely bleak, Burt," Sue smiled. "Due to his high intelligence and the sudden onset of his disturbance two years ago, we thought he might be able to make rapid progress if we could provide the right environment. You and Gus seemed best for the job."

Gus turned to Burt. "Now we know the reward for being good child care workers," he said ruefully. "Just tell us how," he added, looking back at Sue.

"First, let me do a quick recap of his history," she replied. "He was an adopted child and was first seen at the child guidance clinic when he became withdrawn and depressed following the death of his younger sister. He was very attached to her and, as you know, they were swimming together when she drowned. Even though he had to be rescued himself, he apparently felt responsible and withdrew from social contacts. Unfortunately, the parents refused to go for help, claiming it was just Tony's problem. Incidentally, Tony won't talk about his sister's death, although he claims to understand that he couldn't have saved her.

"In any case, he gradually began to act out—at home, at school, everywhere. He was defiant and had severe temper tantrums. One day when his parents were out, he broke every window in the house and a neighbor called the police. That's how he first came to the attention of the juvenile court. After several suspensions from school, he was finally expelled. There's more detail in the record," she concluded, "but now I'd like us to discuss Tony's treatment plan and how it's working. Would you like to start, Dr. Benson?"

"Tony is something of a special case," he replied. "Usually things don't appear so clear-cut. His guilt over his sister's death seems to be the direct cause of his pathology, or at least the trigger. I would predict that he can work this issue through in therapy, but only if we can provide a safe, nonthreatening environment for him. Therefore he must be sheltered from too much stress. You two," here he looked at Gus and Burt, "must help Tony develop trust in the people here and in himself. This is extremely important."

"It seems to me," Sue added, "that as difficult as Tony has proved to be, the one thing we've learned is that we can't predict what his precise problem areas will be. Therefore I would suggest that we keep meeting each situation as it arises and make whatever program adjustments seem necessary to sustain him while I try to reach him in therapy."

"I guess we can try to do that," said Gus, "and we'll keep you posted on our latest adventures, but what I'd really like to know is this. What should we do when, like yesterday, he goes from throwing a kettle of cooked cereal against the wall at breakfast to pouring four filled garbage cans all over the cottage yard before bed? We just don't seem to be getting anywhere."

"Admittedly," added Burt, "that was a bad day. But you have the reports. Even on one of Tony's good days, it might take an hour to get him out of the shower, or into bed, or out of bed for that matter."

The assistant director Phil Gordon, who was sitting in on the meeting in the absence of the child care supervisor, replied. "We realize this puts a great strain on you two," he said, "and we know how patient you've been under trying circumstances. However, we should begin to see some results soon, and in the meantime you can only do your best. We'll try to support you as much as we can."

Dr. Benson nodded. "You've both been handling Tony and his outbursts well," he agreed, "and all we ask is that you try to continue to cope with him. Remember, he should have as little stress outside his therapy as possible. As Sue said, just keep meeting each situation as it arises." After a brief discussion of Tony's school program, the meeting was adjourned.

"Hell, Gus," Burt snapped as they walked back to the cottage, "that 'treatment plan' isn't real and you know it! We've got nineteen other kids in the cottage and we owe them something, too. Tony is taking almost all our time and attention now and the prescription is for more of the same. Suppose the others decide Tony has a good thing going and that's the way to get tender loving care and attention? I know different kids have different needs, but we've got limits, too!"

Gus nodded ruefully. "I know it. We've still got Tony and we've still got the others, and we have to try to give something to all of them without running ourselves into the ground. So where do we go from here?"

(Supplementary discussion questions, page 345)

11.5 WHO OWNS THE CHILD?

"Again?" asked Jack Cunningham into the telephone. "I'll look for him and send him over if I find him. Thanks."

"Damn!" he added to himself after angrily slamming down the receiver. He had spoken with Ken Glidden over and over again about the importance of school and the boy was not there for the second time this week.

As he started up the stairs to the second floor of the cottage, Jack saw Ken sitting quietly on the landing. "All right," snapped Jack, "what are you doing here? Why aren't you in school?"

"I don't know, Mr. Cunningham," responded the boy dully, "I just didn't feel like going. You know, like I've told you, I'm depressed. Fred's gone and he's the best friend I've ever had."

Jack was obviously annoyed. "Look, Ken," he said, "we discussed this yesterday and the day before that, too. Fred has been released. It's over and done with. The best thing you can do is try to get out of here instead of deliberately messing yourself up by staying out of school and all the rest. Then you can see Fred at home and do a lot of other things, too. The way you're acting now, you'll just spoil everything."

"Who cares?" asked the boy, staring at the floor.

"I care. The school cares. And," continued Jack, in a softer tone, "I think you care, too. Remember? Yesterday, you said part of the reason you felt so badly about Fred being gone was that he was out and you were in. The best way to help that is for you to work on getting your discharge, too. It's only about two more months!"

"Maybe I said that yesterday," replied Ken, "but when I got up this morning, all I could think about was that my only real friend was gone and I'd probably never see him again. I can't go to school when I feel this lousy."

"You'll simply have to try," said Jack firmly. "School will help get your mind off it, anyway. I'll walk you over."

Ken did not object further and walked silently with Jack to the school building, where Jack left him and went to meet some friends in the staff lounge.

That evening, Jack was standing outside the cottage day room when he heard Ken being asked about a baseball game that had been telecast in the afternoon.

"We never had a chance," Ken concluded. "Baxter walked the first three guys, then came the homer, and we never caught up."

"Boy," said George, in a mildly envious tone of voice, "I don't care how much they beat us by, I wish I could have seen a grand slam!"

"You're lucky!" Tom added. "You didn't have to sit in school all day."

"I still don't see how you got out of it," said George. "I saw Mr. Cunningham bring you into school himself."

"Sure," drawled Ray, "but then Ken saw his social worker and told her how depressed he was. He got off for the whole day!"

"Jeeze," said George, "anytime you want to cut school around here, all you gotta do is go tell your social worker a sob story!"

(Supplementary discussion questions, page 345)

11.6 TRANQUILIZERS AND OTHER DRUGS

Sam Greene slumped into a chair and fumbled in his pocket for a pen. It sure felt good to sit down.

"Some night!" he remarked to Beth, the evening nurse. "It's a good thing they're not all like this." Beth nodded in agreement and turned back to her notes. "I guess I might as well get started with my notes, too, and get them over with," Sam continued, as he recovered his pen. "Say, Beth, what was that dose of Thorazine you gave Michael? I'd better put that into the log."

Beth looked through her prescription list.

"Let me see. Oh yes, 50 mg," she read, "to be given only if he or a staff member feels he needs it. Really knocked him out, didn't it?"

"It's a good thing, too," Sam replied. "That kid's rough when he starts acting up. I'm surprised he's not on regular scheduled doses like Alan and some of the others. It sure would make him easier to handle."

"Some of the kids need medication to calm them down and make them more open to therapy," Beth said, "but it really upsets me when we use drugs just to keep them quiet because we can't manage them. Sometimes we do have emergencies, but I think it should be considered a drastic alternative and used only once in a while."

"But what about a case like tonight's?" Sam asked. "I was so tired and fed up when I called you and Leon that I just might have given up and walked out if you hadn't come over. This is the third blowup Michael's had this week. It's not fair to the other kids or to us to have one kid take up so much time and energy."

"Well, maybe a kid like Michael shouldn't be in a place like this if it takes so much medication just to keep him under control," Beth replied. "After all, there are some kids we can't help here."

"What's supposed to happen to Michael then? Should we send him to some place where he'll just sit around a day room watching TV for the rest of his life?" Sam was getting pretty excited. "Isn't it better to keep him here where there's at least a chance of helping him even if we have to give him Thorazine ten times a day?"

Leon had come in during the conversation and was listening intently. "I wonder, Sam," he said, "whether it really does a kid any good to be here if he's on tranquilizers all the time. Take Alan, for example. He's usually walking around in such a daze that I don't see how we can be helping him. What'll happen to him when he leaves here? He'll either have to stay on the drugs or wind up in a hospital anyway. And there's another danger in giving kids drugs just to keep them here. We get too used to it ourselves, and we may not try as hard as we should to develop the kind of program that can really help the kids if we have such a convenient crutch. You know, it's a lot easier to have ten docile, passive kids watching TV than to go through what we went through tonight."

"But aren't you assuming that the medication is just to make it easier to manage the kids and not a part of the treatment process as well?" asked Beth. "Wouldn't both of you agree that tranquilizers can have important therapeutic effects? When the kids are calmer, they can deal with their problems more readily in therapy. They don't act so crazy, which helps to change their self-image. And they develop more confidence in their ability to handle real-life situations. Don't you think that drugs can be a very important part of the help we offer, at least for some of the youngsters? That's different than using them just to keep the kids under control and to make our jobs easier."

Sam and Leon both started to answer at once.

(Supplementary discussion questions, page 346)

UNIT FOUR

WORKING RELATIONSHIPS

12. WORKING WITH COLLEAGUES

Effective work with institutionalized youngsters requires high staff morale and close coordination among child care workers and between them and others on the staff. As has been mentioned before, the special nature of the institutional setting may create more stress than there is in many other job situations, which tends to increase the difficulty of maintaining high staff morale and effective coordination. Related issues involving specialized noncottage personnel have been portrayed in Chapters 10 and 11. The cases in this chapter deal with relationships among child care workers themselves and between them and other colleagues who relate to youngsters in similar ways despite differing job titles.

TABLE OF CASES

12.5 A Different Drummer

A recreation assistant whose values and standards are different from those of the child care worker pushes a youngster to the brink, and the child care worker sees his efforts going down the drain.

12.1 A CONFLICT OF PRINCIPLES

Jim Masterson was enthusiastic as he began his first child care job. He liked the boys in his cottage and it was reassuring to know that Herb Knight, an older child care worker with many years of experience, worked in the next cottage and would be there to advise him when unexpected problems arose. Herb was the accepted leader of the child care staff and seemed to be on good terms with the administration as well.

As Jim anticipated, the first few weeks were difficult. His relationships with his group developed surprisingly smoothly, however, and he found that this helped him when problems arose. As much as possible he tried to organize his cottage along the lines of a partnership or family, working toward individual and common goals. Each person had his own clearly understood rights and responsibilities. It did not take Jim long, however, to notice that Herb Knight's way of doing things was vastly different. Herb had established a pattern of almost military discipline in his cottage, and the group seemed to have an intense feeling of exclusiveness.

One day Herb suggested that Jim should establish the same system with his boys, who were about the same age. Although Jim felt that this was contrary to the treatment philosophy emphasized by the director, he was forced to admit that Herb's cottage was probably the cleanest and best organized in the institution, and the boys did seem very well disciplined. As a result of this conversation, Jim began to watch Herb's group more closely for ideas that he could use in his own cottage.

It quickly became evident to Jim that Herb's boys lost much of their organization and control whenever Herb himself was absent. When Jim was called on to handle Herb's cottage one day due to a staff shortage, he found it difficult to maintain order. Once or twice when the group was left alone for a few minutes, the result was complete chaos. Meanwhile Jim felt that his youngsters were learning to be as dependable when left alone or with another counselor as they were when he was there himself. Also, he thought they were beginning to develop trust and affection for him and for each other.

About two months after he started working, Jim was sick for a few days, and Herb was assigned to help cover Jim's cottage. When Jim returned, he found his boys restive and unhappy. They complained that Herb had been to strict and unfair, and two of the youngsters claimed that he had slapped them around. Even allowing for a degree of exaggeration, Jim felt there must be some truth in their complaints and decided to talk to Herb about it.

They happened to meet on the way to lunch, but Jim was hardly prepared for Herb's enthusiastic greeting. "Hey, buddy," Herb called as he approached, "I sure whipped your little punks into shape for you, didn't I?"

Startled, Jim stared at him for a moment. "What do you mean?" he asked.

"They had no respect for authority," Herb replied. "Those kids hardly know what discipline means."

Jim got angry at this and told him about the complaints the boys had made, but Herb laughed it off. "They're bigger babies than I thought," he said. "I didn't hit anybody—just pushed them around a little. These kids have to be a little afraid or else they don't respect you. You'll learn," he continued, interrupting Jim's protests. "You're too idealistic."

A few days later, two boys from Herb's cottage came to Jim to tell him that Herb had blown up and hit them. Jim realized that his own boys must have told Herb's that it would be "safe" to tell Jim. The two youngsters, badly frightened, wanted repeated assurances that Jim would not tell Herb that they had spoken to him. They asked Jim to talk to the director about it without mentioning their names. Jim listened, not knowing quite what to say. He finally agreed to see what he could do, adding that he could make no promises.

About an hour later, Jim saw three boys from his own cottage running toward him. "Mr. Masterson," called one of them, "Jack just took off." Jack Simpson was one of Jim's boys who had complained that Herb had slapped him around when Jim was sick.

"Take it easy," replied Jim. "What do you mean?"

"Mr. Knight slapped him when he was slow getting in line for gym," the boy said, "and he ran away. Mr. Knight went after him. That louse'll really beat him up when he catches him."

"He yelled at us, too," another of the youngsters added. "He said,

'Don't go squealing to Jim like sissies. Take it like men!' What are you going to do, Mr. Masterson?"

(Supplementary discussion questions, page 346)

12.2 DIVISION OF LABOR

"Damn it, Steve, sit down!" said Bill Scott, the child care supervisor. "I know you're angry, but you've got to cool off so we can talk about it!"

Steve smiled a little sheepishly as he fell into the chair beside Bill's desk. "I guess I did get carried away," he admitted. "But I was serious about quitting. It's just not fair to expect me to do all the dirty work even if Jim has more experience working with individual kids!"

"I'm not disagreeing with you on that," replied Bill. "But first, just let me make sure I have things straight. You feel that Jim isn't doing his share of the work. He spends too much time with individual kids and leaves you to deal with the rest of the group by yourself. Right?"

Steve nodded vigorously. "It just isn't fair to expect me to take care of nineteen kids while he . . ."

"O.K., Steve," Bill interrupted. "I understand that. Did you ever talk to him about it?"

"Talk to him?" Steve was getting upset again. "He explained it all to me the first day I was here. Told me he'd been working with kids for years and that he worked best with individuals and small groups. He explained how he and the guy I was replacing had always divided the work so Jim handled the kids' individual problems. He said it worked out well, and maybe we could follow the same arrangement. It sounded fine to me then, since I had some experience working with groups at a community center. Frankly, I guess I was a little scared of getting too close to these kids on an individual basis anyway. But it hasn't worked out," he continued, shaking his head. "Not at all."

"Have you mentioned it to him since?" Bill asked.

"Sure—just last night. I told Jim I was getting tired of having to play policeman all the time, and maybe we could change roles every once in a while. He just smiled and said not to worry, when I got better at handling the group I wouldn't have to act like a policeman so much. In a way he almost had me convinced. But then when I had to get the kids to bed by myself while he was talking to two of them about some complaint they had, I really blew and thought about quitting. But it seemed only fair to discuss it with you before I did anything."

"I'm glad you did," Bill replied. "It would be a shame for you to quit over this kind of thing when you've hardly given the job a chance. Besides, I've watched you work a few times, and you have a good way with kids. I think child care work is a good field for you."

Just then, they heard a knock at the door, and Bill glanced at his watch. "I'm sorry, Steve," he said, "I've got to leave for a meeting in town. Let's talk about this again on Monday, and I'll be able to get into it then. In the meantime, just do the best you can. Remember, it's rough for everybody the first six months."

Steve got up slowly and smiled. "I think I feel better, anyway," he said. "It was good to get it off my chest."

When Steve arrived at the cottage to go on duty that afternoon, he was greeted by Andy Green, a relief child care worker assigned to the cottage. "Where's Jim?" Steve asked after they had said hello.

"In Marshall's room," replied Andy. "Something happened in school today and the boy's been pretty upset since he got back. Jim really has a way with these kids, doesn't he?" Steve nodded blankly. "Well, I better take off," Andy continued. "I have to go to Cottage 4."

A few minutes later, after Steve had told the boys that it was time to get ready for dinner, he knocked at Marshall's door. Jim opened it. "Half an hour to dinner," Steve said, trying to sound casual.

"Thanks, we know," Jim replied, and lowered his voice. "Marshall had a bad time in school today and his therapist couldn't see him, so I've been helping him work it through. Is everything under control?"

"I guess so," answered Steve.

"Good," Jim said, still whispering. "We'll be done soon."

Steve was about to say something when he heard shouting from another room and hurried down the hall. Two of the boys had gotten into an argument over the ownership of a shirt and by the time Steve could straighten it out, it was almost time for dinner and only half the boys were ready. "Come on you guys, hurry it up!" he shouted, and angry now, he knocked again on Marshall's door and opened it. "It's time for dinner," he said curtly.

"We know, Steve," Jim replied in measured tones, obviously annoyed at the intrusion, "but we're in the midst of an important discussion. Why don't you and the others go along and we'll catch up in a few minutes. Is anything wrong?" he added, stepping outside the room and lowering his voice. "Do you need help with the group?"

"Nothing unusual," Steve replied tightly. "I just feel like I'm doing two jobs instead of one."

"Wait a minute," said Jim looking at his colleague. "I thought we agreed that this arrangement would be best all around."

(Supplementary discussion questions, page 347)

12.3 MAKING THE TEAM

Tom Denton had graduated from the community college near his home, where he specialized in child care services. He was looking forward to his first job in the institutional field.

He was offered several positions and accepted one with the institution that had impressed him the most. Mr. Marks, the director, welcomed him enthusiastically. "You'll be assigned to Cottage 4," Mr. Marks told him. "There's one thing I want you to know about, though. The rest of the Cottage 4 staff is a little worried about having a college man working with them. They're older, they don't have your educational background, but they've been a team for a long time. They have their own ways of doing things and they run a good cottage. So don't come on too strong."

Things were working out well, Tom felt as the weeks passed.

Although he didn't agree with everything he saw being done, he said little about it for the first month or so and found that gradually other members of the staff began to ask him for his opinion. However, he still tended to hold back in staff discussions, and he rarely took a stand against anything on which the rest were united.

One day he caught sight of Mr. Talbott, the chief child care worker in the cottage, hurrying up the walk. Quickly opening the front door, Mr. Talbott strode into the cottage. "Tom," he called out briskly, "are you busy?"

"No," replied Tom, walking out into the hallway, "What's up?"

"I just wanted to discuss something that came up at chief child care workers' meeting," said Mr. Talbott. "It's about the dress and personal appearance code. You know the institution's policy is pretty much to let the staff in each cottage interpret the code. Well, at the meeting I just left, there seemed to be some kind of pressure to let the kids decide things like this for themselves."

Tom thought this sounded like a pretty good idea, but he could tell that Mr. Talbott was angry about it and he said nothing.

"Apparently," Mr. Talbott continued, "that student council thing of theirs asked for it and Mr. Marks told them he would bring it up with the staff. All of us in Cottage 4 feel that the regulations on haircuts and neat clothing are important, but I'm sure the boys will do all they can to change the rules over the next few weeks and I want us to be ready! Tom, what do you think would be the best way to go about fighting this kind of thing?"

(Supplementary discussion questions, page 348)

12.4 HELP FOR A COLLEAGUE

Scott Arnold yawned again before starting up the steps to the cottage. "Man, this rotating night-watch shift is too much," he wearily thought to himself. He was assigned to take it one week in every six, and it seemed to turn his life upside down each time. By the time he became accustomed to the change in schedule, the week was practically over and he was back working days. Still mulling this over in his mind, Scott unlocked the door and entered the darkened cottage.

"Bernie?" he called softly, but no one answered. "That's strange," he thought. Bernie was almost always waiting to give him the daily log before leaving with a friendly remark about not falling asleep on the job.

The first floor was deserted, so Scott started upstairs, where he met his co-worker heading toward him. Bernie, obviously agitated, was cursing under his breath. "Hey," Scott said, "hold on. What's the matter?"

"Damn Gerald Powell, that's what," replied Bernie tightly.

"What happened?" asked Scott.

"It started during the weekly cottage meeting," Bernie began, speaking rapidly. "Gerald was being his usual obnoxious self. You know, a lot of talking and wisecracks and stuff. Every time I managed to get a discussion started, he came up with some remark, and everything would be up for grabs again. Finally, I warned him that if he couldn't stay in order, he'd have to leave. He answered with some nasty remark and I told him to leave the room. Well, the kid just sat there. When I repeated the order for him to leave, he just slouched a little lower in his chair and sneered. I think he said something under his breath like, 'You gonna make me, Bernie Bigmouth?' That did it! I really blew up. I grabbed him by the shirt collar and dragged him out of the room. Then he proceeded to go into that temper tantrum bit of his, and you know how that goes!"

Scott nodded. "I know. He can really do it up big once he gets started. Sometimes I doubt that he himself knows whether it's real or not." Scott paused for a moment. "But that must have been at least an hour ago," he added. "What's been happening since then?"

"Guerrilla warfare," answered Bernie. "I thought I had him straightened out when I put him in his room, but there have been periodic outbursts all night. He comes flying down the hall, trying to tackle me, then we're into something like a wrestling match for a few minutes. When I finally overpower him, I march him back to his room where he sits until he builds up another head of steam and comes out fighting. The other kids are in their rooms. I told them to stay there."

"He's quiet now," said Scott. "Why don't you get ready to leave? I'll take over with Gerald if there's any more outbursts tonight."

"Hell no," Bernie replied, anger flashing in his eyes. "He started this and I'm going to finish it. I'm going to make damn sure that kid is settled down if I have to stay here all night. You just stand by, in case I need some reinforcements."

Before Scott had time to tell Bernie to cool it, they heard a loud yelp from down the hall. Bernie nodded grimly and they both ran toward the boy's room. Arriving an instant behind Bernie, Scott just managed to duck in time to avoid being hit with a flying ashtray. As he looked inside the room, he could see the sweat begin to pour down Bernie's forehead as he wrestled with the youngster, trying to gain control of the boy's flailing arms and legs. Securing a hold on the boy, Bernie pinned him to the floor. "See?" he gasped, "this is where he stays. No more rest periods, no more ashtray throwing, no more crap from this kid! He stays pinned until he's ready to throw in the towel!"

Just then the boy jerked his arms out and almost broke Bernie's hold, but Bernie regained his position quickly. Scott could see him tightening his grip on Gerald's arm and realized that they were going through the same pattern that Bernie had described. As the boy quieted down, the child care worker would ease his hold, then Gerald would erupt—kicking, screaming, and cursing. Bernie would react by furiously tightening his grip on the boy, which, in turn, would force him to quiet down. Then the entire cycle would start again.

Scott finally interceded. "Bernie, let me take over for a while," he said firmly. "You go out and cool off."

"I told you before," Bernie replied, tightening his grip on the boy, "I'll take care of this kid!" It was obvious that Bernie meant what he said, but Scott thought that his co-worker was much too angry with the boy, and the boy with him, for them to come to any good resolution. The other boys were edging out of their rooms in an effort to see and hear what was happening as Scott glanced at his watch and wondered what to do.

(Supplementary discussion questions, page 348)

12.5 A DIFFERENT DRUMMER

"Mr. Armstrong," said Mark Wilson to his child care worker, "I have a lot of work to do for school. Can I work in the cottage after dinner instead of going to gym tonight?"

Bud Armstrong eyed the youngster thoughtfully before replying. Mark had been a withdrawn, fearful boy when he arrived at the institution about a year before, but Bud had worked closely with him and felt that the youngster was beginning to respond. The other boys no longer teased him as much and he was no longer regarded as the cottage "sissy." At least not until last week, Bud recalled. The teasing seemed to have started again about that time. "What kind of schoolwork do you have, Mark?" Bud finally asked.

"Oh . . ." The boy hesitated nervously. "I'm getting behind in everything," he finally said. "I just want to catch up."

"Any tests coming up this week?" Bud asked.

"Yes," replied Mark, "I mean, . . . not this week, but soon, I think."

"Then why the sudden concern? Can't you catch up if you do a little bit each night? We only get gym night once a week," Bud continued, "and everyone's supposed to be there."

"But I can't go, Mr. Armstrong," protested Mark. "I mean . . ."

"What's eating you?" interrupted Bud, "Maybe you better tell me the whole story."

"I can't," the boy replied. "Can't you just let me stay back in the cottage?"

Bud decided to try a different approach. "What's been going on with you this week, Mark?" he asked. "The kids seem to be hassling you for something."

"That's why I can't go tonight. You gotta believe me," pleaded the boy.

"What do you mean?"

"It's that new rec assistant they got. You know, his name is Mr. Johnson. He used to be a kid here, then he played in the minor leagues." Mark was near tears now, and he was talking quickly, as if to keep himself from crying. "Anyway," he continued, "I'm not as good as the other guys in sports and he called me a fairy and threw me off the court. Then the guys began to get on my back again and it's a big mess. Don't you see? How can I go back there?"

Suddenly the picture was clear and Bud was shocked. He could see his hard work and Mark's progress going down the drain as the boys picked up on Mr. Johnson's remark. "But if you don't go, Mark," he finally said, "it'll only be worse. The guys'll make it even harder for you. I'll talk to Mr. Johnson after dinner tonight, so don't worry about it. Meanwhile, don't forget how much progress you've made. You've really come a long way, and Mr. Johnson probably just didn't think about what he was saying. I'll take care of it, but I do want you to go tonight."

"If you're sure that's best, Mr. Armstrong, then I'll go," replied Mark reluctantly, "but that business with the kids when I first got here, I couldn't go through that again!"

After dinner, Bud walked back to the gym with Hal Johnson. "My kids are scheduled for gym tonight, Hal," he said, "and they mentioned that there was a little trouble last week. What happened?"

Hal thought for a moment before he replied. "Nothing much that I can recall," he finally said.

"What happened with Mark Wilson?" Bud asked.

"Wilson? Oh, that's the little fruit I threw out of the game, isn't it?" Hal continued. "He was just messing things up because he's so slow and awkward, so I told him to sit it out. Why?"

"Well," Bud began, "maybe you don't know about Mark." Bud proceeded to tell Hal about the boy, his background, the progress he had made, and what had happened to him after last week's incident in the gym. "So," Bud concluded, "I think we have to be careful that the little bit of confidence he's built up so far doesn't get destroyed."

"I don't know about that," replied Hal, "but these kids have got to learn to face reality. I grew up here, you know, and I never would have made it in sports if they hadn't told me straight out when I was good and when I was lousy. Besides, I can't let one kid spoil the game for the others. I'll let him play tonight, but if he screws up, out he goes! I'll find a game of checkers or something for him to play on the side. Or do you think hopscotch would be better?" Hal added with a chuckle.

(Supplementary discussion questions, page 349)

13. WORKING WITH SUPERVISORS AND ADMINISTRATORS

Supervisors and administrators usually have a dual relationship to child care workers. They represent, first, a source of guidance, perspective, and support that may be needed almost as much by experienced child care personnel as by new workers. The pressure and intensity of child care work are great, and the supervisor's greater distance from the situation may be as important an element in his ability to be helpful as his special training and experience. Supervisors and administrators also represent institutional policies, authority, and evaluation—in short, "the boss." The cases that follow illustrate both these leadership roles, how they interact, and how they relate to the job of the child care worker.

TABLE OF CASES

13.1 DOUBLE BIND

The two child care workers were standing outside the administration building in the snow waiting for their ride to town.

"So," continued Russ, "you like the job and the kids. Any problems in the cottage?"

Pat stamped his feet in the cold before he replied. "Well, after two weeks here, I guess I can see a few shaping up."

"Just a few?" laughed Russ.

"Take fighting, for one," said Pat. "This morning at breakfast I heard some of the kids whispering about a fight Toby Wilson and Stanley Maxwell had last night after lights out. They must have been pretty quiet, though, because there wasn't anything about it in the log."

"Did either of them look banged up or hurt?" asked Russ.

"Not that I could see. I've caught those two starting to fight once or twice before, though, and I reminded them what might happen. I guess I'll talk it over with Mr. Compton at my next supervisory conference."

"What do you mean?" asked Russ.

"Well, I think he should know about it so they can consider it in planning for those two. Besides, maybe Mr. Compton can give me some clues for handling them."

"Don't report it," advised Russ.

Pat looked surprised. "What do you mean? I have to! During orientation they told us . . ."

"Listen, will you?" interrupted Russ. "This place hired you to settle a lot of these things by yourself—not to dump them on the bigwigs. The best thing you can do is talk to those kids and give them a clue that you know about last night's fight. Throw a good scare into them!"

"But the director told me to bring my problems to Mr. Compton," objected Pat. "He said I'd never learn if I didn't give Mr. Compton a chance to help me, and Compton said I shouldn't wait until small problems grow into big ones."

Russ shrugged. "Suit yourself. I just don't want to see you get the reputation of not being able to handle a couple of unruly kids. They wouldn't need child care workers if they wanted to handle every little thing themselves. The more they don't have to get involved in," he added as the car drove up to get them, "the better they like it."

On the way to town, Pat was lost in thought. "What if I don't mention it and things really get worse? Then the kids might get shipped, but if I tried to get Compton's help now, maybe we could nip it in the bud. Or" he wondered, "would Compton think I'm a lousy child care worker."

(Supplementary discussion questions, page 349)

13.2 LOOKING UP

"What's the matter, Frank?" asked Larry White as the two child care workers met outside the administration building. "Why the long face?"

"Thompson just asked me to work overtime again," replied Frank Brooks. "He wants me on duty this Sunday because they're short a couple of child care workers. I was scheduled to be off this weekend and we were planning to go camping."

"So tell him you can't be here!" Larry said.

"It's not that easy," replied Frank. "If Steve Moore was still my supervisor, there wouldn't be any problem. Besides, I guess I'd be glad to do it for Steve. But when Steve left, they brought this Thompson guy in and it was just my luck to get him for a supervisor. He's kind of nag and I don't think he'd like it if I told him 'no.' "

"I heard he wasn't too bad," said Larry. "I was talking to some of the older workers in your unit and they didn't seem to mind him that much. What's the problem?"

"I can give you my opinion, anyway," Frank replied. "He used to be a child care worker here, you know. Then he got his degree, studying part-time, and got a job as a supervisor at an institution somewhere out of the state. When Steve left, the boss remembered Thompson and offered him the job. I just don't think Thompson knows that the place is different now. Besides, I think he has it in for me."

"What makes you say that?" asked Larry. "You sound pretty discouraged."

"I am," Frank replied, almost bitterly. "I think he figures the younger child care workers are just errand boys around here, so he keeps riding my tail about extra work and any other shit details he has. It happens all the time. He wouldn't try that with the older guys."

"Have you tried talking to him about it?"

Frank shrugged his shoulders. "It doesn't do any good," he said. "He just listens, nods, and then goes on doing the same thing. I don't think he really cares how I feel about it."

"Have you thought about talking to the boss?" asked Larry. "He knows you're not the kind of guy to come bitching to him over nothing."

"He'd probably just be polite and laugh it off. What could I say—'my supervisor doesn't like me'? But I better do something soon. It's really getting me down and I can feel that I'm starting to take it out on the kids, too."

"I can understand that, Frank," said Larry sympathetically. "You really need some time alone to give it some thought. Maybe you'll come up with something."

"That's part of what the camping trip was all about," nodded Frank. "But now I have to work on Sunday. Maybe I'll go fishing on Saturday—at least I still have one day off this weekend!"

That Saturday, the institution seemed far away as Frank pulled in his oars and prepared to cast his line into the cool water. Well, he thought as he felt himself beginning to relax, what about my job?

(Supplementary discussion questions, page 350)

13.3 WHERE THE ACTION ISN'T

"Where are they getting them, Bert?" asked Ed Frey. "If it's only a problem in your cottage, your kids must have found their own source of supply. Won't any of the kids tell you where the cigarettes are coming from?"

"Not a word," Bert Green replied. "They get punished when they get caught, but they don't talk."

"Are they always the same brand?" Ed asked. "If they are, it might help you track them down."

Using this as a starting point, Bert soon concluded that John Tebbits, the cottage night worker, might be responsible. One night he asked John about it. "Hell, Bert," John said, "what's the big deal? Some of these guys have a mean habit, and they need a smoke now and then."

"But John," Bert protested, "it's against the rules and it's getting the kids into trouble. You're really not doing them a favor."

"Look, Bert," John finally said, "it's your cottage and I'll do what you want. But I think you're making a big deal over nothing."

After a few weeks, the cigarettes began to appear again and Bert felt sure that John was still responsible. Reluctantly, he spoke to his supervisor, Chuck Donnelly, also describing his earlier conversation with John. "John's one of the real old-timers here," Chuck said, "and it's not an easy thing to handle. If I confront him, he'll deny it, so you should have some kind of proof. And John has a lot of friends here, too, who won't be very happy. But I'll follow up on it and see what we can do."

The smoking problem continued, and several of the boys in Bert's group were punished repeatedly. Bert finally spoke to his supervisor again. "I can't go on punishing these guys, Chuck," he said. "It doesn't mean a damn thing as long as John goes his merry way passing out cigarettes to them."

"Wait a minute," retorted Chuck, a little annoyed. "Don't try to protect the kids, Bert. They know the rule as well as we do. No one's forcing them to smoke. You just go on doing your job the best you can and we'll all be better off!"

(Supplementary discussion questions, page 351)

13.4 BEING HEARD

Mr. Russell, the new director, was nearing the end of his get-acquainted speech to the boys and the staff. "And I want you all to understand," he said, "that my door will be open to anyone who feels that I can be helpful. That includes you boys, of course. Just come to my office and if I can't see you then, my secretary will give you an appointment. Let me close with an expression of my hope that working together we will be able to make this even a better place than it is now!"

As the boys left the gym, they began to move toward the cottages in small groups, discussing what they thought the new director would be like. The child care workers, too, walked in two's and three's, sharing their initial reactions.

"Seems nice enough, doesn't he?" Jim Harris asked one of his co-workers.

"Look out, pal," replied Arnie Brown. "I don't know how nice he is, but our lives are going to be hell on wheels from now on."

"I guess you mean that open-door policy," said Jim.

"You bet! If these kids think for one minute that they can appeal, how long do you think they're going to listen to us? He just knocked our authority out the window with one loose tongue!"

"But shouldn't the kids have the feeling that there's someone they can ask if they think things are unfair?" asked Jim, still not convinced.

"Look," Arnie retorted, "when my father told me I had to do something, I didn't have anyone to go to. Wait and see what'll happen when the kids catch on. Every decision's going to have to be made twice—once by you and then when they see Mr. Russell. If Russell changes it, you're going to want to use that open door yourself."

In the days that followed, Arnie's prediction turned out to be true. Some of the boys attempted to use Mr. Russell's invitation to undermine unpopular cottage regulations. When they appealed child care workers' decisions, however, Mr. Russell usually supported the child care worker. When he did not and the worker complained, he usually reversed himself if they could justify their position. The major effect seemed to be a drain on everyone's time and on the workers' morale, but Mr. Russell felt it was important that the boys retain their pipeline to the top, anyway.

"I guess you were right, Arnie," said Jim one day. "I can't take this kind of pressure any more. It's like working in a goldfish bowl. But how can we deal with it?"

(Supplementary discussion questions, page 351)

13.5 WHO OWES WHAT TO WHOM?

The child care workers were talking intensely among themselves as they gathered in the staff lounge. "Let's get started," interrupted Frank Burbank, chairman of the group they had formed. The room quieted down quickly and everyone turned toward Frank.

"Many of you have heard this and that about our negotiations with the administration," Frank began, "but let me review where we stand so we can start our discussion from the same point of departure. I think the job action we took last week really shook them up. No one got hurt, but the administration got the message. The biggest thing still at issue is paid time off and tuition for those of us who want to enroll in the new child care training program at the university. They still claim they can't afford it, and they say the time off would make scheduling too difficult."

"Frank," called out Ralph Fagan angrily from the floor, "that's a lot of bull. They talk all the time about making child care workers professional but now that we have a chance for real training, they don't want to help. I think they should put their money where their mouths are!"

"I've been negotiating with them, Ralph," replied Frank, "and I'm convinced they won't buy it. The extra time off thing really bugs them."

Ralph took a deep breath. "Then I think we have to talk about a strike," he said. "Let's face it. Behind the fancy words, the place is trying to keep us down, and they only move when we show them we mean business. If we get degrees, we might be offered better jobs elsewhere, and they don't want to take any chances."

"Wait a minute," objected Hank Jensen, "wouldn't we really be striking against the kids? Maybe the scheduling thing really is a problem for them."

"You can't think about it that way, Hank," replied Ralph. "First of all, the more training we get, the better it'll be for the kids. Second, you have to think about the kids who'll be coming through in the future. The only way child care work is going to become a real profession is if we insist on getting professional training whenever we can. But all that's beside the point, anyway. We have every right to think about what's good for ourselves. That's the idea of this group we formed. If we don't look out for ourselves, the institution isn't going to get us what we need. We've got to take a stand!"

"I'll go along with whatever you decide," Frank said, "but I think there should be an open discussion before we vote. What do you think we should do?"

(Supplementary discussion questions, page 352)

UNIT FIVE

THE WORLD OUTSIDE

14. PARENTS

The amount of direct contact between child care workers and the families of the youngsters in their care varies greatly among institutions. Past and present family influences on the development of youngsters are great, however, and child care workers can expect to be confronted with a variety of situations directly or indirectly involving family relationships and concerns.

TABLE OF CASES

14.1 "IF I KNEW YOU WERE COMING . . ."

"Mr. Harris," said Jim Scott as he entered the cottage office, "my mother would like to see you."

"Fine, Jim," replied Sam Harris, noticing that the boy looked a little concerned. "I'll be right out."

Emerging from the cottage a few minutes later, Sam saw Jim and his mother sitting together on one of the benches that dotted the campus. It was Sunday afternoon, the usual visiting hour, and other boys with their guests were scattered nearby. "Hello, Mrs. Scott," Sam said as he approached. "Good to see you."

"Mr. Harris," Jim's mother replied, "they called me this week to tell me that Jim was caught trying to start a fire again. They said they might have to send him away."

"We're working with him, Mrs. Scott," said Sam. "I think Jim is beginning to realize how serious it is, too. Aren't you?" he added, looking at the boy.

"Listen," barked Mrs. Scott without waiting for Jim to answer, "I told you last time that you have to beat him. That's the only language he understands."

"Mrs. Scott," Sam replied softly, "we believe . . ."

"I heard all that before," the woman interrupted. "You can keep all that psychology stuff. I brought up six kids and they all turned out right except Jim. He'll be O.K. too, if you just do what I say. Beat him when he gets out of line, so he'll learn."

"But mother," protested Jim, "they're trying . . ."

"Shut up!" roared Mrs. Scott, turning toward her son and slapping him across the face. "Can't you see I'm talking to Mr. Harris?"

The boy reeled backwards as the other boys and their visitors stopped their conversations and watched.

(Supplementary discussion questions, page 352)

14.2 GREAT EXPECTATIONS

Marty Taylor and Neil Thurston were walking back to their cottages from the weekly child care training seminar. "They really hit the nail on the head today," said Neil.

"You mean the discussion about unreasonable complaints?"

"I sure do. I was thinking about that Henry Robb kid in my cottage. Remember? He had a birthday last month and when his parents came to visit without some wild stereo set he'd asked for, he cursed them out and then refused to even say goodbye when the visiting hours were over. His poor mother really looked heartbroken."

"The Robbs are on welfare, aren't they?" asked Marty. "And didn't you tell me they brought Henry a nice present?"

"Sure," replied Neil, frowning, "and they must have really scrimped to save the ten bucks or so it took to buy the three records they presented to their ungrateful son! I think they spend most of what they get on Henry's father's medical expenses."

"I know how you feel," said Marty. "It really turns me off, too, when kids make unrealistic demands, even though I know that sometimes they can't help it." Neil looked up suddenly. "Say," he asked, "do you suppose I could talk to Henry about this before his folks come up to visit him again and maybe help him see things more clearly?"

"Sounds like it's worth a try," answered Marty thoughtfully. "If you could help him see his parents' circumstances more objectively, it might be easier for him to come to terms with the way things are."

"Henry's parents are scheduled to visit again on Sunday," said Neil, "so I'll try to talk to him this week."

That evening Neil asked Henry to come into the cottage office with him as the youngster was leaving the recreation room to put his records away. "The guys really enjoy that music, Henry," Neil said as they sat down.

The youngster smiled briefly. "Yeah, it's pretty good," he said. "What'd you want to see me about, Mr. Thurston?"

"Well, I was remembering how upset you and your parents were the last time they visited. I thought you might want to let them know how much you and the other guys are enjoying the records and maybe thank them when you see them on Sunday."

Henry shook his head. "No chance," he said flatly. "I asked for a stereo phonograph for my birthday and those cheapskates brought me three crummy albums!"

"Look at it this way," suggested Neil. "A stereo set would cost your parents more than half the money they get to support your whole family for a month. You know there's no way they could make it on half that money. As it is, they probably deprived themselves plenty just to buy you the records. Don't you think you're expecting too much from them?"

"Look, it's really none of your business," said Henry emphatically, "but the way I see it, if they really cared about me, they would've found some way to get me what I asked for. Is that all you wanted to talk to me about?"

(Supplementary discussion questions, page 353)

14.3 STIFF UPPER LIP

"Come in, Nancy," said Milt Green, as the social worker entered the cottage. "What's up?" he added quickly, noting the serious expression on her face.

"I got a letter from Oliver Herman's mother this morning," she said as she took off her coat. "She doesn't want Oliver to come home on his Christmas leave."

Milt whistled. "Wow!" he said, shaking his head. "That kid has been talking all fall about going home for Christmas. Why can't he go?"

Nancy Simmons handed him the scrawled note, and Milt read it in silence:

Dear Miss Simmons:
   Please make other arrangements for Oliver's Christmas vacation. His brother will be home and Oliver is a bad influence on him when they are together.
                        Sincerely yours,
                        (signed) Mrs. Herman

After slowly folding the note and handing it back to Nancy, Milt finally spoke. "That's all she says?" he asked sadly.

"That's it. I called to discuss it with her but she didn't even want to talk about it."

"Now what?" asked Milt.

"We have to tell him. I think you're closer to him than anyone else around here, so it might be best if you did it."

"How do you tell a fourteen-year-old boy his mother doesn't want him?" Milt replied, half to himself. "I'll do it, Nancy," he continued. Any suggestions?"

After they had talked about it for a while, Nancy stood up to leave. "One other thing, Milt," she said. "Oliver's record suggests that he sometimes becomes self-destructive when he gets depressed, so keep an eye on him. He smashed his fist through a window once and cut himself badly on the glass, and there were some other things like that, too."

Oliver showed little emotion when Milt told him. "Hell," he said, "I didn't want to go home anyway," but Milt could tell from his eyes that he was deeply hurt. He tried to get the boy to talk about it but Oliver brushed him off.

"Well, maybe you need some time to think about it by yourself," Milt said, finally. "Remember, I'm always available to talk if you want to." The days passed and Oliver went through the routines of living without any of his normal spirit. A number of times Milt broached the subject, but Oliver insisted that he was glad he was not going. Nancy had no luck in drawing him out, either. Both she and Milt were worried about him.

As the boys packed their suitcases on the day before Christmas leave began, they talked eagerly about their vacation plans. Even the ones who had been reluctant and anxious about going home seemed to catch the feeling and were talking about what they would do and what they hoped to get for Christmas. As Milt joined in the conversation, he noticed that Oliver was sitting silently on his bed and watching.

(Supplementary discussion questions, page 354)

14.4 STAND-IN

"What does the A stand for, Mrs. Saunders?" asked Sally Thompson as she ran her finger across the label on the front of her child care worker's record book.

"It stands for Anne," the woman replied. "That's my first name, Sally. Hurry and get ready for bed, dear. It's getting late."

Sally hesitated. "Anne," she finally said softly. "That was my mother's name. Mrs. Saunders," she continued after another pause, "can I call you 'mother'?"

Anne had been working at the institution for only two weeks and she had not anticipated a situation like this. "Sally," she replied as she looked into the girl's plaintive eyes, "it's a good feeling to know you want to think of me that way, but it really wouldn't be a good idea. All the girls here call the ladies on the staff 'Mrs.' or 'Miss.'"

Anne thought about their conversation while the girls were getting undressed. Sally had lived briefly in a series of foster homes after her mother had died and had finally been sent to the institution. Anne felt she had responded the right way, because it had been explained in the orientation program that it was important for child care workers not to take the roles of the youngsters' real parents. However, she made it a point to linger for just a moment near Sally's bed when she said good night to the girls in Sally's dorm. As the girls said good night, Anne heard a whispered "good night, mother," from Sally's bed. No one else seemed to have heard and she decided to ignore it.

During the next few days, Sally continued to address Anne as "mother" from time to time, almost as if by accident. Although Anne was concerned, she continued to ignore it. Finally, she mentioned it to her supervisor.

Mr. Meyer nodded understandingly. "I'm not surprised," he said, "but we'll have to stop it." He went on to explain why he felt it was important.

"I hate to hurt her feelings, though," Anne replied. "What do you think would be the best way to do it?"

"I think the most important thing is to try to make sure she knows you still care about her just as much no matter what she calls you," Mr. Meyer suggested.

When she got back to the cottage, Anne called Sally aside and talked with her. "Remember, it doesn't mean I like you any less," she concluded. "It's just that we've found it best for all the girls to call us by our names."

Sally tried to hold back the tears. "Oh, Mrs. Saunders," she sobbed, "it's just a little thing. Why should anybody else care? I don't feel as lonely when I can think of you as my mother. The other kids don't really mind. Please don't say I can't do it any more!"

Anne shook her head. "I'm sorry, Sally," she said, trying to sound firm and understanding at the same time, "but it really wouldn't be fair. Please remember."

Sally took her hands away from her face and stepped closer to Anne. "Look, she said, lowering her voice, "I'll call you Mrs. Saunders all the time when we're in front of other people. But if there's just the two of us, let me say 'mother,' please!" I'm going to think of you as my mother, anyway. There's nothing wrong with that, is there?"

(Supplementary discussion questions, page 354)

14.5 BAD NEWS

"Thanks, Rev. Melton," said Chris Fuller, as he got up to leave the chaplain's office. "See you on Sunday."

Rev. Melton nodded. "Good. In the meantime, just try to remember what we talked about, Chris. Everything usually works out for the best." When Chris had closed the door, Rev. Melton picked up the telephone and called the boy's cottage. "Could we get together for a few minutes this afternoon?" he asked Ben Holmes, the senior child care worker. "I just spoke with Chris Fuller, and I want to bring you up to date, too."

"Sure," replied Ben, "what time would be good for you?" They agreed to meet about half an hour later.

"How does Chris seem to be taking it?" asked the chaplain when Ben had seated himself.

Ben shrugged. "It's hard to say. I guess it's never easy to accept the fact that your father has a terminal illness. I think you've helped him, though. He talks a lot with me about it, too. He doesn't seem nearly as depressed in the cottage as he was when he first found out."

"That's my impression, too," said Rev. Melton. "I spoke with the family again. Mr. Fuller has been moved to the intensive care unit in the hospital. It doesn't look good."

Ben looked at the chaplain for a moment. "Did you tell Chris about that?" he asked. "He was very quiet when he got back to the cottage, but he always is after he talks about his father."

"No," said Rev. Melton, shaking his head. "I thought about it but decided it would just increase his anxiety without doing any good. Mr. Fuller was in intensive care a couple of times before and managed to pull through. It could happen again." There was a brief silence, with each man momentarily lost in his own thoughts, until Rev. Melton spoke again.

"Well, Ben," he said, "I'm going to be out ot town until Saturday and I know you'll be here, so I wanted to bring you up to date. Let's hope you won't need it."

With a rueful nod, Ben stood up and turned toward the door. "I hope not," he agreed, and he left the office.

Ben was in the cottage the following evening when the news reached him. As he replaced the telephone receiver and stood up to call Chris from the recreation room, Ben suddenly felt queasy. How, he wondered uncomfortably, do you actually go about telling a kid that his dad is dead?

(Supplementary discussion questions, page 355)

15. CONTACTS WITH OUTSIDERS

In most institutions, situations arise when the youngsters go off grounds for recreational trips, special medical attention, and other purposes, and there may be frequent visits from outsiders as well. Even staff members on their time off must sometimes confront the reaction of neighbors to an institution near their community. The cases that follow illustrate some of the major issues.

TABLE OF CASES

15.1 MAIL CALL

Brand new, the institution was scheduled to admit its first youngsters the following week. The basic staff was there already and the director, Larry Shaw, had established a staff council that he hoped would facilitate communication among the various departments. This group had been meeting frequently to help establish rules and procedures.

"One thing we haven't discussed yet," said Mr. Shaw at one of the meetings, "is what we're going to do about the kids' mail. Some institutions read all that comes in or goes out, some are more selective, and others don't read any. Assuming we have a legal right to do it, how do you people feel about it?"

Bill Webster spoke first. "From a security point of view," he said, "my experience is that you use all the information you can get. Drugs get smuggled in by mail, you can learn about a lot of runaways and head them off, things like that. And even news from home, like the death of a parent. It's good to know in advance so you can break it to the kid better."

"But you pay a price for that," replied Joan Sanford, one of the social workers. "The kids would be inhibited. They need to feel they can communicate privately with the people at home, so they can complain or whatever they want without being afraid they'll get punished for it. Otherwise a place like this can be unbearable. What our kids need most is to feel like worthwhile individuals, and you lose that if you know that even your mail isn't private."

"Let's face it, Joan," responded Bill, "you lose that when you get shipped to an institution. And the kids don't have to know their mail is being read. Besides, where I worked before we once picked up a letter from a kid who said she was planning to kill herself the next day and gave all the details. That kid might be dead now if we hadn't read the mail."

Irv Richter, an experienced child care worker, shook his head. "Bill," he said, "I think you've got to assume that, sooner or later, the kids will find out. But maybe it would be a good idea to pick out the kids who seem to have special problems and read only their mail. And we could have a list of incoming mail to be read, too, like from parents whose letters upset their kids too much. That happens a lot."

"I just don't see how we can," said Joan. "I know the risks involved, but I think we just have to watch the kids closely enough so we'll pick up the danger points in other ways."

"Look," suggested Bill, "we don't have to act on every little thing. If we can just prevent a few kids getting hurt bad or maybe even killed, it seems to me it would be worth it."

Mr. Shaw had been listening closely. "These are the kinds of issues that always come up in this area," he said, nodding. "Now I'd like to see us develop a policy on incoming and outgoing mail, so it can begin when the kids arrive. What do you think we should do?"

(Supplementary discussion questions, page 355)

15.2 SENSITIVITY

Erv Visk replaced the telephone receiver and turned to the office nurse. "It's all right to delay Raymond's appointment for an hour, Mrs. Clarkson. I checked with the school and explained that Dr. Sorensen would be late. Guess it's simpler to wait here than to make another special trip to get Raymond's eyes checked." Turning to the seventeen-year old boy sitting in the waiting room, Erv added, "Ray, I'm going to run down to the drugstore and get some pipe tobacco. Want to come with me?"

"Naw," the youngster replied, "I'd rather sit here and look at this new magazine on racing cars." Erv nodded and, as he turned to walk out, had to step aside quickly to avoid colliding with a rather dour, matronly looking woman and her teenage daughter, who were entering the office.

When Erv returned to the waiting room about ten minutes later, he saw that the young girl who had arrived as he was leaving was seated cozily next to Raymond and they were engaged in a low, almost animated conversation. No one else was in the room.

"Will wonders never cease," he thought. "Our Raymond has made a conquest!" Raymond was usually on the quiet side in the cottage, and Erv would have expected him to be especially shy with girls.

Erv slipped into a chair near the door and began to read one of the office magazines. The minutes ticked by and he was beginning to doze, aware only of the pleasant murmur of the young people's conversation across the room, when a voice rang out from the doorway. "Linda!" her mother called, entering the room. "What are you doing?"

Just then, Mrs. Clarkson emerged from the inner office. "The doctor will see you now," she said, nodding at Raymond. He quickly whispered something to the young girl, slowly got to his feet, and walked into the doctor's examining room. "We'll be with Linda soon, Mrs. Evans," the nurse concluded before returning to the inner office and closing the door.

Erv watched with interest as Mrs. Evans, still muttering sounds of annoyance, sat down beside her daughter in the spot just vacated by Raymond. They began to talk in low voices, but it was clear that Linda's mother was beginning to question the girl angrily. Suddenly the woman snatched a small piece of paper from the girl's hand and read it. Casting a scornful glance at Erv she quickly rose to her feet, strode to the inner office door, and knocked. Without waiting for a response, she pushed the door open, and Erv could see Raymond in the room as Mrs. Evans begain to upbraid the doctor.

"Dr. Sorensen," she cried, "how can you expose my daughter—or any innocent child, for that matter—to that. . . that delinquent over there." She gestured toward Raymond. "He was sitting in the waiting room, bold as brass, when we walked in, and the minute I turned my back he had the gall to give Linda his name and address—so they could correspond! He actually admitted that he used to skip school and go around stealing with a gang of other hoodlums. If you must have criminals here, the least you could do is schedule things so that people like that don't have to come in contact with decent people. . . ."

Catching full sight of Raymond's appalled and agonized face, Erv jumped to his feet.

(Supplementary discussion questions, page 357)

15.3 A BOWLING TRIP

Will Borden pulled the station wagon into a parking place and stopped. "Just a minute," he said, as the six youngsters eagerly began to climb out of the car. "Don't forget the ground rules. Any horsing around and we'll have to pack up and leave. Understand?"

Richie Pratt, who had somehow managed to slide out of the car unnoticed, appeared in the window next to Will's face. "Man," he declared, "we'll be cool! We'll be so cool they'll be asking for our autographs—us, the Champeen Bowlers of America'!"

After he had been bowling with the boys for about half an hour, Will remembered that he had promised to telephone his girl friend to discuss where they would be meeting that evening. He excused himself from the next game and walked to the outside entranceway where the public telephones were located.

A few minutes later, his conversation was rudely interrupted when he heard high angry shouts cutting through the usual reverberating booms of the bowling lanes. Running from the booth to the inner doorway, Will could see at least three boys from his group engaged in what looked like an all-out brawl with some older boys right in the middle of the highly polished alleys. Pulling the door open, Will lunged into the room just in time to sidestep a bowling ball that had been thrown by Richie, who was standing on top of a nearby ball rack.

"Richie, get off there!" demanded Will. "For God's sake, what's going on in here? What happened?"

"Stay away!" yelled Richie, holding a bowling ball in the air. "When you walked out, those guys in the next alley told us to watch out and we said we wasn't doing nothin' and the manager came over and called us 'fresh bastards' and Carl said, 'Like that?' and dropped a ball on this other guy's foot. They all started fighting, and the manager shoved me and I jumped up here!"

Trying to collect his wits, Will started to speak when he heard the piercing blast of a police whistle and saw three uniformed policemen framed in the doorway with the infuriated, wildly gesturing bowling lane manager at their side. The room had quieted considerably and one of the policemen stepped forward. "O.K.," he barked, "that's enough! Who's in charge of those kids?"

(Supplementary discussion questions, page 357)

15.4 BIG MEN ON CAMPUS

Ed Lang could hardly suppress a smile as he noticed the unusual tidiness of the institution's grounds. "You can always tell when the governing board's annual visit is scheduled," he thought, shaking his head. His thoughts were interrupted by Joey Ziff.

"Hey, Mr. Lang," Joey asked as the group lined up on the outdoor basketball court, "can't we use the gym today? We want to take the mats down and tumble. Nobody wants to play basketball!"

"No, Joey," Ed replied, "not today. We're going to be practicing basketball with Mr. Catlin's cottage. They'll be here any minute."

"Basketball," groaned Joey, "I'm lousy at basketball. Why can't we use the gym?"

"Yeah," chimed in Patrick, "we've been playing too much basketball lately and we're tired of it."

"I bet it's because those old guys are here today, and we're supposed to play outside so everything stays quiet and nice lookin' inside," offered Jerry.

"The hell with them," said Joey disgustedly. "I don't want to stand out here and make a fool of myself in front of a bunch of strangers. I want to use the gym."

"Cool down, Joey," advised Ed. "Come on, boys," he continued, "let's try a few shots until Mr. Catlin's group gets here."

As the still somewhat disgruntled boys waited in line for their practice throws, Ed saw Grant Catlin, the counselor from the adjoining cottage, approach with his group. "What's going on today, anyway?" asked one of the newcomers as the boys began to mingle.

"Oh, we just gotta hang around out here to show off for a lot of old geezers!" replied Joey.

"That's enough, Joey," warned Ed, and he and Grant began to get things organized.

Within a few minutes, they saw Mr. Marlin, one of the institutions most important benefactors, leading several members of the governing board across the grounds.

"Guess he's acting as official tour director today," commented Grant quietly to Ed.

"Looks that way," Ed agreed. "Do you know Mr. Marlin very well?"

"No, not really," responded Grant. "I've heard that he can be rather pompous, though."

Pausing a minute before replying, Ed stiffened as he began to hear some of the comments Mr. Marlin was making as he described the cottages and the children they housed to the people around him.

"Hey, Mr. Lang, what's that guy saying about us?" demanded Joey indignantly.

"He's just showing them around the grounds, Joey," Ed responded, then tried quickly to divert the group's attention. "Who's next? Come on, boys, let's get with it."

Brushing aside Ed's attempts to change the subject, Joey persisted. "Come on, Mr. Lang, listen to him!"

By this time the group being led by Mr. Marlin was much closer, and he could be clearly heard saying, "Here on the left are Cottages 7 and 9. They house boys between twelve and fourteen who suffer from emotional problems that make residential placement necessary. Most of them have been adjudged to be delinquent. As you can see," he continued, waving his arm toward the basketball court, "these youngsters are outside now with their counselors, enjoying athletic activities!"

"Say, Mister," shouted Joey, as he pointed to Mr. Marlin, who was now practically abreast of the court, "are you showing off all the freaks today? Or just us?"

(Supplementary discussion questions, page 357)

15.5 THE NEIGHBORS

It was snowing hard and there was an icy wind blowing, so Wayne decided to wait inside Frank's Bar and Grill for his co-worker, Dan Hooper, instead of waiting in front. He sat at the bar, ordered a beer, and looked around.

Wayne had been at the Brookville Training School as a child care worker for less than a month, and he had been too involved in orientation and getting settled in his new job to give the nearby town more than a passing glance. That was why Dan Hooper, who had worked at the school for two years, had suggested that they meet at Frank's tonight for a drink. At least Wayne might meet some of the people who lived in Brookville there.

Feeling a blast of cold air on his back, Wayne turned to see if Dan was coming in, but the newest arrival was a tall, sandy-haired man whom Wayne thought he recognized as the owner-operator of the local cab company.

"Is this seat taken?" asked the newcomer, indicating the stool next to Wayne.

"No," replied Wayne. "I'm expecting a friend, but there's plenty of room. Go ahead and sit down."

"Hi, Red," was the barman's greeting. "The usual?" Without waiting for a reply, he placed a shot glass of whiskey and a bottle of beer in front of Red.

"Here's to you," Red called out to the room at large, before downing the whiskey. Turning to Wayne, he asked, "New here? Are you with that electronics place out on the highway?"

"No, I'm not," replied Wayne. "I'm working out at . . ."

"Good," interrupted Red, apparently misunderstanding. "Thought you might be one of those jerks from the training school."

"What do you mean?" asked Wayne, puzzled.

Red answered with an air of disgust. "Oh, that's the place for delinquent kids outside of town. Oh, excuse me," he amended sarcastically. "We're supposed to call them sick!" He spat the word out. "Those punks belong behind bars. Listen, I take people up there in the cab all the time, and you wouldn't believe what those kids do! They're being babied by a bunch of jerks who don't know their left foot from their right. Boy," he added, lowering his voice a little, "could I tell you stories about that place!"

"Like what?" asked Wayne, deciding he'd like to hear what Red thought he knew about the institution.

Red kept his voice low. "For instance, they got boys and girls living there, some black and some white, and they're all mixed up together. You can guess what goes on."

"Has there ever been any scandal?" asked Wayne.

Red snorted. "Shit! They keep it all hushed up. Some of the teachers are probably in on it. You know how it would be with them all locked up together. There's a lot of them mixed up with drugs, too." His eyes took on an almost satisfied air as he thought about it for a second or two. "It's pretty bad, all right," he concluded, shaking his head.

"Let me add my two cents," said a short, heavy man, one of several who had stopped to listen to Red. "Those damn kids come here to take the bus to the city for some kind of home visits, and they're the worst kind of hoods. We've had a real problem with property destruction here in town. Radio aerials on cars get snapped off, hub caps are stolen, vending machines are rifled, the street lights get broken, they write all over the bus station walls . . ."

"Yeah," Red chimed in quickly, as the others nodded their agreement, "They write all that filthy stuff about. . ."

"Wait a minute!" interrupted Wayne. "Are they really responsible for all the vandalism in town? Doesn't this area have a pretty big teenage population of its own? It doesn't seem right to blame every broken street light on the kids from the training school."

At this point, the bartender stopped in front of them. Dropping his voice, he leaned over and said, "I don't like to knock any of my customers and a lot of people from the school stop in here, but the kids in this town are decent, God-fearing young people. They wouldn't do that kind of thing."

"I'm sure that's true of most of them," said Wayne, "but I've seen a couple of local teenage characters hanging around out here . . ."

"Yeah," declared Red triumphantly. "That's the difference, isn't it? Our kids are out—those kids are in! What more can I say?"

As the men standing around joined in laughter and Wayne fumbled for a response, the door opened again, and Dan came in. His head was covered with snow. "Sorry I'm late, Wayne," he called. "I forgot you had your car tonight, so I waited up at the school until the duty officer came by and told me you'd left."

(Supplementary discussion questions, page 358)

UNIT SIX
PUTTING THE PIECES TOGETHER

16. FUNCTIONING IN REAL SITUATIONS

Each of the cases presented in the previous chapters was selected to highlight a particular kind of issue that frequently occurs in child care work. Actual situations on the job are much more complex, however, and child care workers must usually confront several important situations at the same time. The case that follows is presented to help prospective child care workers begin to get the "feel" of this kind of complexity, but only direct experience in child care can illustrate it fully.

TABLE OF CASES

16.1 ALL IN A DAY'S WORK!

Several of the child care workers at the institution had enrolled in an experimental course in child care at the local community college. After the last class, they went out for lunch with the instructor, Bill Neilson.

"I'd like to know what you thought of that case book we used in the course," said Bill after they had ordered. "You're experienced child care workers and I wondered if it seemed real enough to you."

Jack Philipps spoke first. "I must admit," he said, "that I've found myself in many of those situations from time to time. Like the one where the kid found that speeding ticket right after the worker gave him a lecture about not breaking rules. Same damn thing happened to me once. Embarrassing as hell!"

The others laughed, then turned their attention to the waitress as she began to put their lunches on the table. "I guess you were right, Bill," said Gary Hartman after they had started to eat, "when you said it's better for us to figure the answers out for ourselves, but I still wish they had some of the answers in the book instead of just the problems. Take that case where the worker finds the kids sniffing glue in the basement. What the hell is he going to do? You didn't give us many answers, either," he added, looking at Bill with a smile.

They ate in silence for a minute or so, and Danny Page was lost in thought. "One thing bothers me about the cases," he said, finally. "In one way, they do reflect what really goes on, but in another way, they don't. When you're on the job, six or eight of those cases might be happening at the same time, and how you handle each one depends on what else is going on."

The others agreed enthusiastically. "My cottage is a good example of that right now," said Jack. "First of all, I think we're almost on the verge of a race riot. Buddy Ross is the only kid in there who's strong enough to keep things cool, and he's scheduled to leave the day after tomorrow. Also, we still haven't licked the drug thing, and some of the kids are high as a kite, which doesn't help any. The Stockley kid ran away again yesterday, and we finally found him late last night. His therapist keeps warning me that he might be suicidal. Is that enough?" Jack asked, hardly pausing for breath. "Well, there's also that new compulsory religious program that starts this weekend and the kids don't want any part of it, and Sam Lewis, my co-worker, leaves next week. They said they *think* they'll have a replacement for him in time. I know this sounds worse than usual, but it's a good example of how these things can get mixed up together. Sort of like a bad dream."

"Some months are like that," sympathized Gary, "and there are usually several things going on at once even when it isn't that bad. My kids are down on that skinny Sanford kid, saying he's stealing stuff from them. I still can't get them to clean up the cottage, and the boss wants me to let them make more of their own decisions! That doesn't sound like a hell of a lot, but when it all comes at once along with the routine problems—well, all in a day's work, I guess."

"The thing that's hard for me," added Danny, "is not so much that everything's happening at once, but that some of the problems seem to be in conflict with each other. Like when you're trying to work on a problem with one kid, someone else wants attention, and you have to get the kids to lunch all at the same time. That's the thing the cases didn't seem to catch."

They had finished eating by now, and Bill smiled as they stood up to leave. "Maybe they can't put that part in a book," he said shaking his head. "It's a matter of training yourself to see the issues and how important they are. Then you have to set priorities. Supervision can help you unravel these things, and the cases can help you see them more clearly. But there's only one place you can learn how complex and hard the job really is, and that's under fire."

Later that day, as Danny was trying to break up a fight in the cottage and get the group to dinner, he wondered what would happen next. A smile of satisfaction crossed his face as he realized that two of the boys were helping him stop the fight. A few months before, they would have piled into it instead. "Those two are really on the way back," he thought, "and I guess that's really why I'm here. It makes the whole thing worthwhile."

These pleasant thoughts were rudely interrupted when one of the boys ran into the cottage. "Hey, Mr. Page," the boy shouted, "Tommy just fell off the porch. I think he's hurt bad." Just then, the telephone began to ring.

Well, thought Danny, as a grim smile crossed his lips, I guess Bill's right. This is where it's really at!

A final word

Rather than have you attempt to analyze this final case in the usual way, the authors bid you to take its message to heart as you go to work in the child care field. The job is more complex than you may realize, and often frustrating. But equally important, remember and savor the deep feelings of warmth and satisfaction that help make the experience of serving institutionalized young people worthwhile. You may find that you get as much from it as the youngsters, or even more. Good luck in your important work.

Part Three

Supplementary Discussion Questions

1.1 BLOWING UP:
WHO PAYS THE PRICE?

1. Did Tom handle the confrontation with Mike about the radio well? Did he handle the group well? Could the situation have been handled in a better way? If so, how?

2. Since Tom apparently did not want Mike to be sent to the discipline cottage, why did he record the incident in the log the way he did? Was his log entry appropriate? Should he have said more? If so, what?

3. How should Tom handle the boys facing him now?

4. Should Tom take up the matter with his supervisor? With the administration? Or with both? On what basis? What kinds of incidents should be reported? Why?

5. What should he say to Mike about the incident, either now or when Mike is released from the discipline cottage? What factors should he consider?

1.2 TO CLEAR THE AIR?

1. Should Jeff have said to the boy what he felt like saying? Why or why not? What do you think would have been the result?

2. How else might Jeff have shown his displeasure? Would the results have been different? If so, how?

3. To what extent should a child care worker feel free to share his feelings about a youngster's behavior with him, such as when the worker is angry or feels that the youngster is lying? Why?

4. If a child care worker does not like a youngster, should he tell him or try to hide this feeling? Why? How can he handle the problem best?

5. What information would you want to have about a youngster to help you decide how to respond to him?

1.3 MY MISTAKE!

1. What should Hal say to Carlos about this incident when the boy returns from the trip? Besides the boy's wrist, what should be the main concerns?

2. Assuming Carlos frequently does try to manipulate adults to get what he wants, how could Hal have handled the situation more effectively?

3. How can Hal help Carlos deal with the issue of his credibility without Hal appearing to be trying to avoid the fact that he has made a mistake?

1.4 A LOSS OF FACE

1. How was Joe able to get control of the cottage so quickly? If Ted had acted as Joe did, could the incident have been avoided? Why or why not?

2. How could Joe have handled the situation more helpfully? When Ted said "Thank you" to Joe, could he have said anything else that would have given him control of the group? If so, what?

3. What should Ted say and do now? Why?

4. Did Steve give Ted good advice? Would you admit to the youngsters that you feel you are not in control yet? Why or why not?

5. How can a new worker successfully handle youngsters who are "testing" him? What are they looking for? Are experienced workers "tested" as well? If so, why and how? How should they handle it?

1.5 ONE OF THE BOYS

1. Are Mr. Conrad's expectations unreasonable? Why or why not? What is a "good" cottage?

2. How might Roger's personal needs be influencing his behavior with the boys? To what extent, if any, is this appropriate?

3. What do most of the boys probably think of Roger? How might this influence his effectiveness on the job? How might it affect the rest of the staff?

4. Can personal or group loyalty be the basis for effective group motivation? Why or why not? Suppose the loyalty is based on something in conflict with institutional philosophy, policy, or regulations? Does this give the boys sanction to act out in other ways? Why or why not?

5. Under what circumstances, if any, would a child care worker be justified in promoting, accepting, or hiding behavior that both he and the youngsters know is contrary to established institutional policy or regulations? Why? Can special privileges granted by the child care worker contrary to institutional rules ever be justified in working with institutionalized youngsters? Why or why not?

1.6 CARING TOO MUCH?

1. Is Fred trying to help the boys in appropriate ways or is he doing too much? Explain.

2. How might Fred's personal needs be influencing his behavior with the boys? To what extent is this appropriate?

3. What do most of the boys probably think of Fred? Why? How might this influence his effectiveness on the job?

4. Assuming that institutionalized youngsters have special needs both for adult attention and help and for learning to accept the consequences of their own behavior, how can the child care worker handle the resulting dilemma?

5. If a child care worker is off duty but on grounds, how should he handle youngsters who approach him? Might this vary depending on the youngster and the circumstances (other than in an emergency)? If so, how?

6. Should Fred confront Tommy with what Jess said about the boy's bragging about the basketball net incident? Why or why not? If so, how?

1.7 CULTURE SHOCK

1. Should Vic attempt to force Miguel to relate differently to female staff members? Why or why not? What are the alternatives? How should Vic proceed?

2. How should a child care worker handle a situation in which some of a youngster's cultural behavior patterns are personally offensive (or shocking) to the worker?

3. To what extent can a child care worker or an institution ethically and realistically attempt to change cultural patterns that youngsters bring to the institution? If at all, how?

4. How can a child care worker identify behavior as reflecting cultural patterns? What areas of behavior among institutionalized youngsters are likely to reflect deeply ingrained cultural patterns?

1.8 "DID YOU?"

1. How might the youngsters react and what would it mean to them if Tod answered "Yes"? If he answered "No"? If he responded that the question was really too personal and not something he felt he wanted to discuss with them?

2. Why did the boys ask? In this context, how can Tod respond most constructively?

3. Did Tod help to create the situation? If so, how? Should he have tried to avoid it? Why or why not? If so, how?

4. What should a child care worker share with youngsters about his private life and what should not be shared? Why?

5. What are the implications of this case, if any, for the child care worker's role in the area of values?

1.9 A CASE OF BLACK AND WHITE

1. What kinds of thoughts are probably going through Earl's mind? What should he do about them?

2. Does the marked list indicate that the institution is biased? Why or why not?

3. When special programs are established, what provisions should be made for youngsters who seem likely to benefit but whose participation might disrupt the program? Suppose they happen to be minority group youngsters?

4. Does Mel appear to be primarily a constructive or a destructive influence in this instance? How? Are his criticisms of Earl fair and appropriate? Explain.

1.10 ACCEPTING FAILURE

1. Was it a mistake for Jim to report the incident? Why or why not? Since he feels so strongly about the situation, should he take further action? Why or why not? If so, what?

2. Is Jim too emotionally involved with Brian? Why or why not?

3. What might Brian's behavior mean? Should he be given another chance? Why or why not?

4. What criteria should be used to determine when a youngster's acting out can no longer be tolerated and he should be removed from the setting? What consideration should be given to the needs of the others in the group in making the decision?

5. How can child care workers best handle the frustration and guilt involved when their hard work with youngsters results in failure? What are the criteria by which we can evaluate the success of a child care worker in such situations?

2.1 CONFIDENTIALITY

1. Was Mike right in encouraging Tommy to tell him about the dream? Why or why not?

2. Was Mike right in reporting the incident and the details of the dream, since he did not say he would not? Why or why not?

3. What are the limits of confidentiality, if any, in an institution? Why? How can appropriate confidentiality be maintained?

4. Are there issues that a youngster should be able to share only with his child care worker? If so, what are they? If not, how should the worker communicate this to the youngster?

5. Should therapists ever withhold information from child care workers? Why or why not? If so, under what circumstances?

2.2 THE MISSIONARY

1. Should a child care worker tell the youngsters where he stands on value issues? Why or why not? If he is not asked, should he tell them anyway when a value issue comes up? Why or why not?

2. How important is it that a child care worker avoid sounding "preachy" when he presents his values to the youngsters? Why? If it is important, how can he do it?

3. What effect might talking to the youngsters about values have on a child care worker's relationship with them? Why? How should this be handled? Why?

4. Is it reasonable for a child care worker to think that he might be able to influence youngster's values? Why or why not? Should he try? Why or why not?

2.3 "CAN SHE DO THAT TO US?"

1. Was the punishment appropriate? Why or why not? If not, why might Mary have selected it? What does this suggest about effective child care work? Can or should such situations always be avoided? Why or why not?

2. Should Sue have intervened when Mary punished the children if she thought Mary was wrong? Why or why not? If so, how?

3. Under what circumstances, if any, should child care workers disagree openly with each other in front of the youngsters? Why?

4. Can Sue change Mary's decision now without talking to Mary first? Why or why not? If so, how?

2.4 AFTERMATH

1. In view of Ralph's relationship with the youngsters, should he have been dismissed or should some kind of compromise been arranged? Why?

2. Should Stu have been the one to inform the group of Ralph's dismissal? Why or why not? If not, how should the group have been informed? Did Stu handle the situation well? If not, how could he have handled it more effectively? How can a group's anger best be handled?

3. Should Stu tell the group how he feels about Ralph's dismissal? Why or why not? Should he tell them that Ralph had made the job more difficult for him? Why or why not?

4. Should Ralph be permitted to meet with the group before he leaves? Why or why not?

5. Is there any way in which the boys can try to get Ralph rehired? If so, how? Can or should Stu help them? Why or why not? If so, how?

6. Under what circumstances, if any, should the youngsters be consulted before a child care worker is dismissed? Why?

7. How can this situation be used constructively with the group?

2.5 "GLAD YOU'RE HERE!"

1. Are Andy and Harry still testing Paul at the end of the case or are they expressing their real feelings? How might this affect how Paul should handle the situation?

2. Should Paul report this exchange to his supervisor? Why or why not? Should he tell George about it? Why or why not?

3. How should a new child care worker be introduced to his group?

4. What kinds of language, if any, should not be tolerated among institutionalized youngsters in general and when they are talking about staff members in particular? Why?

2.6 COMPLAINT DEPARTMENT

1. Is griping good for the youngsters? For the workers? Why or why not? To what extent is it inevitable? How should it be handled?

2. What kinds of clues can child care workers derive from listening to

youngsters' gripes? What are some possible meanings of youngsters' gripes? Should gripes be reported up channels? Why or why not?

3. Should child care workers share their feelings with the youngsters or simply help the youngsters deal with their own feelings? Why? To what extent, if at all, should workers support youngsters in their gripes? Why?

4. Should a child care worker share such reasons as "budget problems" with youngsters? Why or why not?

5. What is the child care worker's role as a mediator between the youngsters and the institutional "system"? How can he help them learn to deal with the "system," and systems in general? If the youngsters wanted to picket, go on a hunger strike, and so forth, what role should he play? Why? Could he suggest it? Why or why not?

2.7 GIFTS

1. What should Charley have done when he found Donald crying in bed? Why?

2. Should institutions have a policy of "no gifts" from staff members to individual youngsters? Why or why not? If not, how would you explain to a youngster why you have given a present to someone else but not to him? (This might lend itself well to role playing.)

3. Should a child care worker be permitted to give something to his group (for example, a pizza party) as a special treat? Why or why not?

4. How could Donald have been given special recognition in addition to receiving the cake and without a present? Would this have been a good idea? Why or why not?

5. Should arrangements be made to mark youngsters' birthdays and other special occasions or achievements in the cottage? Why or why not? If so, how should this be done?

2.8 MY BROTHER'S KEEPER?

1. Could Max have questioned the boys more closely without making them feel he did not believe them? If so, how? Should he have questioned them more closely? Why or why not?

2. How can a child care worker tell whether youngsters are telling him the truth? (This and the preceding question can be explored in part through role playing by enacting Max's conversation with the boys.)

3. Should Max be considered to be responsible in any way for the accident? Why or why not? If so, what should he have done to prevent it?

4. Why was Fred angry? Was he responsible in any way for the accident? If so, how?

5. At what point or under what circumstances should a child care worker become involved with youngsters from another cottage? How and to what extent? Why?

6. Should child care workers have the same authority over all the youngsters in an institution? Why or why not?

2.9 VOICES OF EXPERIENCE

1. Was Woody right in confronting Liz and Randy? Why or why not?

2. If Liz and Randy do smoke marijuana, would it necessarily impair their ability to work with Terry? Why or why not? Might it be helpful? Why or why not?

3. Is there any reason why staff members should not be permitted to smoke marijuana when they are off duty if there is no such restriction on their drinking? Why or why not?

4. If a youngster confronted a child care worker with the fact that the worker used drugs, how should the worker respond? If he acknowledges it, how can he justify a double standard, since it is not permitted to the youngster?

5. In what ways can a child care worker separate his personal life from his child care practice? And how can he not do so? Why is this important?

2.10 MIXED MESSAGES

1. Is Paul's point a valid one? Why or why not?

2. What can Chuck do to be helpful to him?

3. How can a child care worker best deal with youngsters who "act out" while working on their emotional problems?

4. Should child care workers respond in the same way to the same behavior regardless of which youngster is involved? Why or why not? (Cases 6.9 and 11.4 may be helpful in considering this question.)

3.1 TEACH ME TO LIKE ME

1. Should Marshall have tried to bring Stewart back to the group right after the incident occurred? Why or why not? If so, how?

2. What kinds of help does Stewart need in the cottage setting? What can the child care worker do to help him get it?

3. Should Stewart be shielded from activities that have competitive overtones? Why or why not?

4. What techniques can be used to help a boy like Stewart feel more important?

5. Can or should Mr. Olsen be involved in handling this situation? Why or why not? If so, how?

3.2 THE DEBUT

1. Should Bob try to arrange for Kevin to help with refreshments? Why or why not? Should Bob encourage Kevin to participate at the dance? If so, how? Should he try to force him to participate? Why or why not?

2. What kind of "help" is Kevin asking for? How should Bob respond to this need?

3. What would be helpful for Bob to know from Kevin's case history? Why?

4. Would Kevin's problem be appropriate as the topic of a cottage discussion? Is it too personal? Is it too uncommon? Why or why not? If such a discussion is held, how should it be introduced and handled?

3.3 FOR LOVE OR MONEY?

1. Should Carol have taken the money as she did when she found it? Why or why not? If not, what should she have done?

2. Who should confront Terry about this incident? Why? How should it be approached?

3. Would it be better to wait to see if Terry approaches the staff about it, since the staff feels that he knows they know? Why or why not? If so, how long should they wait? Why?

4. When youngsters steal, what are some of the likely reasons that should be explored? If Terry stole the money, why might it be that he hid it in such an obvious place? What are the implications, if any, for how the situation should be handled?

3.4 THE REFORMER

1. Is Chuck needling Ted because of the inconvenience and the "lousy smell" alone or for other reasons? What might be some likely other reasons that should be considered? How should Chuck be handled?

2. Might it help Ted if Emil told him that Chuck had been a bedwetter? If so, how? What might it do to Chuck? Why?

3. Should Emil ask Chuck how he would feel if Ted were told that he (Chuck) used to be a bedwetter? Why or why not?

4. Should Chuck and Ted be brought together to discuss what has been going on? Why or why not? If so, should the focus be on the bedwetting, on the fighting between the two boys, or both? Why?

5. How could Emil mobilize Chuck to help Ted with his bedwetting so

as to help Chuck at the same time? (It might be helpful to enact a possible conversation with Chuck through role playing.)

6. How should bedwetting be handled? Why? What related problems often arise and how should they be handled?

3.5 "WOULD I LIE TO YOU?"

1. Knowing Richard as he did, was Donald wise to trust him in this situation? Why or why not? If not, how should Richard be handled in situations like this? Why?

2. Could the explanation for Richard's lying that appeared in the report be helpful to the child care workers? Why or why not? If so, how?

3. What, if anything, should the child care worker tell Richard about the explanation that appears in the report? Why?

3.6 TRIAL BY FURY

1. What aspects of this situation should be handled immediately and what aspects should wait? Why? If part should wait, when and how should that part be handled?

2. What facts, if any, besides those presented would you need to know to handle this situation effectively? Why? Should a child care worker know these kinds of information about all the youngsters in his cottage? Why or why not?

3. In a situation where two youngsters are calling each other liars, how would you decide which of the boys to believe? How would you handle the situation of one boy feeling favored and the other feeling rejected because of your choice, particularly if the choice were wrong? Why?

4. Once you have decided which boy is lying, how would you react if he asked, "What if you're wrong?" Why?

3.7 OFF AND RUNNING

1. Should Tom have chased George as he did? Why or why not? Should he really try to catch him? Why or why not?

2. What do you think would happen if Tom just got up and walked back toward the cottage? Why? Should he do it? Why or why not?

3. What does this case do to explain George's position as a scapegoat in the group? What could Tom do to help?

4. Would it be a good idea to transfer George to another cottage? Why or why not?

5. Why do institutionalized youngsters run away? What can be done to prevent runaways? How, in general terms, should runaways be handled?

3.8 GRACIOUS LIVING

1. What specific kinds of negative consequences "back home" is Ted concerned about? Are they realistic concerns? Why or why not? If so, what should the child care worker do?

2. Is it a good idea to expose a youngster like Wally to the kinds of values, practices, and way of life suggested in the case? Why or why not? Should he be expected to adapt to them? Why or why not?

3. When setting objectives with regard to a youngster's progress, to what extent and in what ways should a child care worker take into account the youngster's "back home" environment? What other factors should be considered? Why?

4. What should be the general goals of the institutional program in working with a boy like Wally? Should the institution try to develop his behavior and aspirations along the lines accepted by the larger society? Why or why not?

3.9 DADDY?

1. Should Fred participate in this discussion or call Al aside and talk with him about it privately? Why? If the latter, should he also make it a point to discuss the topic with the group? Why or why not? If so, how?

2. If Al says he does not want to do anything about his girl's being pregnant, what, if anything, should Fred do? Why?

3. Is this an area in which Fred should give advice? Why or why not? Should he refer Al to his therapist? Why or why not?

4. What provision for sex education should be made for institutionalized youngsters? What kinds of information should be provided? Should information about birth control be included? Why or why not? What role, if any, should child care workers play in this area? Why? How should they be prepared?

5. Suppose a similar situation occurred in a girl's cottage, where one of

308/Critical Incidents in Child Care

the girls learned that she was pregnant. How should the child care worker handle the issues raised above and in the case? Why?

3.10 TOO GOOD?

1. Can a youngster be "too good"? Under what circumstances, if any, should a child care worker be concerned about a boy who is not a management problem?

2. Under what circumstances, if any, should a child care worker encourage a youngster to act out in the cottage? Why?

3. Is therapy "the place for him to let out his excess anger"? Why or why not? How can the child care worker and the therapist work together to help a youngster in a situation like this?

4.1 HOW CLOSE IS TOO CLOSE?

1. Did Mr. and Mrs. Arden handle the situation well as it developed? Why or why not?

2. Was it right to separate the girls, thus creating a situation disturbing to both? Why or why not?

3. Should one or both of the girls have been sent to another institution? Why or why not? Should both girls have been sent to different cottages instead of only one? Why or why not?

4. What is "normal adolescent sex play" that should be expected among institutionalized youngsters? How should it be handled? Should Gail and Marsha be considered to be homosexuals? Why or why not? What might have caused their behavior with each other?

5. How might the relationship between Gail and Marsha be affecting the other youngsters in the cottage individually and the group as a whole? What are the implications of this, if any, for handling the case?

4.2 THE FINK

1. What kinds of group pressure were likely to emerge in response to the approach used by Greg and Jack? In light of this was their handling of the situation appropriate? Why or why not?

2. Should the child care workers focus their attention on the "ratting" issue, on the damage in the recreation room, or on the two together? Why?

3. In what kinds of situations, if any, should "ratting" be encouraged and when should it be discouraged? Why?

4. Should "ratting" be handled differently if the "fink" is a victim of the misbehavior he reports rather than a bystander? Why or why not? If so, how?

5. How might a child care worker's approach to "ratting" relate to his effectiveness in promoting the goals of healthy social and emotional development?

4.3 "REALITY THERAPY"

1. Why did Mark wait so long to express his problem to the cottage life director and then throw away the note? Was this wise? Why or why not?

2. Was Mark too sensitive to failure? Was he too emotionally involved to handle the situation well? What should he have done?

3. Should a child care worker share with a youngster the worker's feeling that they are not "making it" with each other? Why or why not? Does this weaken the worker's position in the eyes of the youngsters? Is honesty the best policy in a case such as this? Why or why not?

4. Was Gene helpful to Mark? If so, how? Could he have been more helpful? If so, how?

4.4 HELPING THE SCAPEGOAT

1. Should Chet let the boy "get his lumps and grow up"? If so, why? If not, what should he do? What is the role of the staff in protecting weaker youngsters from stronger ones?

2. Should Bruce be transferred to a different cottage? Why or why not? What are the pros and cons of moving a youngster to a different living group to avoid trouble? And under what conditions should this be done?

3. What kinds of goals should Chet be setting for his group as a result of this incident? For Bruce? For JoJo? How should he proceed?

4. Was Chet's little speech to the boys about "I'll do the teaching around here" appropriate? Why or why not?

4.5 THE LACKEY

1. How might Maynard have seen earlier how the situation was developing and acted before it reached this point?

2. Can Maynard handle both Eddie's problem and the disciplinary situation resulting from the bottle of wine on grounds at the same time? If so, how? If not, which should take precedence and why?

3. How can a child care worker become aware of relationship patterns among the youngsters in his group on a continuing basis? How can he best use such knowledge in planning room assignments, assignment to leadership roles, and so forth?

4.6 "I CAN'T GO BACK"

1. Might Bob and John be overly concerned? Do situations like this have a way of resolving themselves satisfactorily? Why or why not?

2. Should consideration be given to assigning Ralph to a different cottage? Why or why not?

3. How can Ralph's attackers be identified if Ralph continues to refuse to name them? What should Bob and John do if they learn who did it?

4. How can they handle the situation so that Ralph will be protected? What is the appropriate role of the child care worker in protecting a boy in a situation like this?

5. Is it important to know who the attackers were? Why or why not? What can be done without knowing their identity?

5.1 PEER CULTURE

1. Assuming that Frank is right about how things are where most of the boys come from, should Barry and Bill expect it to be any different in the institution? How should it be different, if at all? What should Barry and Bill do about it?

2. Is it "natural" for the toughest youngsters to run the cottage? Is it acceptable? Why or why not? What are the implications for institutional goals?

3. How effective was the approach used by Barry and Bill? How else might they have approached the situation?

4. Would the child care workers' job be easier if they enlisted the cooperation of the cottage "toughs"? How could this be done in a way that would promote institutional goals?

5.2 ON THEIR OWN

1. Under what circumstances, if at all, should a child care worker enlist the help of natural cottage leaders in managing the cottage?

2. Can strong-arm tactics be avoided if natural cottage leaders are involved in cottage management tasks? If so, how?

3. What should Barney do, if anything, if he learns that Rocco is using strong-arm tactics? Why?

4. What role, if any, do natural cottage leaders play in cottage management when they are not "appointed" by the child care worker as Rocco was in this case? What are the implications of this, if any, for the job of the child care worker?

5.3 THE CRUDE AWAKENING

1. Should Stan intervene immediately or hold off? Why? If he delays, what should he do in the meantime? Why?

2. When Stan takes action, how can he protect Fred from reprisals?

3. What would be an effective way for Stan to work with Mackie toward solving the problem and helping the boys involved?

4. Could the problem in Stan's cottage be solved by assigning Mackie to a different cottage? Why or why not? What does this suggest about the nature of group problems?

5. What kinds of indications might alert a child care worker to the possible development of a shakedown in his cottage so he can "nip it in the bud"? What should he do if he suspects it?

6. How should Fred be handled? Why?

5.4 EVERYBODY GETS HIGH ON SOMETHING

1. What kinds of approaches might be most effective in handling a negative leader like Charley? Why?

2. Can Del disregard or avoid dealing with Charley's accusation? If so, should he? Why or why not? Is the accusation relevant? If so, how? If not, why not?

3. Should there be differences between how a child care worker lives his personal life and what he expects or requires of the youngsters in his care? Why or why not? If so, what are the potential problems and how should the child care worker explain and interpret such differences to the youngsters?

4. Does Del appear to be well informed about drugs? Why or why not? If not, how would he have reacted if he were better informed?

314/Critical Incidents in Child Care

5. What kind of drug control program might be most effective with institutionalized youngsters? What should the role of the child care worker be in this area? Why?

5.5 HELP!

1. What are the greatest dangers in this situation? How can Lew minimize the dangers?

2. Should Lew consider this as primarily a homosexual behavior problem or as something else? What else might it be?

3. How can a child care worker judge what is "normal" sex play among institutionalized adolescents and what is abnormal? What difference, if any, should this make in how they are handled?

4. Which aspects of the situation should the child care worker handle and which, if any, should be referred to a social worker or other clinical personnel? Why?

5.6 INTERGROUP RELATIONS

1. Should Frank relate to curfew as the issue and postpone dealing with the racial confrontation? Or should he deal with the racial problem now? Why? If he decides to send the boys to bed, what precautionary steps should he take?

2. What, if anything, should Frank do with regard to Tim, the boy who came and told him about the situation developing upstairs? Why?

3. How can racial or other intergroup problems be prevented in institutional settings? How can they be handled effectively when they occur?

4. Can racial quotas to allow "balanced" groups in institutions be justified? Why or why not? Should the racial composition of staff reflect the racial composition of the youngsters? Why or why not?

5.7 FOILED FROM ABOVE!

1. Should Cliff have asked the boys to go inside the cottage or let them stay outside to watch when he spoke with Mr. Hull? Why?

2. What would you have said to Mr. Hull when he said he was not sorry? Why? Would your answer have been any different if you knew the boys were nearby and could hear what you were saying? Why or why not? If so, how?

3. Should the institution arrange to have the garden replaced? Why or why not? If so, how should it be paid for and by whom should it be done? Why?

4. Is planting a garden a good idea for a cottage project even though so many things can go wrong? Why or why not?

5. What can youngsters learn from a situation like the one portrayed in this case? How can a child care worker help make it a constructive experience for them?

5.8 A THIEF AMONG US

1. What might be some likely causes of an outbreak of stealing? How important is it to find out the cause as a basis for handling the problem? Why?

2. If the plan suggested in the case is used, should the boys' rooms and lockers be searched whenever something is reported stolen? Why or why not? If so, how and by whom should this be done? Would the implications of such a search procedure be different if the "insurance" plan were not used? If so, how?

3. What other approaches might be used to control stealing in the cottage?

4. How might the claims and settlement procedure work if the suggested plan is used? (It may be helpful to role play a claim and settlement procedure.) What else might a group learn from this?

6.1 CHALLENGING AUTHORITY

1. Was Bill wrong in not intervening sooner? Why or why not? When is it important to intervene in a developing situation? Under what circumstances might it be better to wait? Why?

2. What is Ted trying to do? What should be explained to Ted about what he is trying to do? How?

3. How important is it that Bill find a way to save face? Why? Should Ted be allowed to save face, too? Why or why not? If so, how?

4. Is it important for a child care worker to be in full control of his group at all times? Why or why not? Are there occasions when a challenge to the child care worker's authority can be helpful? If so, how?

5. Is it a good idea for a child care worker to be strict at first, planning to ease up when the youngsters get to know him and what he expects of them? Why or why not?

6.2 "IF YOU DO THIS FOR ME . . ."

1. Should rewards be used to motivate good behavior? Why or why not? If so, how? How do you differentiate between rewarding and bribing?

2. What are the similarities and differences between Jeff's system and the merit system used for the younger boys? What are the pros and cons of incentive systems in general? Under what circumstances should they be used, if at all?

3. Was Jeff's system effective despite Eddie's challenge? Why or why not? What might the challenge mean and how should it be handled?

4. Was it a mistake to take the boys on a trip before their chores were completed? When should this be done, if ever, and when should it not be done? Why?

6.3 "PLEASE, MR. CAMPBELL, PLEASE . . ."

1. What are the likely consequences for a worker if a youngster is able to "con" him? How is it likely to affect the boy? What about the group?

2. In the above case, should the worker confront Jackson and the group together or see Jackson alone? Why? If alone, should he pull the boy out of the group now or wait until later?

3. How can a child care worker tell when a youngster is trying to "con" him? If the worker is not sure, how should he respond?

6.4 YOUNGSTERS OR ADULTS—WHO'S IN CHARGE?

1. Was the treatment plan—setting tight limits and forcing Billy to work through Jim—a good idea? Why or why not? How should a child care worker deal with a manipulative youngster? Why?

2. Should Bill be "shipped" because he was warned that that would be the punishment for "one more AWOL" or should an effort be made to keep him at the institution? Why?

3. Why do you think Billy went AWOL and came back with Mr. Jenkins? How, if at all, should this affect the decision about what should be done? Why?

6.5 TABLE TENNIS, ANYONE?

1. Was it a good idea for Terry to suggest the ping-pong match to get Joel's mind off his worries? Why or why not?

2. Under what circumstances, if any, is it appropriate to try to change the subject when a youngster is worried about his problems? Why?

3. Should Terry have shared with Joel the fact that he felt uncomfortable in the situation? Why or why not? If so, how?

4. Should Terry let Joel know that he overheard his last remarks? Why or why not? If so, how? What else should Terry do now?

5. What are the implications of this case for the role of the child care worker?

6.6 "DO AS I SAY . . ."

1. Gary's reaction when he finds Keith's ticket may be a natural one under the circumstances, but is his attack on Keith really valid? Why or why not? How are the two situations similar and how are they different?

2. Although Keith may be embarrassed, how can he make this a constructive experience for the youngsters and himself?

3. Does setting a good example mean not getting a ticket? Not letting the youngsters find out about it? Handling it well when they do find out? Or some combination of these? Explain.

4. To what extent should the youngsters be aware of events (such as the ticket) in the private life of their child care worker? Why? How should the child care worker handle such issues when they arise?

6.7 THE DIFFERENCE

1. Should Tom deal primarily with the issue of the boys' boredom or with Herb's accusation? Why?

2. How would you interpret Herb's accusation? Why? How can Tom deal most effectively with it? Why?

3. How should Tom deal with the boys' boredom? Why?

4. Under what circumstances, if any, should Tom now permit Herb to go to the gym? Why?

6.8 ARE YOU A FAG?

1. Was there anything improper about Vince's behavior as portrayed in the case? If so, why was it improper? If not, why did the boy respond as he did?

2. Should Vince focus his immediate response on Mel's calling him a "fag" or on the boy's disappointment about the postponement of his leaving? Why?

3. How should he handle each of these areas? Why?

4. Should his immediate response be any different if other boys are around? Why or why not? If so, how?

5. Under what circumstances can putting your arm around a youngster be helpful? Under what circumstances might it be likely to cause trouble? How can a child care worker decide when to do it and when to avoid it?

6.9 INDIVIDUALIZATION OR FAVORITISM?

1. Was it appropriate for Barry to "miss a meal" when he had a tantrum in the dining hall? Why or why not? Under what circumstances, if any, is it appropriate for child care workers to deprive youngsters of food? Why?

2. Was the procedure Al arranged for avoiding Barry's tantrums in the dining hall a good one? Why or why not?

3. Was Al right in forcing Steve to go into the dining room and "look at the food"? Why or why not?

4. Was Al playing favorites? Is it best, as a general rule, to treat all youngsters alike? Why or why not?

5. If a child care worker does treat some youngsters differently from others, how can he interpret this to the youngsters involved? How much can he explain? Why?

6.10 "IF I GIVE MY HEART TO YOU . . ."

1. Should Frank give up part of his weekend off to stay and help the boy? Why or why not? If not, how can he still show the boy that he cares?

2. Was Frank getting "too close" to John? Why or why not? In general, what are the characteristics of an effective relationship between a child care worker and a youngster?

3. Should child care workers expect to keep to their scheduled working hours as closely as office workers, for example, usually do? Why or why not?

4. Should child care workers always receive additional pay or time off if they stay later than scheduled or arrive early to handle a special problem with which they are involved? Why or why not?

5. Should child care workers always receive additional pay or time off if they are asked by the institution to work overtime to provide

coverage because a colleague is late? Why or why not? In a more extended emergency? Why or why not?

7.1 THE ROAD TO AUTONOMY

1. Who is reflecting Mr. Packard's philosophy and intentions more accurately, Norm or the boys? Why?

2. Should Norm agree? Why or why not? If the boys suggest that they make up a set of rules together, should he agree to support home visit privileges for anyone who follows all the rules? Why or why not? Should he suggest this alternative? Why or why not?

3. Why is the question of home visits a particularly difficult one for youngsters' decisions? What kinds of privileges might be more appropriate? At what point should youngsters lose their share, if any, in decision-making? Why?

4. What are the pros and cons of involving institutionalized youngsters in institutional decision-making processes? Is this really a place to "try out" freedom? Why or why not? Is it better to err on the side of too much freedom or too little? Why?

5. Suppose a child care worker asks newly arrived youngsters in his cottage how long they plan or expect to stay, feeling that this involves them in starting work on what they must do to get out. Does this sound like a good approach? Why or why not? If so, how would you follow up on it?

6. Rumors are a frequent source of information, often false, in an institution. What are some possible effects of rumors? How can they best be handled?

7.2 STICK WITH ME!

1. What should be Larry's primary concerns as he confronts the three boys? Why? How can he communicate these to the boys most effectively?

2. Why did Jimmy share his glue sniffing with Bobby and Van? Of what importance, if any, might this be to Larry as he handles the situation?

3. Should Jimmy be dealt with differently from Bobby and Van? Why or why not? If so, how?

4. Was there a failure of supervision that permitted this incident to happen? If so, who was responsible and how can such problems be prevented?

7.3 PROMISES

1. Did Jim imply that he would not repeat what Craig was about to tell him? Since he did not actually promise that he would not tell, should he report the incident? Why or why not?

2. How should a child care worker answer the question, "If I tell you, will you promise not to tell anyone else?" Why? Under what circumstances, if any, should a worker promise to keep something confidential before he knows what it is? Why?

3. Under what circumstances, if any, should a child care worker keep anything pertaining to youngsters in his group confidential from other staff? Why? What is the purpose of confidentiality?

4. If Jim reports the incident, what might be the effect on his relationship with Craig? How should this affect his decision? Why?

5. Why do you think Craig told Jim about this incident "in confidence." Why do you think he told Jim at all?

6. Does it appear that Craig may really want to be "caught" for his offenses? Why or why not? In light of your answer to this and the questions above, how should Jim handle the situation? Why?

7.4 "CARDINAL SINS"

1. Should Tom check the bathroom, since he suspects that Oliver is smoking there, or should he ignore the situation? Why?

2. What should Tom do if he sees Oliver smoking? Does it matter if Oliver knows that Tom saw him? If so, how?

3. Is the rule too harsh? Why or why not? Is it a good idea for the institution to enforce the rule strictly to "set an example"? Why or why not?

4. Should the different needs of individual youngsters be taken into account in enforcing a rule like this? If so, how?

5. How should a child care worker deal with institutional rules with which he disagrees? Should he let the youngsters know he disagrees? Why or why not?

7.5 WELCOME MAT?

1. Does Harry's behavior show the boys that he is concerned about them and will it help their relationship? Or does it make him look like a

"sucker" and give them an unfair picture of how the institution views their behavior? In other words, is it appropriate or is it phony? Why?

2. Is Harry trying to divorce himself from whatever punishment may follow? If not, how can he avoid appearing to do so? What should Gil and Harry do now? Why?

3. Should the boys be punished the following morning? Why or why not? Would that be in conflict with the way Harry is treating them now? Why or why not? Should Harry be involved in whatever happens in the morning? Why or why not?

4. What are the objectives of punishment? How does punishment help reach these objectives? How does a child care worker determine what the punishment should be?

5. Might Harry's handling of the situation encourage other boys to run away? Why or why not? Why do youngsters run away? How should AWOL'S be handled?

7.6 "GIVE US A BREAK!"

1. Is it a good idea to extend curfew occasionally for late television programs of special interest to the youngsters? Why or why not? If so, what kinds of programs should be included? Why?

2. Was Tom fair in not permitting the boys to watch a different program when the game was rained out? Why or why not? Should he have given them a choice of seeing the movie tonight or a game another night? Why or why not? Of what relevance, if any, is the fact that some of the other groups were apparently staying up? Why?

3. What factors should Tom consider in deciding how to deal with this incident?

4. Should Tom return to the cottage to handle the situation now, ignore it now but handle it with the youngsters in the morning, or simply pretend he did not see it? Why?

5. If he decides to handle the incident, what should he do about it? Why?

7.7 PAVED WITH GOOD INTENTIONS

1. Is there any way Albert could justify letting Ronald use his money, even though having it was against the rules? If so, how? If not, what should Albert do?

2. If Albert decides to let Ronald treat the group, should he deal with Ronald privately or should the situation be dealt with in front of the group? Why? Should it be handled differently if Albert decides not to let Ronald treat? Why or why not? If so, how?

3. Should Albert have treated the boys, as he considered doing, since they had already spent the money allotted to them? Why or why not? What are the pros and cons of child care workers spending their own money on youngsters? Under what circumstances, if any, should it be done?

4. How should money belonging to youngsters be handled in an institutional setting? What are the pros and cons of allowing the youngsters to keep some or all of their money with them in the cottage? If money is unavailable, what substitutes are used for it? How should this be handled?

7.8 WHO SHOULD BE PUNISHED?

1. Mike was obviously one of the offenders although he did come to tell Ted about the accident. How should he be handled? Why?

2. How should Brian be handled? Why?

3. Should an effort be made to find out who else was outside after lights out? Why or why not? If so, how?

4. If the others are identified, what should be done? What should be done if they are not identified? Why? What are some alternatives to disciplinary action in this situation and what are the pros and cons of each?

5. Should Ted have held a meeting with the group as soon as he saw that Brian was taken care of? Or was he wise to postpone further action until morning? Why?

7.9 SETUP

1. What was Fred's purpose in punishing the group? Would it have been better, under the circumstances, not to punish anyone? Why or why not?

2. How should the group's new misbehavior be handled? Why? Should the situation be viewed and handled as a problem of the total group? Why or why not?

3. Under what circumstances is group punishment appropriate? How should it be handled when there is a scapegoat or victim, such as Dominick in this case?

4. How should Dominick be handled? Should he be removed from the cottage temporarily? Why or why not? Might this set him up for future scapegoating that would outweigh the immediate relief? Should he be removed permanently? Why or why not? How can he best be handled if he is not removed?

5. Should a child care worker apologize for a punishment, as Fred did when he said he was sorry to have to punish the whole group for the actions of one or two of the boys? Why or why not?

7.10 SHOW NO SCARS

1. What are the pros and cons of physical punishment? How would you rate the relative importance of each? Why?

2. What are the alternatives to physical punishment for a serious offense? What might be the likely results of the alternative Doug selected? Why?

3. Is there a legitimate place for physical punishment in an institutional setting? Why or why not? If so, under what conditions?

4. If physical punishment is to be used, what kinds are acceptable? Why? How and by whom should it be administered? Why?

5. Is it any more or less appropriate for a parent to use physical punishment at home than for it to be used by staff members in an institutional situation? Why?

7.11 CONFINEMENT

1. What effects might the confinement cottage have on Ernie? What might be the effect if he is released after an hour?

2. What might be the effects on Hank of his placing Ernie in confinement? What might be the effects on Hank if Ernie is released after an hour?

3. Should Mr. Goddard have given Hank more support than he did? Why or why not?

4. Can confinement be used constructively? If so, how?

5. Is it a good idea to have a locked discipline or confinement cottage in an institution? Why or why not?

6. Is it a good idea to have an "honor cottage" in an institution? Why or why not?

7.12 A JURY OF HIS PEERS?

1. How can Al intervene without getting Jimmy into more trouble?

2. How should "kangaroo court" situations be handled by the child care worker? Why?

3. Under what circumstances, if any, should institutionalized youngsters decide how others should be punished? Why?

4. Should Al have, in effect, agreed to Lou's gambling debt by letting Lou do Bill's job, as he did? Why or why not? If not, what should he have done?

5. Should gambling be controlled in an institution? Why or why not? If so, how?

8.1 I REMEMBER MAMA

1. Does it seem likely that Joseph's comment reflects a real problem or is Joseph probably just giving an excuse? Why?

2. Should Murray deal with Joseph's remark now, ignore it, or deal with it later? Why? Should he talk with either his supervisor or Joseph's therapist about it first? Why? Can he realistically ignore it for the moment? Why or why not?

3. Should Murray communicate with the school about this incident? Why or why not? If so, how should he proceed? Why?

4. What are some common reasons why it may be especially difficult for some institutionalized youngsters to get up in the morning? How can a child care worker be helpful?

8.2 WHY SHOULD THEY?

1. How much stress should be put on having a clean cottage? Why? On having the cleanest cottage in the institution? Why?

2. What are the pros and cons of giving a prize for the best work at the cottage cleanup or elsewhere? What special considerations, if any, are entailed with youngsters who have emotional problems and handicaps?

3. In general, is it better to give youngsters something special for being "extra good" than to take something away if they do not do what is expected of them? Why or why not? If so, does that justify the idea of giving a prize for the cleanest cottage? Why or why not?

4. What kind of system would you want to use to promote effective cottage cleanups? Why?

5. Under what circumstances, if any, should youngsters living together be urged to compete with each other? Why?

8.3 COME AND GET IT!

1. What are some frequent reasons for weight loss in institutions? How would you determine the reasons in an individual case?

2. What do you think might be the reasons that Tommy is losing weight? Why?

3. Should Tommy be left alone on the assumption that he will eat when he gets hungry and will gradually begin to eat enough to gain weight again? Why or why not?

4. If not, what would you do to help the situation? Would you suggest any changes in food service procedures? Why or why not? If so, what changes would you suggest?

5. How would you deal with a youngster who was considerably overweight? Consider Questions 1, 3, and 4, above, with reference to a youngster who had gained too much weight rather than lost it.

6. To what extent should child care workers concern themselves with matters like these? Why?

8.4 BEDLAM

1. How much further should Mac push this conversation before discussing it with his supervisor or Joey's therapist? Why?

2. What are some of the common reasons why youngsters may have trouble getting to sleep at night?

3. How can a child care worker make it easier for youngsters to get to sleep?

4. Should "lights out" time be flexible or should it be rigidly enforced? Why? What kinds of exceptions, if any, should be permitted? Why?

5. What are some of the common reasons why youngsters awaken during the night and cannot get back to sleep? How should such situations be handled? Why?

8.5 TIME'S UP!

1. Does it appear that the boys were trying to manipulate the workers? What else might explain the fact that this conversation developed when it did so soon after Fred and Will had confronted the group?

2. How important is it to enforce the 9:30 P.M. lights out under the circumstances? Why? Might an alternative deprivation make sense? If so, what? And how might it be introduced?

3. How appropriate was the way Fred and Will handled the lights out problem? Why? What are the pros and cons of deprivation as a disciplinary technique in an institutional setting?

4. Should Fred and Will have accepted Tim's suggestion of a compromise, 9:30 P.M. for "a couple of nights," instead of their own plan at the afternoon meeting? Why or why not?

5. What should Fred and Will have said or done, if anything, at the end of the afternoon meeting when Matt said, "You stink!" Why?

8.6 STUDY HOUR

1. How should a change in rules be presented to the group? Why?

2. Should the youngsters be involved in the process of developing all changes in rules? Some changes in rules? Why or why not? If so, which ones and how should they be involved?

3. Should child care workers be involved in the process of developing institutional rule changes that affect cottage life? Why or why not? If so, how should they be involved?

4. Can a child care worker tell a youngster that he does not necessarily agree with a rule he is enforcing? Why or why not? (It may be helpful to explore this situation through role playing.)

5. Can a child care worker fail to enforce a rule if he strongly disagrees with it? Why or why not? If so, how should he handle the situation with the younsters? If not, what should he do about it?

9.1 NEW MAN IN TOWN

1. Why are youngsters sometimes reluctant to undress in front of other youngsters? How are the others likely to react to this? Why? How can a child care worker help?

2. What are some other common concerns of youngsters when they arrive at an institution?

334/Critical Incidents in Child Care

3. How can a child care worker help a newcomer to the cottage get started on the right foot?

4. Is it a good idea to assign one of the youngsters to orient a newcomer? Why or why not? If so, how should he be selected and prepared for the task?

5. Is it a good idea to have an "orientation cottage" for newly admitted youngsters in large institutions? Why or why not? If so, how should it be used? Why?

9.2 WELCOME TO THE CLUB

1. Under what circumstances, if any, can informal initiations be a positive force in the development of the group and for the newcomer? Why? Should they be permitted? Why or why not?

2. How should child care workers deal with such practices? Why? If something is to be done, would it be better to deal with the boys individually or as a group? Why?

3. If Mort takes action, can he avoid setting Dean up for rejection by the group? If so, how?

9.3 SUDDEN DEPARTURE

1. Is it likely that Michael is right about the prison farm? If so, does this mean that the staff is taking the easy way out for themselves? Why or why not? What should they do?

2. How can Ralph help Michael between now and the time he leaves? What should he do?

3. What criteria should be used for "shipping" a youngster to a more secure facility?

4. Under what conditions, if any, can a youngster who has attempted physical violence on others, youngsters or staff, be retained in an open setting?

9.4 DOING TIME

1. What might be some reasons why the girls are acting out at this time? What are the implications for how they should be handled?

2. How would you help the girls deal with the reality that they may not be able to leave if they continue to act out? Suppose they reply that it is the institution's fault for keeping them so long?

3. In general, how can you help youngsters deal with the problems at hand when they might otherwise get sidetracked into acting out what may be justified feelings of anger, guilt, etc., in ways that would be self-defeating?

4. Is it good practice to set a release date as a goal for a youngster and to tell him about it, or is it better if the date is kept indefinite? Why?

5. What kind of special plan or program, if any, should be established for youngsters approaching discharge? Why?

6. Is it a good idea to have an "exit cottage" for youngsters approaching discharge? Why or why not? If so, how should it be used? Why?

9.5 NO PLACE LIKE HOME

1. How can a child care worker help a youngster deal with his anxiety about going home? How should the worker handle the situation if the youngster's apparent reaction is to act out so that he will not be released?

2. Should a youngster be forced to go home against his will if it can be avoided? Why or why not? If so, under what circumstances?

3. What are the crucial steps and issues that a child care worker should consider in preparing a youngster to leave the institution?

4. How long before a youngster is scheduled to leave should a child care worker begin to help him prepare for it? What issues should be dealt with at what intervals before the youngster's departure?

9.6 THE VACANCY

1. If Eric is correct, should he and Dennis hold an election to select a new leader for the group? Why or why not?

2. Should a child care worker ever try to designate a leader? Why or why not?

3. If a youngster is a strong leader in the cottage, does that suggest that the child care workers are not doing their job well? Why or why not? Is it desirable to have a "natural leader" among the youngsters? Why or why not?

4. If there is no "natural leader" in the group to take over when a leader leaves, what is likely to happen eventually? Why?

5. What other roles appear in most groups? How do they affect group functioning? Why? What are the implications for the child care worker?

6. As an exercise, prepare a sociogram based on your own observation of a cottage group you know well and, if possible, compare it with one based on the youngsters' actual sociometric choices. What are the implications of the results for the child care worker?

10.1 LEISURE IN THE COTTAGE

1. In this case, why might the youngsters have wanted Leo to leave them alone? Does this suggest that Tom is right that the youngsters need as much freedom from adult supervision and involvement as possible? Why or why not?

2. How should a child care worker decide when to be involved with the youngsters in activities? When to observe them? When not to be present?

3. What are the purposes of direct involvement of child care workers with youngsters in activities? What is required to make such involvement successful?

4. Can a child care worker realistically expect to develop the kinds of relationships with youngsters that will enable him to participate comfortably with them in activities as well as to work effectively with them toward the goals of the program? If so, how can he best work toward this objective?

10.2 AS THE REAL WORLD TURNS

1. Why do youngsters watch television? Why do they sometimes watch it more than seems to be good for them?

338/Critical Incidents in Child Care

2. What are the pros and cons of television for institutionalized youngsters? Of using it as a reward? How can it be used constructively?

3. Should Del and Mark force the boys to do something other than watch television if they choose not to be on the basketball team? Why or why not?

4. Is taking away one activity an effective way of getting youngsters involved in something else? Why or why not? If not, what might be more effective?

5. What are the pros and cons of having a cottage basketball team?

10.3 "WHERE IS IT WRITTEN?"

1. In general, what kinds of programs should be compulsory and what kinds should not? Why? How should attendance at and participation in compulsory activities be enforced?

2. Should attendance at religious services be compulsory? Why or why not? If so, how should it be enforced?

3. Should participation in a religious program be compulsory, as in this case? Why or why not? If so, what can Andy do to encourage Hardy and Joe to participate? If not, what should Andy do now?

4. What are the pros and cons of having youngsters attend religious services at the institution versus going to services off grounds?

10.4 THE WORKING CLASS

1. What are the values, if any, of assigned work responsibilities in an institutional program?

2. How should work programs be interpreted to the youngsters? Why?

3. Should youngsters be paid for such tasks? Why or why not?

4. On what basis should youngsters be selected for particular work assignments (for example, taking turns, skill, reward, punishment)? Why?

5. On what basis should particular jobs be selected to be included in the work program? Why?

10.5 PROGRAM FOR WHAT?

1. Assuming it could be arranged, what would be the best solution in terms of Lillian's needs? Why? Could such a solution be arranged? Why or why not? If so, how?

2. How could you let Lillian go to rehearsal and still hold her responsible for her cottage chores? Should this be done? Why or why not?

3. Might Lillian be "using" this situation, whether or not she realizes it, to get what she wants? If so, how, and what should Ethel and Virginia do about it?

4. What kinds of criteria should be used in making program decisions concerning institutionalized youngsters? What other criteria are also used and sometimes interfere? How can such conflicts be resolved?

10.6 THE GOAL OF THE GAME

1. Is there any way that Tim could let Paul go to practice? Could he let Paul make up the "grounding" another night or be punished in some other way so that he could go to practice? Why or why not?

2. Should Paul be on the team at all? Why or why not? In terms of the discussion between Hank and Tim, how should the varsity team be chosen and what should be the requirements for playing on it? Why?

3. What are the pros and cons of having varsity teams in an institution? Under what circumstances, if any, would you favor having a varsity sports program? Why? What might a good institutional sports program look like?

4. How should special privileges be allocated among institutionalized youngsters? Why? What kinds of problems may arise when some youngsters are identified as "privileged characters"? Why? How can such situations be handled most effectively?

10.7 THE ACID TEST

1. What might be the results if John intervenes in this situation? What might be the results if he does not intervene? How would you weigh them against each other?

2. As it stands is this situation acceptable or unacceptable? Why? Should John let Terry know if he disapproves? Why or why not? Should he take further action? If so, what should he do? Why?

3. If John decides to intervene and the test results are reversed, how should he handle the resulting situation with Terry? Why?

4. Is the rule that youngsters must stay at an institution until they have

a job or a school program to go to a good idea? Why or why not? How might it affect the child care worker? And what can he do to help?

10.8 DETOUR

1. As things stand at the end of the case, what are the greatest dangers in the situation?

2. Was it a good idea for the child care workers to encourage Karen's efforts to read comic books instead of trying to get her to read the kinds of things that were favored in school? Why or why not?

3. In view of the way the situation has developed, should the child care workers involve themselves directly with the school? If so, how can they try to avoid making things even more difficult for Karen and how should they proceed? If not, what else should they do?

4. In general, should child care workers involve themselves directly with the school with regard to the school performance of the youngsters? Why or why not? If so, in what ways?

10.9 STUPID AGAIN

1. What is the crucial difference between this case and the preceding case, 10.8? What are the implications of the difference for how the two situations should be handled?

2. What major problem appears in this case in addition to Duane's difficulties in school?

3. Should Al refer this situation to the school guidance counselor? If so, should he remain actively involved in it himself? Why or why not?

4. What should Al say to Duane's parents if they come to visit? (It might be helpful to enact this conversation through role playing.)

5. What are some common reasons why youngsters may find it difficult to attend school, or to succeed in school, or both? How can they be helped?

6. What are some frequent problems related to mail from home and how should they be handled? (Case 15.1 on mail censorship may be of interest in connection with this question.)

10.10 THE CIVICS LESSON

1. Is an institution really a place for democracy and for involving youngsters in decision-making? Why or why not? If so, in what area and to what extent? Should it be viewed primarily as a learning exercise or as an exercise of the youngsters' rights? Why?

2. How can a child care worker let youngsters participate in decision-making in a meaningful way without giving up his responsibilities and authority? How can the worker avoid creating a situation in which the youngsters feel that they are victims of a "con job" and have no real decision-making power?

3. Was Bill's group really ready for involvement in decision-making? Why or why not? How can a child care worker tell when his group is ready?

4. What are the pros and cons of having an institutional "student council" representing the living units? What kinds of functions might best be given to such a group? Why?

5. What role, if any, should child care workers play in various areas of institutional decision making, determining policy, and so forth? Why?

11.1 HOW MUCH THERAPY?

1. At this point, would it be best to try to get Patty back to sleep or to try to talk to her? Why? What should Eileen do about this tomorrow? Why?

2. Should Eileen have approached Patty differently? If so, how? How long should a child care worker wait to approach an "uncommunicative and aloof" youngster? Why?

3. Did Eileen make a mistake in approaching Patty at all? Why or why not? Should the situation have been referred to Patty's therapist instead? Why or why not?

4. How can a child care worker determine what kinds of situations he should try to handle himself and which should be referred to clinical specialists?

5. How familiar should child care workers be with details of the case records of the youngsters in their care? Why?

11.2 "THANKS A LOT!"

1. Despite the way things turned out, did Bert do the right thing by convincing Jim to see his social worker as scheduled? Why or why not?

2. Did Bert speak to Jim effectively in convincing him to go? Should he have spoken to him differently? Why or why not? If so, how?

3. What should be Bert's primary concerns now? Why? What should he do? Why?

11.3 CONNING THE THERAPIST

1. Should Mr. Palmer involve himself at all in what the boys say about their therapists? Why or why not? If so, should he discuss the incident with his supervisor first? Or should he confront the group immediately? Why?

2. If he confronts the group, should Mr. Palmer share with them his feeling that the others are afraid to differ with Alex? Why or why not? What about his feeling that they are more concerned with therapy than they admit? Why or why not? What about his feeling that the new therapists are too concerned about being liked? Why or why not?

3. Why else might the therapists be letting the boys work on models in their therapy sessions? Should Mr. Palmer discuss this incident with the therapists? Why or why not?

4. If the circumstances were reversed—that is, if the youngsters told their therapists how they were conning their child care worker—what would you, as a child care worker, want the therapists to say and do? Why? How is this relevant to the present case?

5. What, if anything, should Mr. Palmer do about Jimmy, the boy who appeared to be disturbed by the things the other boys were saying about their therapists? Why?

11.4 HOW MUCH IS TOO MUCH?

1. What criteria can a child care worker use to determine when an individual youngster's acting out can no longer be tolerated in a group setting?

2. Should Gus and Burt explain to the group why they seem to tolerate behavior in Tony that they would not tolerate in the other boys? Why or why not? If so, how?

3. If the institution continues to make so many special arrangements for Tony and to grant him so many special privileges, will this make it harder for him to go back to life outside the institution where people may not modify rules and procedures to suit his convenience? Why or why not? What else might special privileges do to Tony?

4. Is it fair for the most difficult youngsters to be assigned to the best child care workers, as appears to have happened in this situation? Why or why not? How is this related to the professionalization of child care?

11.5 WHO OWNS THE CHILD?

1. Was Jack right in forcing Ken to go to school? Why or why not? Was the social worker's action appropriate? Why or why not?

2. Who should decide whether Ken should go to school in a situation like this—his child care worker or his social worker? Why? Should either make the decision by himself? Why or why not? How should communication be maintained?

3. Should Jack tell the boys if he thinks the social worker was wrong? Why or why not?

4. Should Ken be reprimanded for going to his social worker to get

excused from school after his child care worker had refused him? Why or why not? Can situations like this realistically be avoided? Should they be avoided? Why or why not? If so, how?

5. Was Ken probably manipulating, really depressed, or both? How should this affect the handling of the situation? Why? Can you tell? How?

6. In what ways might an incident like this be important?

11.6 TRANQUILIZERS AND OTHER DRUGS

1. Is it appropriate for a child care worker who feels that he can no longer manage a particular youngster to request that medication be considered as an interim measure to calm the boy down? Why or why not?

2. Under what circumstances, if any, is it acceptable to use medication just to calm a disruptive youngster down? What should the child care worker do once the youngster is more relaxed? Why?

3. As a general rule, do you think it would be better to keep a youngster and provide him with regular medication or to transfer him to a more secure facility if he cannot function most of the time without such assistance? What criteria should be used in making such a decision? In what ways, if any, should child care workers be involved in such decisions?

12.1 A CONFLICT OF PRINCIPLES

1. Should Jim talk to Herb again? Why or why not? If so, what should he say?

2. What will be the likely consequences for Jim if he reports Herb to their supervisor? How should Jim handle the consequences if he reports Herb?

3. Under what circumstances, if any, should a child care worker go to his supervisor to criticize a colleague? Suppose the problem involves youngsters in the colleague's cottage only?

4. What would you want a substitute child care worker to know before he began working in your cottage? Why?

5. Under what circumstances, if any, is it all right to hit an adolescent youngster? (See also Case 7.10.)

12.2 DIVISION OF LABOR

1. Do Steve's feelings appear to be justified or does he seem to be oversensitive? Why? Of what immediate significance, if any, is this? How should he respond to Jim now? Why?

2. What are the pros and cons of having this kind of division of labor between two child care workers in a cottage? Under what circumstances might it be a good idea and when might it be a poor idea?

3. What are the essential elements in a good working relationship between two child care workers who work together? How can such a relationship be developed and sustained?

4. How should a child care worker deal with a situation in which one or a few youngsters in an emotional crisis appear to need immediate attention that would pull the worker away from the group, perhaps making them late for dinner or otherwise disrupting the schedule?

12.3 MAKING THE TEAM

1. Should Tom express his true feelings to Mr. Talbott on this issue? Why or why not? If so, what possible reactions should he be prepared for? And how should he handle them? (Role playing might be helpful here.)

2. Did Tom reduce his effectiveness by not expressing himself sooner and more forcefully about cottage practices that violated what he had been taught? Why or why not?

3. Could and should this incident have been avoided? If so, how?

4. What are the responsibilities of the older, experienced worker and the younger, formally trained worker to each other in a situation like this? How should the younger worker approach the situation? The older?

12.4 HELP FOR A COLLEAGUE

1. Should Scott permit Bernie to continue to handle the situation? Why or why not? If not, what should he do?

2. If Scott tells Bernie that he is too "hot" and forcibly moves into the situation, what follow-up actions should be taken with Bernie and the group later? Why?

3. How can child care workers who work together regularly handle situations like this effectively?

4. What kind of advance preparation might contribute to effective handling of such a situation involving child care workers who do not work together regularly or know each other well?

5. What are the pros and cons of a rotating night-watch system, such as is portrayed here, compared with the employment of a separate group of night shift child care workers?

12.5 A DIFFERENT DRUMMER

1. Under the circumstances, should Mark be encouraged to go to gym night? Why or why not?

2. Is the problem one that can be avoided by avoiding the situation? Why or why not? If so, is this a good way to handle it? Why or why not?

3. Whose approach is more likely to help Mark adjust to the real world, Bud's or Hal's? Why?

4. Was Bud forceful enough with Hal? Why or why not? Does he have the right to "interfere" in the recreation program in this way? Why or why not?

5. What can Bud do to change Hal's attitude if that seems like a good idea? What else can he do? What should he do? Why?

13.1 DOUBLE BIND

1. Should Pat try to deal with the problem on his own before taking it to his supervisor? Or should he discuss it with his supervisor now? Why?

2. What should a child care worker expect of his supervisor? What is the appropriate role of a supervisor of institutional child care workers?

3. What would be the most difficult kind of experience for you to share with your supervisor? Why?

4. Should it be required for a child care supervisor to have had direct child care experience? Why or why not?

13.2 LOOKING UP

1. What seems to be the basic problem in this case?

2. If a child care worker feels that his supervisor is treating him unfairly, what kinds of action are appropriate? Why?

3. At what point is a child care worker justified in taking an issue to his supervisor's supervisor? How should he do it?

4. Using role playing, enact a conversation between Frank and Mr. Thompson about the problem when Frank gets back to work. Enact a conversation between Frank and the director about it. In general, what are the likely consequences and the pros and cons of each approach?

5. Should Frank try to get the other child care workers to support him? If so, what kind of support should he seek? What might be the consequences for all concerned?

6. Should Frank consider seeking another job? Why or why not? If so, what, if anything, should he try first? Why?

7. To what extent should a child care worker feel obligated to work overtime in an emergency? Why?

13.3 WHERE THE ACTION ISN'T

1. Was Bert right in reporting John to Chuck as he did? Why or why not? Under what circumstances, if any, is it good practice for one worker to report another?

2. What might account for Chuck's inability to handle the situation? Under the circumstances, what should John consider doing now? Why?

3. Should a child care worker expect to get direct help with a problem like this from his supervisor? Why or why not?

4. What kinds of help should a child care worker expect from his supervisor? What should he not expect? Why?

13.4 BEING HEARD

1. Is it good practice for the top administrator to be available to the youngsters? Why or why not? If so, should he refuse to talk with youngsters unless the child care worker is present? Why or why not?

2. Is it good practice for the top administrator to have an open door policy for all staff? Why or why not?

3. What are the values of having a formal "chain of command"? How rigidly should staff adhere to it? Why?

4. Do you know the complete "chain of command" at your institution? Does it operate as it appears on paper? Why or why not? If not, what are the implications for the child care worker? For the youngsters?

5. What should child care workers do if they disagree with an administrative policy to which the director seems deeply committed?

13.5 WHO OWES WHAT TO WHOM?

1. Should child care workers strike to enforce their demands if other methods have failed? What are the pros and cons? What might be the consequences for the youngsters in care?

2. If the issue were the "shipping" of a youngster, and the child care staff felt he was being shipped unfairly, what kinds of staff action, if any, would be appropriate? Why?

3. If the issue were the firing of a popular child care worker for reasons considered by the child care staff to be questionable, what kinds of staff action, if any, would be appropriate? Why?

4. What are the potential values to the institution of advanced training for child care workers? What are the potential problems, if any?

5. What are the potential values of advanced training to the child care worker himself? What are the potential problems, if any?

14.1 "IF I KNEW YOU WERE COMING . . ."

1. What should be the child care worker's primary concerns and objectives in handling this situation? Why?

2. Should the child care worker intervene immediately? Or should he

wait to see what Jim does? Why? If he intervenes immediately, what should he do? Why?

3. If Jim does nothing, should the child care worker then intervene? Why or why not? If so, how? Why?

4. What, if anything, should Jim do to follow up on this incident? Should he report it? Why or why not? If so, to whom?

5. Should Jim's mother's visiting privileges be restricted in any way? Why or why not? If so, how? What should Sam do if she wants to see him again? Why?

6. What are the purposes of visiting days, if any, beyond providing a chance for youngsters and their families to get together? Is it a good idea for child care workers to talk with parents on such occasions? Why or why not? How should such contacts be handled by the child care workers? What kinds of objectives might they try to accomplish?

14.2 GREAT EXPECTATIONS

1. Should Neil have involved himself in this situation? Why or why not?

2. When he confronted Henry about it, should he have indicated his own feelings about it more strongly? Why or why not?

3. Is Henry really ungrateful? Explain.

4. Should Henry be asked to thank his parents even if he does not feel gratitude? Why or why not?

14.3 STIFF UPPER LIP

1. Should the child care worker or the social worker have been the one to tell Oliver that he could not go home for the vacation? Why?

2. How should Oliver be told that he will not be going home for vacation? (This question can be explored in part through role playing by enacting the conversation between Milt and Oliver.)

3. What else, if anything, should the child care staff have been doing about the situation between the time Oliver was told and the start of the vacation period?

4. What kinds of preparations should be made by an institution when many of the youngsters are leaving for a vacation period? What are the major concerns that should be taken into account?

5. Should Oliver's mother be pressured to let Oliver come home for vacation? Why or why not? If so, how? (It might be helpful to use role playing to enact a meeting at which Milt and Nancy try to convince Oliver's mother to let him come home, and to enact the situation with both Oliver and his brother at home.)

14.4 STAND-IN

1. Should an exception to the rule have been made for Sally in this case? Why or why not?

2. If no exception is made for Sally, should Anne explain the specific reasons? Or would it be better for her to be vague in this situation? Why?

3. In general, what form of title, if any, should youngsters use when they talk to child care workers? Why?

4. Should all child care workers in a cottage be addressed in the same way as a matter of policy (for example, Mr., Miss, and Mrs., or first names), or should differences be acceptable? Why?

5. Whatever the the policy is about addressing child care workers, how should the limits be enforced? Why?

14.5 BAD NEWS

1. Should Chris have been told that his father was in intensive care again? Why or why not?

2. Who should tell an institutionalized youngster the news that one of his parents has died? Why?

3. Assuming that Ben is the one who must tell Chris in this situation, how should he do it? Why? (Role playing may be helpful in relation to this question.) What should be done later to follow up?

4. Under what conditions should a youngster be told that his parent is dying? Why? Under what conditions should he not be told? Why?

5. If the death is sudden, such as in an accident, rather than expected as in this case, should the situation be handled differently? Why or why not? If so, how?

15.1 MAIL CALL

1. Is mail censorship in an institution really an invasion of privacy? Why or why not? Assuming it is legal, is it justifiable? Why or why not?

2. What are the pros and cons of reading mail, or of withholding it, or of both, assuming that this is legal, in an institutional situation? How important is this issue for treatment purposes? Why? How important is it for custodial or security purposes? Why?

3. Consider a specific institution (real or hypothetical) and the kinds of youngsters it serves and formulate an appropriate policy on mail censorship. Should outgoing mail be read routinely? Sometimes? By whom? What about incoming mail? Under what circumstances, if any, should mail be withheld? What should the youngsters be told? If mail is read and something significant is discovered, what should be considered in determining how such information will be used? Explain the reasons for each aspect of the policy.

4. What rights, if any, does a child lose when he is admitted to an institution? Why? On what grounds, if any, can this be justified?

15.2 SENSITIVITY

1. Was it appropriate for Erv to leave Raymond in the waiting room the way he did, assuming that the boy was not considered dangerous to himself or others? Why or why not? Should Erv have stopped Raymond's "cozy" conversation with Linda? Why or why not?

2. What should be Erv's primary concern? Should he confront Mrs. Evans? Why or why not? If so, should he do so out of Raymond's hearing? Why or why not?

3. How might this incident affect Raymond? What can Erv do to help?

4. How might this incident affect the institution? What should Erv do in this connection?

5. Should Erv have accompanied Raymond into the doctor's inner

office? Why or why not? What are the responsibilities of the child care worker when he takes a youngster off grounds?

15.3 A BOWLING TRIP

1. Should Will talk with the police in front of the boys or in private? Why?

2. How should institutionalized youngsters be prepared for an off-grounds trip? Why?

3. What, if anything, should the people at the destination of an off-grounds trip (for example, the bowling alley manager) be told before a group of institutionalized youngsters arrives? Why?

4. What kinds of off-grounds trips are appropriate for institutionalized youngsters? What should be considered in deciding whether a proposed trip is appropriate?

5. With what should a child care worker be concerned when leading an off-grounds trip in addition to his usual concerns? Why?

15.4 BIG MEN ON CAMPUS

1. What would probably be Ed's immediate impulse? What should he do? Why?

2. Should Joey be asked to apologize to Mr. Marlin? Why or why not?

3. Why does an institution sometimes arrange a special cleanup when

the board or other visitors are coming? Is this good practice? Why or why not?

4. What is the role of the board? How, if at all, should child care workers relate to the board? Why?

5. Should the role of the board be interpreted to the youngsters? Why or why not? If so, how?

15.5 THE NEIGHBORS

1. Is it important that Wayne report this conversation to his supervisor? Why or why not?

2. What might be the causes of townspeople's animosity toward a nearby institution? How should this be handled?

3. Is it important that child care workers actively involve themselves in establishing good relationships between the institution and the local community, or should this be primarily a function of the administration? Why? How can child care workers help?

4. Should a child care worker act as a spokesman for his institution when he is off duty? Why or why not?

APPENDIX

A FEW WORDS FOR
SUPERVISORS AND INSTRUCTORS

As institutional expectations for child care personnel have broadened from simple custodial care, through benevolent parenting and milieu therapy to the present emphasis on the integration of custodial and rehabilitative tasks, the skills needed by child care workers have become more sophisticated and complex. Standards for personnel have been unable to keep pace, however, since economic and social constraints have prevented the implementation of professional requirements for child care work comparable to those in such fields as teaching, social work, and psychiatric nursing. This has led to an increasing disparity between expectations and performance, and only recently have major, widespread efforts been initiated to bridge the gap.

Early training efforts were concerned largely with the essential custodial and administrative elements of the job—the daily routines such as getting the youngsters to meals and to bed on time, preventing or ending disruptive outbursts, and the like. A limited amount of published text material is available in these areas and provides concrete guidelines as well as, in many cases, reflecting a great deal of sensitivity to the challenges and opportunities provided by such situations. Elements of child care philosophy are also included—implicitly, if not on a planned basis. As more formal training programs have been developed other forms of content including activity resources and an orientation to the institutional field have been introduced into child care training curricula. Such material should be read and understood by child care trainees, of course, but more than "how to" formulations and descriptions of the field are needed if trainees are to be able to perform more effectively as new situations arise on the job.

More recently, particularly with the development of a professional or paraprofessional conception of the child care role, child care workers and trainees have been presented with behavioral science principles—material from psychology, sociology, anthropology, education, child development, and so on—in an effort to help them introduce insights from such fields in their work. A wide variety of general resource materials in these areas is available, and such material is usually included in child care training programs. Partly because such principles are particularly difficult to apply on the job if learned only in the abstract, however, practicum programs have been developed; these provide opportunities for trainees to learn to use the relevant contributions of behavioral science. It should be noted, however, that in the absence of sensitive supervision and self-criticism, field experience may be counterproductive, thus reinforcing negative attitudes and practices.

Although there is no fully adequate substitute for effectively supervised field experience in the training process, cases provide adjuncts with certain advantages at particular stages. They are, in most situations, more convenient for classroom use, and they can be used as "dry runs" to help prepare trainees for field assignments. More significantly, they provide the advantages of stop-action photography, and situations are available to be "re-run," reviewed, and discussed. In real life, critical situations are imbedded in the ongoing stream of behavior and are often lost to reflective, retrospective analysis as a result. Furthermore, there is little opportunity to identify and deal with the ways in which real situations may be distorted in recall, whereas cases provide consistent stimuli that can be checked for distortion as needed. This may suggest areas in which a trainee or a worker is particularly in need of help.

Whereas field work can be expected to provide a wide variety of experiences for the trainee, it does not offer systematic exposure to the range of situations normally encountered on the job. Thus there may be significant gaps in the experience, although this depends somewhat on the extent of the field work. More important, since the experience is not systematic, there is normally less opportunity to identify classes of situations, common threads, and the implications of a particular situation for others that may be encountered in the future. The cases included here have been chosen to reflect, insofar as possible, the full range of situations that normally confront child care workers, and they are categorized and presented so as to facilitate generalization and the application of the insights and principles developed from each in other similar circumstances.

In training programs for novices, cases have the further advantage of relative safety: there are no youngsters involved who might be hurt by faulty handling. They also provide trainees with a chance to prepare themselves under less stressful conditions for the kinds of incidents that are likely to occur on the job and that might otherwise appear overwhelming. Thus they can be used to "desensitize" prospective child care workers to the extremes of behavior with which they will be expected to deal as calmly and rationally as possible. For practicing child care personnel, appropriate cases may shed new light on real situations with which they need help by presenting similar occurrences without the emotional pressures accompanying the real event. Thus insulated the worker may be able to analyze the situation as it is portrayed in the case more objectively and apply the resulting insights in his own behavior. Of course, the cases are also useful when opportunities for observation or practical experience in connection with a training program are limited, because they provide trainees with examples of significant "on the job" situations and with a chance to formulate and evaluate their own reactions and prescriptions in concrete terms.

Thus the cases provide vicarious experience that simulates the crucial elements of child care work as the basis for field experience and the development of a body of concrete, directly applicable knowledge. "Answers" are not provided with the cases, reflecting the authors' conviction that effective child care practice is a function of interpersonal interaction and relationship and therefore must be learned through a problem-solving process rather than through the rote learning or memorizing of a cookbook-type formulation.

As a result the case study method requires more of the instructor or supervisor—as well as of students—than do more traditional teaching techniques. The instructor should be a sensitive leader, actively involved and closely attuned, yet with enough patience and internal security to permit learners a large measure of freedom. Using his knowledge of child care practice and institutional philosophies as the foundation and the cases as his raw material, he should be able to stimulate the problem-solving approach and the generic application of new insights and skills that mark the development of effective child care workers. The process of case analysis through which this can occur is described in Part One of the book.

GROUP ANALYSIS OF CASES

Perhaps the instructor's or supervisor's greatest contribution to enhancing child care practice through the case method can emerge when he serves as the leader of discussions about the cases. In this role he can focus the group's attention not only on the case being discussed but also on the development of human relations and interaction patterns in the group itself. Thus trainees can be helped to examine parallels between the cases and their own interpersonal behavior, and the implications for their performance on the job with youngsters, colleagues, and supervisors. For example, group analysis of cases with instructors or supervisors involved sometimes dramatically helps trainees to recognize and overcome irrational fears of authority. Thus the very mutuality between teachers and learners that can be fostered by the analysis of cases through group discussion can play an important role in the learning process.

Small groups seem to be most effective for case analysis since a variety of viewpoints can be expressed and there is ample opportunity for all to participate. When larger numbers are involved, such as in some college classes, it may be best to divide the class into groups of more convenient size for discussion. If there is more than one discussion group, it is often helpful to compare conclusions at the close of the discussion period. If the group includes clinicians, supervisors, or others who are not child care personnel, it may be especially important that the instructor make sure that the discussion is neither inhibited nor monopolized by a single perspective. When practicable, it may also be illuminating to include institutionalized or other youngsters in selected group discussions.

The technique of "role playing" provides an effective method of realistically portraying a variety of viewpoints and presenting them for consideration. The roles of characters portrayed in a case are assigned to various group members, who proceed to "act out" the case, while any remaining members observe. Each "actor" may be given a few minutes beforehand to think about his role. After the role playing experience, the situation can be discussed and the feelings of the various participants and observers compared. This method has proved to be effective in stimulating increased sensitivity and insight in human relations.

There are many variations and adaptations of role playing that may be used to further facilitate learning. Some groups will wish to enact a given case more than once with the roles rotated among different group members. It is frequently helpful to keep all characters constant with the exception of one (the child care worker or a youngster, for example) on whom the group may wish to focus its subsequent discussion. Conversely the group may wish to keep the enactor of a key role constant while other roles are rotated in an effort to observe how the same person's feelings and behavior may vary depending on how others act toward him. Role playing is, of course, a learning technique with much deeper and more complex potentialities than can be indicated here. More details are provided in some of the references listed at the end of the book.

Additional techniques may be introduced as desired to enhance learning. For example, it is often helpful for group members to serve on a rotating basis as discussion leaders to gain leadership experience or as nonparticipant observers. Such observers can then report to the other members how they performed individually and as a group as seen from "outside." This may help to provide new insights for all concerned. Other variations of the basic approach outlined above, such as the use of selected "encounter" techniques, may be used in connection with the cases as well. The pros and cons of these methods as well as the specifics of their application in this context lie beyond the scope of the present discussion. Readers seeking further information about case study methods may find the suggested references helpful.

In short, the cases provide a focus for discussion and for the "cooperative competitiveness" of ideas that stimulates thinking and the progress of any group toward its goals. Group members learn to look at problems from the points of view of various other people, to defend their own views in the competition of ideas, and when and how to accept gracefully the ideas of others. Experience suggests that this process can lead to growth in the personal attitudes and insights of motivated participants, and thereby greatly enhance their effectiveness in institutional child care positions and elsewhere.

ORGANIZING TRAINING CURRICULA

For use in a training curriculum, this book provides a reservoir of case material that is adaptable to a variety of kinds of programs. For a one-term or a full-year course or a more concentrated workshop, the units appear in logical sequence. For a two-year curriculum with specialization in child care, a model being implemented increasingly in community colleges and other settings, the individual units can be used separately to provide case material in appropriate courses. Thus, Unit One might find its place as part of the survey course in human services, illustrating the basic demands of a child care position. Unit Two is appropriate for a course in the therapeutic management and control of institutionalized youngsters, individually and in groups. The cases in Unit Three, illustrating institutional life as it affects the child care worker, may relate most clearly to the introductory course on the nature of institutions. Some of the other chapters provide cases for more advanced, second-year courses in institutional child care.

In most situations the instructor will want to select cases on which to focus, since a single course or workshop could not consider all of them in depth. In this connection the chapter headings provide a course outline within which key cases can be chosen from the descriptive tables of cases by chapter. Thus the instructor can build a course to meet his specific requirements by selecting cases that illustrate the areas he wishes to emphasize. In a single semester course, for example, one week could be devoted to a case or cases chosen from each chapter or, in a few instances, two chapters.

The chapters that might best be combined may vary with the composition and goals of the group involved, but some areas seem to fit together particularly well. Thus questions of formal treatment (Chapter 11) might be considered together with other parts of the institutional program that occur outside the cottage such as the school program and work details (Chapter 10). Chapter 11 might, alternatively, be considered together with Unit Four in the context of the child care worker as part of the institutional team. The two chapters comprising Unit Five might also be considered together.

In a year course, at least one week could be devoted to the subject of each chapter, using selected cases, and two or even three weeks could be devoted to some chapters. A workshop might best concentrate on one or two of the units, leaving the others for detailed attention elsewhere, although it is suggested that some attention be given to Unit Six, "Putting the Pieces Together," as the culmination of any training sequence.

USING CASES IN INSTITUTIONAL SETTINGS

Finally, the cases can be used within institutional settings in a variety of ways. Selected cases presented to applicants can be helpful in screening for child care positions, for example, and in identifying likely areas of weakness for special supervisory attention. In preservice training the cases can be used much as has been suggested above with regard to workshops, with the selection of cases and the discussion leadership oriented directly to the nature and philosophy of the particular institution. Likewise, in-service training can be built around case analysis, either with the cases discussed in sequence or with particular cases chosen to reflect issues that appear to be in the forefront of institutional attention or importance at a given time. Finally, as has been suggested above, supervisors of child care may find that particular cases can help to objectify a situation with which a worker may be struggling at a given time, or workers may be able to use the book in this way to help themselves. In institutional settings the material presented in Part One may be of interest particularly to supervisors as a basis for orienting child care workers to the productive use of the case material.

As they become familiar with the nature and uses of open-end case materials, instructors may wish to prepare additional cases based on their own experience. Trainees can be encouraged to submit their own relevant cases for discussion as well, perhaps using the case material in this book as a model. These approaches may provide especially useful case study resources specifically related to the problems of a given setting. The preparation of cases can also serve as a valuable training experience since it requires a conscious effort to perceive and present complex human relations situations clearly and objectively.

SUMMARY

In summary, there are several ways in which child care workers may learn their jobs. They can be taught principles, but principles alone seem to offer relatively little help. They can be simply exposed to the situation and learn through experience, although what is learned in this way in the absence of analysis and thoughtful supervision may consist largely of stereotyped, ineffective group management techniques. A blend or integration of principles and actual situations in a problem-solving process mediated by an effective instructor appears to be more promising, however, and cases such as those given here appear to be useful vehicles in the attempt to translate philosophy and principles into effective practice.

BIBLIOGRAPHY

Beker, J. *Training camp counselors in human relations: A case book*. New York: Association Press, 1962.

Besaw, V. E. (Ed.). Proceedings and discussion: National conference on curricula for the career ladder in the child caring professions. Pittsburgh: Department of Child Development and Child Care, School of Health Related Professions, University of Pittsburgh, 1969.

Broten, A. *Houseparents in children's institutions*. Chapel Hill: University of North Carolina Press, 1962.

Burmeister, E. *The professional houseparent*. New York: Columbia University Press, 1960.

Burmeister, E. *Tough times and tender moments in child care work*. New York: Columbia University Press, 1967.

Child Welfare League of America. *Training for child care staff*. New York: Child Welfare League of America, 1963.

Foster, G. W., Vander Ven, K. D., Kroner, E. R., Carbonara, N. T., & Cohen, G. M., *Child Care Work with Emotionally Disturbed Children*. Pittsburgh: University of Pittsburgh Press, 1972.

Ginott, H. G. *Between parent and teenager*. New York: Macmillan, 1969.

Goldfarb, W., Mintz, I., & Stroock, K. W. *A time to heal—corrective socialization: A treatment approach to childhood schizophrenia*. New York: International Universities Press, 1969.

Grossbard, H. *Cottage parents: What they have to be, know, and do*. New York: Child Welfare League of America, 1960, 1968.

Hromadka, Van G. Child care worker on the road to professionalization. Hawthorne, New York: Hawthorne Center for the Study of Adolescent Behavior, Jewish Board of Guardians, 1967 (mimeo.).

Jones, H. *Reluctant rebels: Re-education and group process in a residential community*. London: Tavistock Publications, 1960.

Kaminstein, P. *Training the residential child care worker: A design for in-service training*. New York: Institute for Child Mental Health, 1970.

Klein, A. F. *Role playing in leadership training and group problem solving*. New York: Association Press, 1956.

Konopka, G. *Group work in the institution: A modern challenge*. New York: Association Press, 1954.

Mayer, M. F. *A guide for child care workers*. New York: Child Welfare League of America, 1958.

McNickle, R. K. (Ed.) *Demonstration programs in education for work in juvenile corrections*. Boulder, Colorado: Western Interstate Commission for Higher Education, 1966.

368/Critical Incidents in Child Care

Neilson, F., & Kaminstein, P. *A step toward professionalism: A dynamic method for training child care workers.* New York: Center for Mass Communication, Columbia University Press, 1967 (audiotape).

Patten, J. *The children's institution.* Berkeley, California: McCutchan Publishing, 1968.

Patterson, G. R., & Gullion, M. E., *Living with Children: New Methods for Parents and Teachers.* Champaign, Illinois: Research Press, 1968.

Pigors, P., & Pigors, F. *Case method in human relations: The incident process.* New York: McGraw-Hill, 1961.

Polsky, H. W. *Cottage six—The social system of delinquent boys in residential treatment.* New York: Russell Sage Foundation, 1962.

Powell, J. R., Plyler, S. A., Dickson, B. A., & McClellan, S. D. *The personnel assistant in college residence halls.* Boston: Houghton Mifflin, 1969.

Redl, F., & Wineman, D. *The aggressive child.* Glencoe, Illinois: The Free Press, 1957.

Schulze, S. (Ed.). *Creative group living in a children's institution.* New York: Association Press, 1951.

Trieschman, A. E., Whittaker, J. K., & Brendtro, L. K. *The other 23 hours.* Chicago: Aldine Publishing, 1969.

United States Children's Bureau. *Staff training for personnel in institutions for juvenile delinquents.* Washington, D. C.: Children's Bureau Publication No. 377, 1959.

United States Children's Bureau. *Training personnel for work with juvenile delinquents.* Washington, D. C.: Children's Bureau Publication No. 348, 1954.

Weber, G. H. *A theoretical study of the cottage parent position and cottage work situations.* Washington, D. C.: United States Children's Bureau, 1962, 1966.

Weber, G. H. Emotional and defensive reactions of cottage parents. In Donald E. Cressey (Ed.). *The prison: Studies in institutional organization and change.* New York: Holt, Rinehart and Winston, 1961 (Pp. 189-228).

Whittaker, J. K., & Trieschman, A. E. (Eds.). *Children Away From Home: A Sourcebook in Residential Treatment.* Chicago: Aldine Publishing, 1972.

INDEX OF CASES

NUMERICAL LISTING OF CASES

CROSS-INDEX OF CASES—SELECTED CASES OF RELATED INTEREST

Many of the cases presented above deal with related issues from somewhat different perspectives or with differing emphases. The following list may be helpful to those seeking to identify additional cases related to particular areas of concern. Readers may also want to add to it in accordance with their own needs as they use the book. (Cases appearing in the same chapter are not cross-indexed since the common thread is reflected in the chapter title and description.)

1.1:	2.3; 12.4	6.2:	1.5
1.3:	6.3	6.3:	3.5
1.4:	6.1	6.4:	3.7; 7.5
1.5:	6.2; 7.6; 8.5	6.6:	1.8; 5.4
1.6:	6.10; 14.4	6.9:	10.5
1.7:	2.2; 3.8; 5.1; 7.12	6.10:	1.6; 9.3; 10.4; 10.8; 10.9; 14.4
1.8:	5.4; 6.6	7.1:	8.6; 10.10
2.1:	7.3; 11.1; 11.2	7.2:	2.9; 5.4
2.2:	1.7; 3.8; 5.1; 7.12	7.3:	2.1
2.3:	1.1; 12.4	7.4:	1.5; 2.7
2.7:	1.5; 7.4	7.5:	3.7; 6.4
2.8:	12.4	7.6:	1.5; 8.5
2.9:	5.4, 7.2	7.8:	4.2; 4.6; 5.3
3.3:	5.8	7.9:	4.6
3.5:	6.3	7.10:	12.1
3.6:	11.6	7.12:	1.7; 2.2; 3.8; 5.1
3.7:	6.4; 7.5	8.1:	14.4
3.8:	1.7; 2.2; 5.1	8.2:	5.2
3.9:	1.7; 2.2	8.5:	1.5; 7.6
4.1:	5.5	8.6:	7.1; 10.10; 12.3; 13.4
4.2:	7.8	9.3:	6.10; 10.4
4.6:	5.3; 7.8; 7.9	9.6:	10.1
5.1:	1.7; 2.2; 3.8; 7.12; 9.6	10.4:	6.10
5.2:	8.2	10.5:	6.9
5.3:	4.6; 7.8	10.6:	12.5
5.4:	1.8; 2.9; 6.6; 7.2	10.8:	6.10
5.5:	4.1	10.9:	6.10; 15.1
5.8:	3.3	10.10:	7.1; 8.6
6.1:	1.4	11.1:	2.1

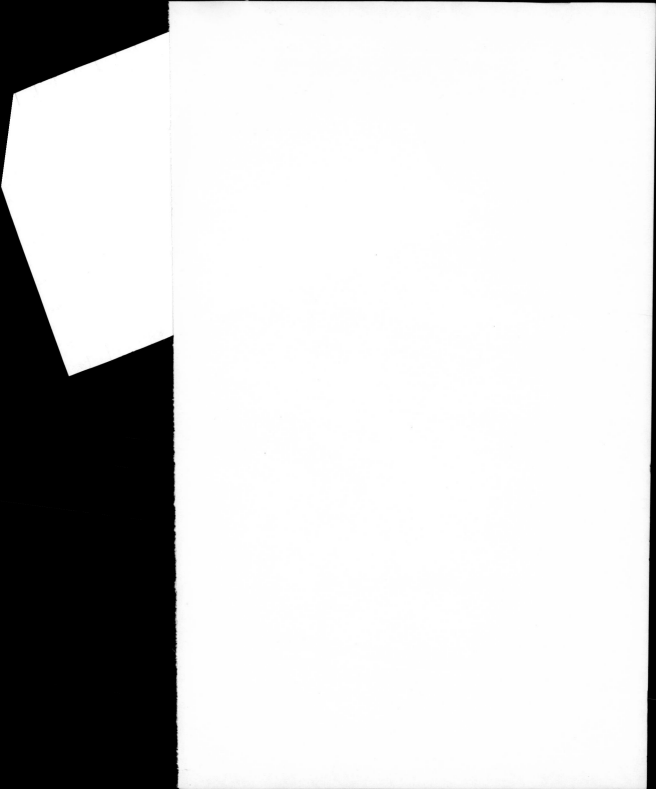

DATE D

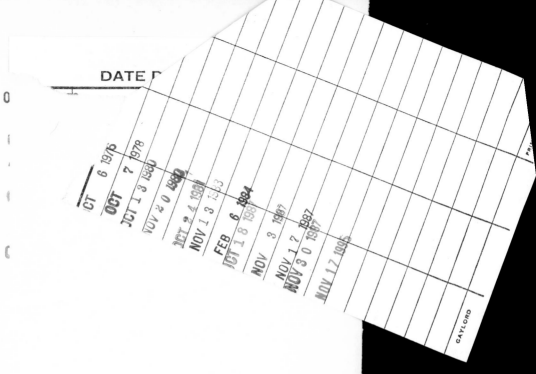

OCT 6 1976
OCT 7 1978
OCT 13 1980
NOV 20 1980
OCT 24 1980
NOV 13 1983
FEB 6 1984
OCT 18 1984
NOV 3 1987
NOV 17 1987
NOV 30 1987
NOV 17 1995

GAYLORD

HV881 .B43   c.1
Beker, Jerome.   100106 000
Critical incidents in child ca

3 9310 00006451 7
GOSHEN COLLEGE-GOOD LIBRARY

HV881 .B43   c.1
Beker, Jerome.   100106 000
Critical incidents in child ca

3 9310 00006451 7
GOSHEN COLLEGE-GOOD LIBRARY

DATE DUE

CT 6 1975		
OCT 7 1978		
CT 1 3 1980		
OV 2 0 1980		
CT 2 4 1981		
NOV 1 3 1983		
FEB 6 1984		
CT 1 8 1987		
NOV 3 1987		
NOV 1 7 1987		
NOV 3 0 1987		
NOV 17 1995		
GAYLORD		PRINTED IN U.S.A.